LANGUAGE PLANNING AND LANGUAGE USE

Language Planning
and
Language Use

WELSH IN A GLOBAL AGE

GLYN WILLIAMS and DELYTH MORRIS

UNIVERSITY OF WALES PRESS
CARDIFF
2000

British Library Cataloguing-in-Publication Data

A catalogue record for this book is available from the British Library

ISBN 0-7083-1579-8

Typeset by Action Publishing Technology Ltd., Gloucester
Printed in Wales by Dinefwr Press, Llandybïe

Contents

List of Figures

List of Tables

I Gymdeithas yr Iaith Gymraeg,
ddoe, heddiw ac yfory

Acknowledgements

We are indebted to both the University of Wales' Board of Celtic Studies and the European Commission for support in undertaking the field work associated with the work reported in this volume. The various meetings of a series of Research Group initiatives funded by DGXXII of the EC have been invaluable by reference to both the survey work and the work on language planning which we report upon in this book. The individuals involved in these groups are the following: Padraig O'Riagain, Hilary Tovey, Miquel Strubell, Joan Romani, Xavier Aixpurua, Josean Undangarin, Durk Goerter, Modesto Rodriguez-Neira, and Manuel Gonzales Gonzales. We have learnt a great deal from them. We also wish to thank the staff of the University of Wales Press for their efforts, and for the smooth and efficient way in which Ceinwen Jones undertook the onerous task of insuring the transformation of our manuscript into the finished product.

Introduction

1. Introduction

This book is about those people living in Wales who use the Welsh language. That is, in sociological terms, it is about a language group viewed as a social group. It is about the extent to which the use of Welsh is possible, and the lengths to which those with the necessary competence go in order to use the language. This means that we are discussing those situations in which individuals are constituted as certain kinds of subjects – as Welsh speakers, thereby establishing a relationship between these subjects and a specific object, the Welsh language.

It is also, however, about a certain activity – language planning – which takes the existence of Welsh as an object for granted. It is an activity that obliges those involved in its practice to think hard about what kind of object it is. For Welsh can mean a number of different things, and the way in which we build these meanings will influence how we proceed to plan its future. We argue that this is a contentious issue and that, as a contentious issue, it will be the subject of disagreement and struggle. After all, if there is an issue in Wales on which everyone would appear to be an 'expert', it is the Welsh language!

In what follows we begin with an overview of the theoretical orientations towards minority language groups within the social sciences, leading to our own particular theoretical perspective. In the second chapter we consider the nature of the available empirical information by reference to Welsh and its use. This overview allows us to consider some of the issues that are essential prerequisites of developing a language use survey, while also allowing us to present one account of the nature of the changes recently operating by reference to the Welsh language group. The second part of this chapter is then taken up by a discussion of the methodological issues associated with the survey which is the main focus of our study. Chapters 3 to 7 are then dedicated to a consideration of this data which is discussed by referring to the various topics associated with language production and reproduction consistent with our theoretical perspective on competence. In pursuing this analysis we try to link competence with use in order to map out the incidence and nature of language use without going so far as to locate this data within an explicit action perspective. Having thus outlined the structure and context of Welsh-language use, we proceed to a consideration of the manner in which language planning is currently being activated to promote language use. Thus, in Chapter 8 we consider the work of the Welsh Language Board and how it is premised upon the implementation of a Language Act which derives from a particular political problematic. This leads us to the final chapter where we consider the current debates concerning social, political and cultural change and their implications for the language group.

Before we begin this overview of language planning and language use, we would like to devote a few lines to how those 'real experts', the academics, have dealt with Welsh. We do this in order to highlight the fact that the academic disciplines are not objective activities that allow the author to uncover 'truth' or 'reality'. Rather we view them as discourses which carry their own biases, allowing certain things to be said while preventing other things from being said. Furthermore, they all have their say in quite different ways.

2. *Academic Discourse on Welsh*

Welsh has been the focus of considerable attention among intellectuals. Given the extent to which the period since at least 1850 has generated a debate about the relationship between Welsh, Welshness and the idea of a Welsh nation, this is hardly surprising. The creation of the different disciplines at the end of the eighteenth century served as the basis for a range of different orientations towards any particular subject and this was no less true of Wales and the study of Welsh. Historians, sociologists, anthropologists, linguists, students of literature *inter alia* have all had something to say about Welsh. True to their disciplinary orientations they have all said what they have had to say in different ways, yet they have all shared the rationalist orientation of the discourse of modernity.

The Classical episteme

Foucault (1966) makes the point that the appearance of disciplines coincides with a complete reorganization of knowledge at the beginning of the nineteenth century. In what he refers to as the Classical episteme, knowledge was analogous to language. The elements of human discourse provided both a representation of phenomena and, in the same operation, an analysis of phenomena. Knowledge is signification, and signification is both representation and analysis. The example he used was the manner in which a representation both signifies and analyses something in the same way a map does. Since representation is also analysis, things could be represented as a discourse, not merely in discourse. Prior to the nineteenth century, philosophy could not be organized as a knowledge by reference of problems either of epistemology or of meaning. The central philosophical questions of knowledge, ontology and meaning did not exist. What became philosophy was very much a function and effect of the organization of knowledges in the nineteenth century. What was written as 'philosophy' within the Classical episteme was an elucidation of the problems of representation in general, tending encyclopaedially to draw together the entire issue of objects of representation. The emergence of philosophy as that which adjudicates claims to knowledge and arbitrates over the status of objects signalled a radical transformation and heralded the end of the Classical episteme. It was replaced by philosophy on the one hand, and the life sciences, the science of labour and of language which began to work at different levels. Philosophy ceased to be the elaboration of these knowledges and these knowledges no longer meshed together, and so became incapable of being elaborated through the category of representation. Rather, they drew into themselves and their concepts became internal to each discipline. The conditions of their truth, their relation to other sciences became a profound problem, leading to the emergence of the modern form of epistemology.

It is recognized that the shift towards modernism in the seventeenth and eighteenth centuries involved a prolonged political struggle within which social philosophy played a central role, leading to the triumph of what was called reason in the idea of modernity. The struggle was to replace an order which involved a monotheistic religion relying on the theme of revelation by a correspondence between human action and the order of the world or nature. It was also a discourse which presented a struggle between the 'domestic grandeur' (Boltanski and Thevenot, 1987) of the royal line and 'the people'. It was this struggle and the discourses involved in the struggle that animated science and its application, that directed social life towards individual and collective needs, and which replaced what modernity regarded as the arbitrary and the violent by the State of law and by the market. As a consequence it was claimed that humanity advanced towards a condition of abundance, liberty and the good life. What is usually missing in the analysis of this particular historical conjuncture is the need to treat the relevant discourses as metadiscourses rather than as the creative works of individual authors.

Language as an object has a particular relevance for such discursive contexts. The Port Royal Grammar established the shift from the conception of language as the signs out of which commentary draws closer to the primary text by establishing language as a relationship of representation. Things and words become separated from each other, and seeing becomes different from reading. It raises the question of the relationship between the sign and what is signified, or how humankind uses signs to signify thoughts. The focus shifts to the mind, to conceiving, judging and reasoning, opening the door on a link between language and a rationalism of the mind. The goal becomes one of directing 'mental vision' to discovering truth as '... the order and disposition of objects' (Descartes, 1970: 14), and intuition becomes the starting point for thought and, together with deduction, it becomes the basis of method.

There is another important development in the Port Royal Grammar, a development that permits the elaboration of a link between language, reason and politics at the end of the eighteenth century. Language teaching shifted from the teaching of the rules of language in the same language, to a situation in which the rule to be applied to the language being taught is formulated in the language already known. This leads to conceptual transformations. An order in any language is presupposed, and that order can be reconstituted with clarity in one's own language. It is also an order that can be penetrated by reason, thereby being capable of reconstitution in terms of general principles without reference to use, and independently of what we would consider to be the linguistic elements that determine use. Languages now have two levels – one of words, phrases and use, and the other of the principles which govern the appearance of the visible level. The other crucial development involved the claim that to speak truly was to speak according to the rules which must be constructed by grammar. There is a proximity between grammar and truth. It leads to a shift from interpretation to analysis based upon comparison and measurement as the search for order. It linked with the claim that humankind had a natural capacity to order the world. This also had a profound influence upon deictics in that both the 'I' and space take a profound turn. A new relationship is established between the 'I' and space, leading to a direct link between 'I', space and time, this being the basis of a conception of order that structures grammar (Clarke, 1997). The 'I' is driven between existence and being. Humankind is located at the centre of a conjectural world that unfolds from the intellect through reason. The centre of this world constitutes the 'I' which is, thereby, located in relation to a surrounding space that is never fixed. The relation between this space and the 'I' is a matter of reflection and intuition related to representation. But it is in perception, where the foreground is presented simultaneously with the representation of the wider world, that a sense of oneself, an 'I in us' is found. Arnauld (1990: 53) presents a differentiation between the 'I' and the self as something other than the 'I'. Thinking becomes perception constituted in the reflective 'I', linking through to the 'self'. It leads to a focus upon the individuality of the self through identity. That self is firmly locked in relation to time and space within a new deictic.

Knowledge came to consist of the correct order of representations, revealing identities, differences and their degrees. Signs become knowledge, tools of analysis and the means of representing order. The world and signs, things and words are divided. It changes the whole basis of the sign. It becomes a binary feature involving a signifier and a signified. The question of the sign is now co-extensive with knowledge and representation. The totality of signs is the corpus of knowledge. It led to the use of tables to represent taxonomies based on differences and similarities and, thereby, identities. This became a science of ordering representations, and the task of knowledge was to produce a system of names which function as a taxonomy. Signs are now modes of representation, not properties of things. For Foucault the difference between how knowledge differs between the Renaissance and Classical epistemes is not a matter of progress, but rather, one of the effects of different epistemes.

It is this awareness that tends to be missing among both Welsh historians and students of Welsh literature. There is an unfortunate tendency among Welsh historians to conceive of the Welsh culture, and the Welsh language as a feature of that culture, by reference to a period of perfection which has subsequently fallen from grace. It is evident in the title of a recent publication (Jenkins, 1997), *Y Gymraeg yn ei Disgleirdeb* (The Welsh Language in its Splendour), which replicates the title of a seventeenth-century Welsh–English dictionary. This is partly a consequence of the reification of language and culture, and the associated inability to conceive of them as pertaining to social groups. Whatever the reason for this, its consequences involve a tendency to treat 'Welsh culture' by reference to a golden age after which it was subject to decline. Culture is treated as a static entity. Consequently there is an inability to conceive of culture as a dynamic and creative entity that is constantly being created and recreated. Associated with this trend is the equally damaging tendency to conceive of culture change by reference to a diffusionist model devoid of any social component, leading to the demise of Welsh culture through contact with forces that derive from the east. '[T]he rugged mountains and the country's crude roads served as barriers which defended the monoglot residents of the north and west from English influences' (Jenkins, 1997: 2).

Yet another problem with historicism is the tendency to conceive of subjects and objects by reference to current meaning structures. Thus the overlap between polity, language and identity is evident in such comments as 'Communities which were Welsh by language were lost to England as a consequence of the restructuring which occurred following the Acts of Union' (Jenkins, 1997: 3). Surely, either the whole of Wales, whatever it was as an object, was lost to England, or the communities which were 'lost' were geographically already in England. The tendency to equate language and nation is far-reaching, even when it pertains to a time when these objects had quite different meanings from those that obtain today. This is not to deny that trends in language use cannot be identified from the historical record, but that the ascription of meaning of these trends requires considerable care. Perhaps such views are inevitable given the reification of language: 'even though the deWelshification process was slow in these regions it was not easy to withstand the power and influence of the English language' (Jenkins, 1997: 3). Certainly such comments oblige us to begin with at least a few lines about language in history and even, perhaps, language and history.

At that time of the modistae, the being of God was responsible for a creating movement or *energia* which was a relating movement. Within this motion creation had the possibility of being, even though it always related back to God as the place of origin or the point of Being. This was the kernel of a deictic which determined all being. Thus the *essentia* of being existed within it and gave rise to the *existentia* of being, the deictic relation that makes all relating possible. The three elements of any deictic – time, place and person – accounted for the possibility of being.

Within this context, the kinship mode of production of pre-Norman Wales established a particular structure. Ownership of land was impossible, only the right of usufruct existing, and that only through the ability to demonstrate inter-generational descent. Thus we have the essential deictic components – time in the form of descent, space in terms of a kinship territory, and person in terms of the different places that open up for being within this system, albeit that it was always a being that was subordinate to the ultimate Being. The entire mode of production was locked into this deictic and mobility out of it was inconceivable, since being was locked in space through time and person. It is this that structured identity, and language was a mere detail of this identity. However, since God was the word, or Logos, while also being the source of *energia*, that word contained power and was the means whereby human being was made possible. Furthermore, since all relationships were discovered through the deictic, then God was always located through the same deictic. It was also the means whereby being related to what it was not. It is therefore not surprising that being was not a polity structured by language, nor by a concept such as Wales, but by the very deictic that revolved around kinship and genealogy, with God at its centre. The world was a constellation of lineages which played a part in determining being and around which the economy was organized, while also being subordinate to it. Not that language was irrelevant for identity, but only as a deictic grammar. Language was something quite different from the way we currently conceive of it with its focus upon the normative of the standard, and the associated link between the world, thinking and expression. This underlines how human being is governed by the relationship between the external world and the knowledge of it. The 'us' and 'them' of being, that which sets the social boundary and becomes the basis of identity, was constituted out of this deictic. As such, identity was far removed from the current conception as it relates to language, territory and time. It does not focus upon the rational human subject freely claiming, 'I feel Welsh therefore I am Welsh'! It is futile to search for a contemporary sense of nationalism in a period when it not only did not exist but, more importantly, could not be conceived of.

Modernism and historical explanation

Welsh was incorporated into the modernist discourse at the end of the nineteenth century. It was this discourse which equated language and reason but insisting upon specific languages, those of the state, as the only languages of reason. It also emphasized moral individualism wherein the individual was responsible for his or her own well-being. Social integration involved these preconceptions but was established through law and education. A considerable range of material concerning the Welsh language and its speakers existed prior to the end of the nineteenth century, including the infamous Blue Books which sought to correlate a knowledge of Welsh with the absence of the factors which were regarded as essential for the promotion of individual and social development. Such material falls within the realm of policy statements made from particular political positions at a particular historical conjuncture. They fall within the general discourse on language which designated certain languages as the languages of reason, leaving others somehow outside of reason. As Calvet (1974), Achard (1986) and Balibar (1985) have shown, this preoccupation with reason as the essence of development, and its link to language, derives from eighteenth-century modernism and its quest for the principles of universal progress. While we have discussed this elsewhere (Williams, 1992a), it is necessary to emphasize the manner in which it has shaped much of the thinking about the relevance of language for Welsh society. The tendency to dichotomize society along the modern/traditional distinction and its link to civilization as the outcome of progress has had devastating effects for many minority language groups (Williams, Nelde and Strubell, 1997). The modern/traditional distinction was extended to encompass the distinction between emotion and reason, with reason being the force which controlled the basic emotional condition of humankind, leading to progress and civilization, a state that was equated with the European nation state. The 'traditional' features included language, and speakers of what were regarded as non-rational languages, that is, languages which were deemed unfit for the lofty state purposes, were conceived of by reference to a propensity for behaviour determined by emotion rather than reason. Thus we find a suspicion of language as a seditious object, capable of undermining the state and the very social order which it sought to confirm.

Among the objects created within the discourse which distinguished between reason and emotion were the economic order and work, which were essentially linked to the idea of both individual and universal progress. Yet economic activity was to a great extent autonomous, linked as it was to the goal of establishing entrepreneurial profit. The link between economic prosperity and universal progress became the cornerstone of the concept of modernization. Development as a correlate of progress was imposed between competing factions and classes as the possible link between economic efficacy and social integration. Moral individualism was conceived of as essential for productive activity, leading to a moralization of collective and individual life. It was the role of the state to ensure that human capital was nourished and promoted in the right manner that would ensure progress. This was done in the name of the nation – the British nation. The link between reason, economy and language was restricted to specific languages. It was a reiteration of the same claim by reference to administration and government, both of which were closely aligned to economic activity, even if liberalism did claim to keep them separate. Furthermore, the concept was that the British polity linked the masses to a leadership which was constructed out of the link between the subject as leader and the space that was the universal space of Britain. Yet within civil society in Wales, it was the same principle which served as the basis for two parallel reactions to such statist conservatism – that of trade unionism and that of Nonconformist liberalism.

This link between economic activity and reason led to two developments. It led on the one hand to the argument for the exclusion of Welsh from the relations of production, and on the other hand to the argument for the exclusion of Welsh from the political practice that integrated social classes within that process of production. The first thrust involved a conception of the relationship between the individual subject, language as an object, and progress within a definable space that incorporated the idea of a relationship between social and geographical mobility. Thus the enterprising individual sought his or her destiny through an enterprise that linked with the language of reason within a spatial context that expanded beyond the limits of the space that defined the Welsh language. A knowledge of English was the prerequisite of success: 'If you want to get ahead, get an English head!' At the beginning of the eighteenth century this awareness led some of the gentry to advocate not teaching English to the Welsh peasantry for fear that they would emigrate *en masse* to the Americas, thereby forcing up the cost of labour in Wales. There were voices raised in support of teaching English, recognizing the value of language prestige as we refer to it, for the survival of the language group. Thus Michael D. Jones, writing in the middle of the nineteenth century, made a strong argument in favour of allowing the entry of Welsh into the market practices of the emerging capitalism (Williams, 1983). This was the basis for an interdiscourse which created language upon quite distinctive preconstructed elements that linked constructively with geographical space. The inherent interdiscursive tension was the basis for political antagonism that was activated in and through social practice.

The discourse which argued for the exclusion of Welsh from the political practice of class integration did not construct language as an object linked to reason, but rather as a force for cohesion and solidarity, as an emotional force. The space wherein that solidarity was activated was, once again, the universal space of Britain. Yet it was a space which accommodated the local or the community within the universal space through the construction of a distinctive object, the universal class-based community. It served as the basis for another interdiscourse where the community object linked with the well-being of the subjects which constituted that community, thereby making community the focus of contestation.

It is essential to recognize the multifaceted nature of nineteenth-century Nonconformist discourse and the specific nature of Nonconformism in Wales, if only because of the profound impact it had upon civil society and political society. Nonconformist discourse spanned a range of subject positions which extended from the individual, through the community to the universalism of religious being. This was sometimes constituted in social practice through distinctive institutional organizations, with some sects giving individual chapels a high degree of autonomy and others generating distinctive administrative structures that encompassed all of Wales. Furthermore, the political discourse of the sects varied from the socialist principles of the Baptists to the more conservative orientation of the Methodists, discourses which varied across time. Clearly it is facile to discuss

Nonconformism as a uniform homogeneous discursive formation. None the less, what is clear is that community in Wales during the second half of the nineteenth century was structured by religion (Owen, 1960). It generated sacred and secular status groups which cut across social class (Jenkins, 1960; Day and Fitton, 1978; Williams, 1983). Furthermore, it was these status groups rather than social class which generated language varieties of Welsh.

The points made in the preceding paragraph apply very much to Wales, yet there were some discursive features that were universal and homogeneous in relation to Wales. Firstly, an opposition was generated between the Church of England in Wales and the nonconformist sects. The Church of England was constructed as an alien force, hostile to Welsh speakers. In this respect it was a representation of the rational universalism of the evolutionary continuum. In contrast, Nonconformism was constructed as the force which protected the integrity of the Welsh-speaking subject within his or her community. Particular subjects were linked to these objects. The landed gentry, predominantly non-Welsh speaking, were aligned with the Church of England, whereas the predominantly Welsh-speaking tenantry and working class were aligned with Nonconformist chapels. The process which embedded these subjects and objects focused upon the notion of patronage and community representation. Nonconformism was constructed as the force of benevolence which represented the unit of the local community, offering a form of welfarism for the needy members. The needy who conformed with the behavioural codes dictated by Nonconformism were deemed worthy of support by those fellow members who could offer it. By mid-century the construct of Nonconformism as a seditious force linked to Chartism had given way to a more explicit political link between Nonconformism and liberalism; the discourse of Nonconformity and that of the Liberal Party achieved a remarkable homogeneity.

In the whole of Wales, but especially in the industrialized regions, trade unionism came to represent a powerful discourse that linked the working class with the evangelizing force of unionism. Once again we encounter a discursive formation which constructs a social body, this time a particular social class, and claims to link that body to another social body, the community, which is represented by the institution – the trade union. In our view, the context in which this discourse linked to social practice in Wales has been oversimplified and misunderstood, largely because the interpretation derives not from a consideration of discourse but from the perspective of a particular discursive formation. There has been a tendency to present social practice by reference to a simple polarization between a progressive, universal working-class movement which focused upon English as the language of reason. This in turn uncovers the ideological nature of class oppression, and a narrow, élitist local movement dominated by a religious ideology expressed through an emotive Welsh language. In this respect it is viewed as a microcosm of the ensuing political struggle between the Liberal and Labour parties.

Within some of the south Wales valleys there ensued a struggle over community welfarism between the Nonconformist chapels and the trade unions. This involved the construction of an external object as a negative force, even if that object was differently constructed in each discursive formation. The local community becomes the local object which represents the different of that external object, and the local chapels and union lodges as the institutions which promoted community welfarism as a defence against the negative externality. However, to present this struggle as universal is misleading. In some of the valleys it is clear that the chapel deaconry and the trade union leadership overlapped, making the construction of an oppositional discourse involving the two institutions impossible. That is, it represents that which cannot be said from the specific place. These tended to be locations where employment focused upon a single employer who was often a local employer. There is an evident need to consider the intricate local nature of knowledge and how it pertains to social practice.

Evidently what is at stake here is the different nature of the 'us' and 'them' distinction, and the identity of the 'them' in each of the two discursive formations. Within unionism, as in the Nonconformist discourse, the 'us' was the community, being integrated and supported from within its own strength and resources. Unionism and Nonconformism differed in that the socialist discourse of unionism constructed a class community, whereas the Nonconformist community was centred upon chapel membership and Nonconformism, that is upon conformity with a morally conditioned behavioural norm. On the other hand for the unions the 'them' was a stranger in terms of social class, and the universalism of proletarian communities was the means whereby the alien force was constructed, not as a political force constituted in space and time, but as another universal component to which it was politically opposed. In contrast, some but by no means all of the Nonconformist discourses saw the 'them' in terms of cultural, or even national, differences. Nonconformism was constructed as the 'we' of the community but in opposition to a 'them' which also pertained to the local if not to the community, but which was also linked at the institutional level to the state, the object which laid claim to nationhood. Thus the opposition came to have nationalist overtones which linked the community, language and nation. We recognize the overgeneralization of this opposition, and that the discourses of the different Nonconformist sects were articulated with quite different political discourses, and await the work of historians in clarifying this diversity by reference to discursive analysis.

Clearly, language was constructed at the point of articulation of quite different enunciative and discursive positions, thereby becoming a contested object that was crucial to the manner in which subject positions within social practice were constituted. It linked with a series of contested objects – the community, the nation and class. What is implied here is that the discourse which sustained much of nineteenth-century sociology was also the basis for sustaining a normativity that linked with social order in the name of the state.

Demodernization

It is now customary in the social sciences to resort to a claim for the existence of a post-modern society. In at least one sense this is puzzling. On the one hand those who make this argument reject the modernist conception of evolutionary development and progress. Simultaneously, however, they argue for the emergence of a new 'stage' of society that has emerged out of the previous modernist stage. In common with much of historical society it establishes typologies of the modern and the post-modern, in order first to demonstrate their difference, and second to seek a rationale for the change from one stage to the other.

Others refer not to post-modernism but to demodernization (Touraine, 1997). Persisting with the evolutionary orthodoxy they claim we are entering a phase of later modernity within which the principles of social order and economic development are replaced by a new conception of rationalization and personal liberty (Touraine, 1997: 162). The claim is made that the drive of economics and the quest for the capitalist goal of sustaining profits lead to certain forms of economic restructuring. This has reached the point where the entire market has been globalized, obliging states to relinquish their modernist practices of economic regulation and monetary manipulation. Since modernism was premised on the equation of each political state with a single society, and since that society was the basis for integrating the economic and the social order, the argument leads towards a new conception of a global society which invades all aspects of public and private life. Technology permits the transmission of messages that are of relevance to everyone across the world. The emaciation of the state means that it can no longer play the role of promoting a homogenization of culture premised upon an equation of reason and language that can no longer be sustained. Thus, it is argued that, in place of cultural homogenization, we are currently entering a period of diversity constructed out of localized, community-based action. The nation no longer designates the collectivity of the citizens of a particular state who share a collective identity. The means of social and political mediation between economy and culture that assured the integration of all elements of social life recede, leading to a rupture of the universe of the market and of civic life. These are replaced by a dynamic of liberalization of exchanges and conditions of production which is simultaneously a process of de-socialization, depoliticization and the weakening of political mediation and its mechanisms of social integration. Beck (1986) maintains that part of this process involves the replacement of certainty by doubt, and the reproduction of order by risk. This leads to an increasing emphasis upon trust. We made a similar argument concerning the relationship between risk and trust and the role of language meaning in this process on a local level some time ago (Williams, 1976). It is argued that such developments are only possible once industrial society, with its close link between social organization and methods of rationalization, which emphasizes the link between the division of technology and the social division of labour, is in decline.

It seems that both of these arguments exaggerate. While it is true that in Europe at least, the role of the state is shifting and the emergence of the proto-European state which seeks to make Europe competitive in geo-political terms presents a threat to the existing state order, this process is still in its infancy. Equally important are factors such as the fiscal crisis and the reconceptualization of democracy. Certainly these are all factors to be considered in any attempt to come to terms with the future of minority language groups.

Whether we support the argument that sociology as a discipline is relevant to the study of language in society (Williams, 1999a), or whether we argue that the discipline has much to offer the analyst but that we must come to terms both with its limitations and the manner in which society is being transformed, it is clear that the study of language in society must take account of such arguments. It is no longer sufficient to resort to the orthodoxies of classical sociology and the works of the founding fathers. For this reason, before proceeding to our own work we would like to consider briefly how the social sciences have been deployed to study the Welsh-language group within Wales.

Modern empiricism and the social sciences

Interpretations of social life in terms of objective, technological, demographic or economic evolution incur the danger of reducing social life to the confrontation of the future with the past, of modernization with tradition, of the outside with the within. All the social sciences in the twentieth century have expressed one form or other of evolutionism. Thus, as we have argued (Williams 1992a), they all carry limitations and biases which are manifested in the way in which they are drawn upon to explain some conception of 'truth' or 'reality' which they are meant to 'explain'. That is, the social sciences play a central role in the manner in which they construct the very subjects and objects which they purport to explain. This has been true of the manner in which the social-scientific disciplines have been used to analyse issues of language in Wales.

A second point to be made is that if, as we have implied above, the nineteenth century saw the emergence of a range of different political positions vis-à-vis Wales and Welsh, it is inevitable that the two objects 'Wales' and 'Welsh' are subject to quite different constructions within the respective discourses. If, on the other hand, the social sciences are themselves merely discourses, it is unlikely that they can be brought to bear upon these differences in order to resolve competing constructions in relation to 'truth' or 'reality'. None the less, analysts have attempted this, while also limiting attempts to conceal their own subjectivity or their own positions as subjects within the resultant discourse. That is, accountability was limited to a faith in the objectivity of the theoretical and disciplinary position and the associated reporting discourse of academic writing. Some have been aware of some of these constraints but, by and large, the work on

Welsh which has carried either a personal or a disciplinary reflexivity has been rare, and the bulk of the work, as with most of the work in sociolinguistics and the sociology of language, has slavishly replicated the work of others, complete with their conceptual and theoretical orientations. All we can achieve here is to outline briefly some of the issues involved.

We have a range of accounts of the nature of Welsh and of its relationship to Wales. These differences are accounted for by differences in disciplinary emphases, by different theoretical orientations and by the political position of the analyst *vis-à-vis* the object under scrutiny. Two evident factors of division and difference involve the manner in which Welsh is constructed *vis-à-vis* Wales. First, the construction of Welsh does not merely construct an object – the Welsh language, but also the subject positions that relate to that object – Welsh speakers. It also constructs that population which is constructed by exclusion – non-Welsh speakers. That exclusion focuses upon the relationship between 'us' and 'them' in such a way that it conveys a sense of being a stranger. Thus when the meaning of 'Wales' and 'Welsh language' are synonymous, it excludes subject places which may pertain to one but not the other of these two objects. There is a lack of stability in the relationship between these two objects which obliges a degree of reflexivity and contestation of meaning. The same is true of the construction of Wales as a 'region' on the one hand, and as a 'nation' on the other. It is axiomatic that a 'region' is part of some larger spatial, usually political, entity. Until recently within Britain the preconstructed (Britain) was stabilized, and it was not this preconstructed that was contested but, rather, the political opposition between 'nation' and 'region'. What is clear is that the different analysts have all been drawn into these difference places as subjects that relate in particular ways to these constructed objects. Thus, much of Marxist analysis gives precedence to class and sees language groups as outmoded. Most fail to see a language group as a social group and merely reify language in analysing it.

At the end of the nineteenth century the initial statements appeared that reflected a trend that has become characteristic of twentieth-century empiricism, and in particular of what has become known as geolinguistics. This was in the form of a book by Southall (1895) which discussed the 1891 language data from the census. By now the raw data from this census is available for analysis, work that is currently being undertaken by the Centre for Advanced Welsh and

Celtic Studies. Prior to the 1991 census, almost all the work on census data inevitably focused upon the limited amount of data available from the published decennial reports. The simple descriptive statistics have tended to be treated by reference to causality rather than relationism. That is, the theoretical perspective guides the nature of the conceptualized variables and, rather than accepting that correlationism merely shows relationships between variables, the work has proceeded to analysis in terms of causal relationships between variables. In a sense this involves an attempt to translate an inductive process into a deductive exercise. It is an issue to which we return in Chapter 2 when we discuss the relationship between census data and sampling procedures.

Most of the work undertaken on Welsh language census data has been undertaken by geographers, largely because of the success of the department at Aberystwyth and because of that department's decision to take a geographic as well as an anthropological direction (cf. Aitchison and Carter, 1994). Whenever the decennial census results were published, the geographers produced a spatial analysis of subjective competence, replete with numerous maps demonstrating the spatial context of inter-censal change in the incidence of reported competence. The main thrust of the early analysis involved reference to 'language zones', the 'heartland' or the 'core', 'Y Fro Gymraeg' etc. There is an assumption that the process from Welsh monolingualism to bilingualism to English monolingualism is an inevitable evolutionary continuum. Sometimes this is openly resented, reference being made to the reduction of the 'heartland' or 'Y Fro Gymraeg' as if it involved the dilution of Welshness. This Welshness is conceptualized as 'a Welsh way of life' (C. H. Williams and Evas, 1998) that is somehow distinct. The tendency to equate culture with the anthropoligical 'way of life' is never outlined nor operationalized, it merely exists as a 'taken for granted'. Whatever it is, its demise is a matter of national concern. Behind these conceptualizations are the familiar analyses of industrialization and geographical mobility. Inevitably, the way in which these concepts are incorporated into the analyses reflects the current modernist interpretations of an inevitable spread of 'modernization' deriving from outside the area. Whether this is regarded as beneficial or harmful varies from one author to another. Unsurprisingly, considering the period when this concept appeared, there was a tendency to superimpose on the spatial the usual configurations of modernism – arguments pertaining to lags in modernization resulting in the persistence of 'tradition', or the romantic tendency to consider the heartland as the pure form of social practice and cultural production, a form that is under constant threat from the external, urban and industrial language and culture. Thus we still find the argument that only those raised within the heartland and its institutions are really Welsh, despite the fact that more facilities for young people through the medium of Welsh exist in Cardiff than in Cerrigydrudion. This is a form of folk–urban continuum which still persists in presenting urban and rural as two different forms of society despite sociology's argument that each state contains only one society. Throughout such studies, the analysis remains focused on the spatial analyses of these processes and almost entirely lacks any sociological input, and certainly no reference to language groups as social groups. Rather, what we have is the reification of language in terms of 'languages in contact', or the reference to cultural area analysis which equates language and culture, often with an explicit support for 'traditional Welsh culture'. Even when reference is made to inter-personal communication, it is referred to by reference to 'code-switching' rather than confrontation between social actors or subjects.

Until the 1960s such analysis, together with dialectological studies, has been the extent of the work on Welsh. In this respect, it is interesting to note that the various community studies undertaken in rural Wales during the 1950s (Rees and Davies, 1960) make little reference to Welsh, merely taking it for granted. The accelerated process of change associated with the rapid economic restructuring during the 1960s and 1970s generated a new urgency and, with it, a new impetus for study. Whereas hitherto the social study of Welsh society was mainly in placid, descriptive, community studies, the rapid change altered things. Geography's inherent discourse and the focus on spatial analysis within that discourse had its effect. It means that while there is a superficial attempt to come to terms with the study of language in society, the understanding of the social is limited, and it tends to take a back seat to the distributional force that drives the orientation. Little mention is made of what the sociologist or economist might consider to be the relevance of spatial analysis – the spatial division of labour or the relationship between location and labour markets. Yet even here the work which geographers have produced with reference to Welsh has been uneven, to say the least.

The same problem of space and evolutionism is evident in the work of political scientists, who have tended to treat Welsh as a survival

from a 'tradition' that has disappeared from the modern, urban/
industrial context, and survives because of a distance from 'modern'
centres of modern/rational communication, most notably London.
This diffusionism is evident in the work of Madgwick, Balsom and
van Mechelem (1984) who crudely established what they regarded to
be indicators of 'Welsh culture', among which was Welsh-language
competence, before proceeding to describe this by reference to a
'tradition' that was counterpoised in time and space to the 'modernity' which had yet to diffuse to these locations and actors. Speaking
Welsh, singing Welsh hymns, and similar activities were denigrated
as outmoded practices related to an irrational adherence to the past. It
is merely another version of the unfortunate tendency to construct the
concept of 'ethnicity' by reference to cultural deviation from the
normative, and the associated labelling of this deviant by reference to
emotion rather than reason. In this respect political science is not
alone in constructing the victim. This line of argument persists in the
work of Balsom (1985) who lays claim to the existence of three kinds
of 'Wales'. His argument is based upon language and 'chosen
national identity' and the effects on voting behaviour. Its weakness
derives from the tendency to equate rationalism with voting behaviour, and to infer specific common 'cultural' features from the
resultant correlations which are then given a spatial or distributional
context. No attempt is made to define the nature of culture and to
show how it generates the different kinds of 'Welshness', nor to
account for the spatial variations other than by reference to 'Welsh
Wales', 'Y Fro Gymraeg' and 'British Wales'. It is precisely the kind
of journalistic venture that gains attention while lacking substance.

In some respects, the work which E. Glyn Lewis undertook at this
time stands out in the sense that it is far more orthodox by reference
to North American sociology of language than any of the other academics who have worked on Welsh. This partly accounts for the
esteem with which his work was regarded in North America. It
encompassed the modernization thesis and the associated structural
functionalist work of mainstream American sociology during the
1960s and 1970s. While his contribution deserves greater acknowledgement than it has received in Wales, we suspect that the persistent
tendency for his studies to portray a gloomy future for the Welsh-
language group was a hindrance in this respect. He was the driving
force behind the early study of language attitudes and Welsh-medium
education (Sharp et al., 1973), and he made numerous contributions

to the main international journals at a time when the sociological study of Welsh was in its infancy. His work certainly inspired further work on attitudes and language to the extent that it has become *de rigueur* in much of what passes as the sociology of language in Wales.

A number of factors contributed to an upsurge in activity during the 1960s and 1970s. The atheoretical spatial correlationism of the pre-1970s gave way to a far more analytical orientation, with the consequence that specific divisions emerged, both in the terms of reference of the analyst, and of the consequence for the description of the social and cultural processes. The rapid process of cultural change associated with the economic restructuring, which involved the relocation of manufacturing activity from the English core to the periphery, contributed to a rapid decline in the percentage of speakers within what had been referred to as the 'heartland'. It followed the replacement of labour by machinery in the agricultural sector and the demise of the slate industry. This generated a crisis and a sense of panic among some Welsh speakers. Analysts expressed concern that the 'heartland' was being fragmented into 'islands' or 'pools'. It led to a heightened political activity involving an increase in the membership of Plaid Cymru, and the formation of Cymdeithas yr Iaith Gymraeg, the Welsh Language Society, which adopted a militant stance in response to the emotive analysis of the data available on Welsh-language competence undertaken by Saunders Lewis. This, in turn, led to an increased willingness to countenance a consideration of what sort of intervention could sustain the language group. Such intervention was, in a sense, the initial step in developing a planning orientation which, in some respects, paralleled the growth in interest in language planning even if the orientation was quite different. Welsh became an explicit political object.

Equally important was a shift in the focus of sociological theory, away from the predominant structural functional and modernization emphasis which had dominated mainstream sociology for some time, towards the neo-Marxism that derived from the dependency theorists critique of Latin America (Williams, 1998b). Dependency theorists argued that the normative tendency to equate development with the traits of the states which benefited from development merely constituted a means whereby the Third World became locked into a dependency relationships with the developed states, a relationship which promoted a persistence of their underdevelopment. This theme was taken on board during the early 1960s by Michael Hechter who drew upon Lenin's concept of internal colonialism in extending the argument to encompass the Celtic nations. His book *Internal Colonialism* (1975) had a profound influence. The expansion of the social sciences within Wales during the 1960s extended beyond sociology to encompass linguistics and psychology, and it was the link between these two disciplines which was the basis for the development of the ethnolinguistic vitality model. It developed from the work of Tajfel (1974) and his associates at Bristol, but was taken up in the case of Wales by Giles, Bourhis and Taylor (1977), who constructed a model of what they called 'ethnolinguistic vitality', which sought to account for changes in the salience of minority language groups. Since both Bourhis and Taylor worked from Canadian universities, and drew upon their Quebecois background in developing their model, it is hardly surprising that the result involved a certain degree of overlap between work on Welsh and the work on French in Quebec. Among those who have been particularly influenced by this body of work are Aitchison and Carter. Perhaps this is hardly surprising since, as we have argued (Williams, 1992a), it is fundamentally a typological rather than a theoretical model, and since one of the main independent variables involves the spatial distribution of minority-language speakers, it fits neatly with the geographical problematic. It also suffers from any clear conception of social structure and an equally weak understanding of the relationship between language and labour markets within the dynamics of economic restructuring.

The work of the geographers and the political scientists points to the constructions of different types of Wales. Perhaps this is inevitable given the manner in which the relationship between language, nation and politics is constituted in discourse. The link between nation and language as related objects which relate to the same subjects has the effect of establishing a closure and exclusion for those subject places which relate to nation but not to language. This would seem to imply that there are competing discourses which create the same object – Wales as a nation – in quite different ways and, in so doing, involve different subject places which open up for interpolation on the part of the individual. This much is evident in the work of Giggs and Pattie (1992) who have pursued and extended our own line of analysis of the 1981 census data (Williams, 1987a) in order to demonstrate the different economic structure of Welsh speakers, non-Welsh-born and Welsh-born non-Welsh speakers. While revealing the progressive reduction in socio-economic status between non-Welsh-born Welsh speakers, and Welsh-born non-Welsh speakers, rather than focusing upon the privileged position of the non-Welsh-born as we have done, they focus upon the other two strata, claiming that the media status of the Welsh speakers betrays an élitism by reference to Welsh-born non-Welsh speakers. The issue at stake here revolves around the issue of language and labour market segmentation and the manner in which it excludes non-Welsh speakers. It is an argument strongly made by the occasional forays of the non-Welsh-born into the debate who, arguing from a universalist British position, claim not only that it is exclusionary but also racist (Denney, 1991; Denney, Borland and Fevre, 1992; Williams, 1994). What is interesting in the argument of Giggs and Pattie (1992) is that it speaks not from the place of the universal, but rather from that of the Welsh person, arguing that it has a divisive effect by reference to Wales as a unifying force or nation. This is partly a consequence of the absence of any conception of power by reference to socio-economic determinants *vis-à-vis* the labour market, something that is not assisted by their Weberian conceptualization. Our own position is that, given the role of rational instrumentality in the modernist discourse which supports capitalist development, it is only by opening the labour market to minority languages that non-speakers will be sufficiently motivated to accommodate the production of the language (Williams, Roberts and Isaac, 1978). Local and regional market segmentation is the consequence, at least until a bilingual society exists (Williams and Morris, 1995). Clearly all the places from which these different studies speak allow certain things to be said about Wales and Welsh while limiting other statements. It is an indication that the question of 'what is Wales' (Williams, 1984) remains unanswered, and may never be answered, given the dynamic nature of social and cultural change. It certainly indicates that no single concept of Wales is stabilized. The various metadiscourses reflect not merely the different theoretical positions and the manner in which they determine what can and cannot be said, but also the political position which the author assumes *vis-à-vis* the construction of the social.

In many respects the work of Giggs and Pattie (1992) reflects the recent preoccupation with the statistical analyses of census data in order to identify social groups which deviate from the norm by reference to the position within the division of labour. Our own position on this has been that this is structurally determined, being a feature of the manner in which state regulatory principles of regional development generate such anomalies. The converse argument is evident in the claims of Menter a Busnes that the culture of Welsh speakers inhibits the development of entrepreneurial activity. Inevitably such culturist arguments lead to a 'blaming of the victim' and an associated hierarchical valuation of cultures, however they are defined. That is, where the social sciences have played a central role in constructing the victim, practitioners now blame the victim.

Inevitably our own work was subject to the same limitations. From the outset, our goal was that of treating minority language groups as normative rather than by reference to deviation from the rationality of normativity which the prevailing modernist sociological discourse claimed was essential for what they called 'ethnic groups' (Williams, 1979). Furthermore, we insisted that the normative was always a matter of struggle between social groups, among which were language groups. These simple observations and objectives had far-reaching implications. What we sought to achieve was to draw upon the conflict perspective of Marxism in order to redress the statist bias that was inherent in the more orthodox structural functionalist and modernization perspectives that prevailed during the 1970s. Thus we adopted the production/reproduction analogy of Gramscian Marxism, and an insistence on not prioritizing class analysis but rather on analysing all forms of social inequality in tandem. Thus language groups became social groups in the same sense as social classes, a position that was assisted by our concept of language prestige or the value of a language for social mobility. In this respect it extracted minority language groups out of the orthodox discourse of the social sciences which presented ethnic groups as non-normative, sustained by allegiance to outmoded, non-rational, emotive cultures. In pursuing this line of analysis we managed to extract the sociology of language from its reifying tendencies and its failure to treat a language group as a social group. This was achieved by seeing the various processes of language production and reproduction as linked to the ongoing processes of economic restructuring. Our insistence upon treating minority language groups as normal in terms of sociological concepts meant that we shifted away from the customary evolutionism of Marxism as well as from the functionalist and conspiratorial tendencies. This led to a focus upon the ideological analysis of the French Althusserians which eventually became the driving force of

French Discourse Analysis (Williams 1987b, 1999b). What we failed to recognize was that Marxism also betrayed a statist bias.

Having worked in Latin America during the 1960s we came across the work of the Latin American dependency theorists early. Equally important was the translation of Gramsci's *Prison Notebooks* (1971) into English. In this respect our work ran parallel to that of Nairn (1975) and Hechter (1975). Hechter's concept of cultural division of labour was particularly important in addressing the relationship between the economic structure and language groups. The link of this concept to the core-periphery argument of the *dependistas* was equally attractive. This orientation generated quite distinctive questions concerning society and culture, an orientation that was equally applicable to language, given its social and cultural constitution. Thus, it was this paradigm which generated the specific questions associated with the sociological dimension of the study of Welsh, an approach which, at the time, broke new ground with reference to the sociology of language. We did not begin with the orthodox sociology of language nor with sociolinguistics, for it was evident that there were profound epistemological and conceptual problems associated with these sub-disciplines which had developed as a sort of American common sense. Rather, we began from sociology, as if language was merely another social phenomenon to be dealt with, and language groups constituted a relevant feature of social organization and social inequality. It allowed us to redress the static and consensual nature of the orthodox concepts of sociolinguistics (Williams, 1992a).

We sought to develop this orientation by taking on board the work of Poulantzas (1973) and Olin Wright (1978). The focus upon the cultural division of labour led to a consideration of how social classes were fragmented by language, resulting in language groups as class fractions within the overall division of labour (Morris, 1990). The main focus was upon the new middle class where the fractioning was particularly evident. The fractioning relied not merely upon the public/private sector division, but also on labour-market segmentation associated with particularist recruitment practices. By the end of the 1980s this perspective had been adopted by others, most notably Colin Williams (C. H. Williams, 1987).

There are a number of limitations to this body of work. It is an explicitly nationalist orientation, blaming the state for forms of economic regulation which disadvantage groups marked off by language and location, and thereby for promoting the demise of language groups. In this respect it remains a conspiratorial argument, even if the state replaces the bourgeoisie as the agent of conspiracy. Despite attempts to avoid it, the argument remains a functionalist one by reference to the relationship between the infrastructure and the superstructure. Such limitations were evident in our forays into the linguistic analysis of ideology (Williams, 1987b), while the structural emphasis of the socio-economic analysis failed to accommodate a coherent link between social structure and social practice.

3. Language Use

At the heart of sociology since its inception has been the centrality of repeatable and predictable social behaviour. In this respect it is surprising that sociologists in Wales have not previously sought to treat language as an institution by focusing upon the issue of language use. On the other hand, much of what is written by sociologists about Wales could equally apply to anywhere in England and the language group tends, at best, to be regarded as a peripheral interest. Thus far the limited studies of language use that have been undertaken have been highly local in nature and have adopted orientations quite distinct from those of the customary language-use survey. Thus our work on a single community in Anglesey (Morris, 1989) and on young non-mother-tongue speakers (Williams and Williams, 1998) have both focused upon social networks. The work of Harrison, Bellin and Piette (1981) involved formal interviews with the mothers of young children in a single community. Aitchison and Carter (1994) sought to polarize language use in two communities - Cardiff and Tregaron - in order to exploit the geographic conception of heartland and urban conurbation by reference to the domain context of Welsh-language use. Useful though these studies are, they fail to give a representative picture of language use in Wales.

It was the Irish case which constituted the first European minority language-use survey undertaken during the 1970s. This was very much the outcome of a state initiative and the general social feeling of unease about the future of a language which held such a large amount of social capital. Since then we can point to other such surveys including the Frisian survey (Gorter et al., 1988). This was somewhat different in the sense that it was not the result of a state initiative but derived from the interests and concerns of a particular individual. Other cases are Catalan (1998), Euskadi (1996) and Galicia (1990). These three all represent the outcome of regional authorities emphasizing the importance of language use surveys as a basis for language planning in the period of autonomization that followed the Franco era in Spain. To these can be added the various small surveys of language use that were undertaken on a range of European minority languages as part of the recent *Euromosaic* (Williams, Strubell and Nelde, 1996) study. It is tempting to suggest that these developments were the result of the diffusion of a planning approach that had been quite common in the Third World, especially the post-colonial Third World. In this respect it was a pattern which went hand in hand with the more general spread into Europe of the neo-liberal principles which had existed for some time in the Third World.

The conception of the need of a language-use survey by reference to Welsh goes back to the 1970s. A familiarity with work in the Third World and the recognition of the understanding of language behaviour that derived from the Irish study resulted in an application to the then SSRC to undertake a similar survey in Wales, an application which, for one reason or another, was rejected. It was not until twenty years later that involvement in the *Euromosaic* study afforded the possibility of undertaking such a survey. In order to supplement the European funding we approached the newly established Welsh Language Board, only to be rejected once again. Funding was eventually obtained from the Board of Celtic Studies of the University of Wales and we acknowledge their assistance in this respect.

The theoretical framework for the *Euromosaic* study derived from the same body of work as that which stimulated the interest in a language-use survey during the 1970s. This allowed us to develop an instrument based upon those principles, and the field work was undertaken by a team of trained interviewers from Research Centre Wales between May and August 1994. The data was analysed, side by side with all the *Euromosaic* data, at the same centre. A short report on the work was submitted to the European Commission in December 1994. This is an extended analysis of the data and a much more far-reaching report on the work.

PART I

Theory and Method

1

The Sociology of Minority Language Groups

1. Introduction

It should be evident that survey research bears a close relationship to the theoretical perspective to which it pertains. That is, the deductive approach is an inherent feature of survey research. It involves developing hypotheses based upon the relationship between measurable concepts, these hypotheses being tested by reference to the statistical relationship between the concepts and their measures. One problem associated with this line of work is that the philosophical assumptions or the problematic of the research is rarely questioned. Theories tend to be adopted from previous pieces of research, and a 'new' approach developed by either drawing on and expanding upon the results of previous findings deriving from these theories, or by making adjustments to the relationship between variables. Rarely do we encounter work which carefully thinks through the problematic, questioning the assumptions inherent in the theoretical approach, the line of philosophy from which this approach derives, and the implications for the meaning of the various concepts that derive from the work. A second problem involves the need to develop a clear understanding of what empirical correlationism can achieve. Correlations merely show relationships between variables; the explanation of that relationship is the work of the theory that is applied, and the associated concepts which the variables measure.

In a recent book (Williams, 1992a) an attempt was made to consider the bulk of the work which falls under the heading of Sociolinguistics and the Sociology of Language by reference to such a critique. It was claimed that these fields are characterized by an approach which is often *ad hoc* in nature and which betrays a particular understanding of the nature of society. This conception of society involved subscribing to the main limitations of eighteenth- and nineteenth-century social philosophy, which was an essentially political philosophy that fed in to the emerging proto-sociology. We

3

argued that there is an inherent sense of statism in the manner in which orthodox sociology has been constructed. This is hardly surprising given that sociology began as a political science, and that its main function was to sustain the new states emerging at the end of the eighteenth century and the beginning of the following century. The work of Adam Smith (1976) makes it abundantly clear that society was constructed as that which could replace a politics of pity constructed around the conception of domestic grandeur (Boltanski and Thevenot, 1987; Boltanski 1993). It was essential to create a society which could be an integral part of the emerging sense of democracy. That society was a unitary society in the sense that there was a single society for each state. Furthermore this society was the basis of a normative order of which the state was a part. It generated the idea of a society conceived of as the legal state, a collection of institutions which functioned according to the principles of universalist and individualist rights. Each individual was conceived of as a rational being, conscious of his or her rights and obligations, and as such would submit to laws which respected his or her legitimate interests and the liberty of his or her private life, while simultaneously the solidarity of society, of the social body, was maintained in good health by the effective functioning of its organs. This classical model was formed by the interaction of three elements – rationalization, moral individualism and the functionalism of institutions. It affirmed that the individual could not be truly human without participating in collective life and in contributing to the functioning of society. That which allowed modernity to hold on to its two supports – rationalization and moral individualism – was the force of the state and its link to what is termed 'national rights'. The common good, the general interest or the 'nation' was the basis for defining the good and the bad, the normal and the pathological, of inclusion and exclusion, replacing the sacredness of tradition.

The problem here is that 'tradition' was measured by reference to distance from a homogenizing normativity that was sanctioned by the state. This sociologism, which assumes the form of a communitarianism, of a moral and legal consensus, is no more than an ideology which serves to disadvantage and exclude while integrating, to affirm a superiority that reduces social distance. The nation appears as the political form of a complex and changing modern society where differences disappear, and where the triumph of reason is translated into administrative laws, systems of communication and educational programmes. This national-democratic model has permitted the combination of a pluralism of interests and opinions and political unity. However, it has also, in the name of progress and law, imposed the same rules and forms of living on everyone. Anything that is deemed archaic, traditional, marginal or minority is forbidden and made inferior because of its distance from an imposed normativity. The imposition of a supposedly progressive and scientific model of society has contributed to the destruction and elimination of language groups. Thus ethnic groups, which often tend to include minority language groups, are treated as part society, as part culture, in effect as the stranger within (Williams, 1996a, 1999a).

We now know that this founding philosophy of society was wrong, but as a discourse it has had enormous effects on social practice. More importantly perhaps, sociology as a discipline has been constructed out of these initial ideas. This creates a dilemma: if we are to draw upon sociology, how do we ensure that the sociological discourse does not carry these implicit and explicit assumptions which construct the minority language groups as deviant, in the process marginalizing and stigmatizing their members?

The critical reflexivity which has allowed us to recognize the statist nature of sociological discourse and its relevance for minority language groups has been paralleled by the work of those engaged in what is called socialist feminism. Beginning from orthodox Marxism, they argue that Marxism itself is a male discourse which contributes to the patriarchy of orthodox modernist accounts of society. They assert that non-waged labour, undertaken mainly by women, maintains and reproduces the labour force and that it is as important as waged labour for any analysis. Furthermore, it is not merely the by-product of class relationships that oppresses women, but also patriarchy and the class structure itself. Within capitalist society, patriarchy assumes forms that are interwoven with capitalism in mutually supportive ways and an awareness of the relevance of gender is as important as social class for an understanding of exploitation and oppression. This is a line of enquiry with which we have engaged by reference to Welsh and gender (Jones and Morris, 1997).

This kind of neo-Marxism operates together with the work that derives from post-structuralism, which claims that any aspect of social structure is conditioned by the social construction of meaning. This has considerable relevance for the work reported upon in this book, since most of the sociological work on class consciousness derives from the same kind of survey method as we use. As a consequence, class consciousness becomes a static and individualistic phenomenon abstracted from reported social action and the context of class practices. Recent work argues that class formation is more than the ideationally bound concept of class consciousness, leading to incorporating the role of language in shaping the construction of meaning.

This thrust takes two directions. First is the post-structuralism which denies the existence of any structure independent of its construction in and through language, while the other draws on the link between Marxism and critical theory. What they both have in common is a critique of positivism which questions the assumptions that academics take for granted when they write and read science. In this respect, the empirical work of Adorno (1969) notwithstanding, there is doubt concerning the possibility of the very empirical social science with which language use surveys are inextricably linked. Where they differ is that the former would tend to dismiss Marxism as merely one of the grand narratives which totalizes history and society. It tends to mistrust social sciences which conceal their own investment in a particular view of the world and the link of that view to its own prehistory. On the other hand, they both reject the possibility of presuppositionless representation, arguing that every knowledge is contextualized by its historical and cultural nature. Social science becomes an accounting of social experience from the places of the different subject positions associated with different discourses. Thus, it can never be the cumulative enterprise of modernist science that is committed to the general principles of social structure and organization. It also has implications for methodology in that it argues that methodology is not simply a technical apparatus but, when considered as a discourse, suggests that it is a rhetorical means for concealing metaphysical and political arguments. This problem arises by reference to committed Marxists who seek to account for language by reference to the presuppositions of Marxism (for example, Fairclough, 1992). Some might argue that what such work misses is the manner in which the state intervenes in protecting capitalism against its own contradictory nature. This moves beyond the claims for the relative autonomy of the ideological order argued for by Gramsci (1971) and Baudrillard (1981), but does not go as far as the post-structuralists who would advocate complete autonomy in claiming that Marxism itself is merely a discourse.

In our critique of sociolinguistics and the sociology of language (Williams, 1992a), we distanced ourselves from the orthodoxies of these subdisciplines, arguing that language groups should be treated as social groups, and that in this respect orthodox sociology should suffice for such an analysis. This means that in what follows orthodox concepts such as domain, diglossia, language maintenance and language shift *inter alia* are not encountered. However, it is also clear that such work must challenge the orthodoxies of sociology and that a high degree of reflexivity is necessary on the part of the analyst. That is, it is necessary to understand why things happen the way they do, and to do so on a critical basis.

One person whose work did not figure in that critique is Pierre Bourdieu. His work derives from the same Marxist framework of social and cultural reproduction as our own but is different in many respects. It did not accommodate minority language groups even though others, most notably Padraig O'Riagain (1997), have used his work on linguistic markets as a basis for such an analysis. Rather, Bourdieu focused primarily upon class varieties and their social status and ideological purchase. Before proceeding to an account of our own orientation, while recognizing the value of his contribution, we offer a brief critique of Bourdieu's work.

2. Bourdieu and Language

Given that this body of work derives from the same neo-Gramscian thrust as our own approach, while also sharing the reproduction analogy and orientation, many of the criticisms applied to his work will also apply there. Bourdieu's work focuses upon the role of culture in the reproduction of the social formation, and in this respect the central focus is upon social class rather than upon language groups, language being treated as a feature of culture rather than being the direct basis of group formation. Thus, it becomes necessary to abstract the idea of a language group as a social group from that perspective, and to apply the principles of Bourdieu's work to such an issue. The problem then revolves around the fact that language *per se* is taken for granted, and the focus for Bourdieu's work is on class varieties. This means that treating language groups as social groups demands the same orientation to minority language groups, many of which lack class varieties because of the extent to which they are disassociated from the main agencies of social reproduction (Williams, 1987a). It is this that O'Riagain's (1997) work has sought to achieve.

Clearly, looking at the role of culture in social reproduction involves a central concern with the role of ideology in social reproduction, and this is a major thrust of Bourdieu's work. In this respect it relies heavily on the Marxist argument that the central ingredient of social reproduction is social class, and that where capitalism exists, then so will social classes which will be constantly reproduced. The main attention then shifts to how ideological forces come to play a role in legitimizing the process of social reproduction to the extent that the inequalities of social class relationships are masked and do not become disruptive. This seems almost quaint today when such functionalist and conspiratorial arguments have been replaced either by the pragmatics of neo-liberalism or by the anarchist strain of poststructuralism.

Central to Bourdieu's work is the relationship between the contrasting features of culture associated with, or available to, the various social classes. That is, the concern is with subcultures of class. It also involves the manner in which culture or subculture serves as the mediating force for the consolidation of social differentiation. Therefore, in a sense, it is the absence of access to the features of the dominant culture that are held to be responsible for the lack of success of lower class members. However, unlike the culturalist arguments, class dimensions of culture are not held to be inherently superior or inferior in themselves. Rather, the problem lies in the manner in which culture is manipulated by the power holders. Where a less conspiratorial view is presented, the issue of the role of culture in the hegemonic order is offered. In a sense, features of culture are akin to aspects of ideological control, with the educational system serving as the primary agency for the transmission of culture whereby the social structure is legitimized.

One of the issues that must be addressed in relation to different language groups must therefore be the relationship between culture and subculture. The more orthodox Marxist approach to this issue would focus upon the Gramscian distinction between state and civil society, treating culture as the universal features of society that tend to be produced and reproduced through state agencies, leaving subcultural elements to the agencies of civil society. The arguments of cultural anthropology, on the other hand, tend to link language and culture in an explicit way, arguing for separate cultures for different language groups. Evidently, this is far too simplistic an argument if we take the relationship between culture and society, and between culture and subculture, seriously. In treating a language group as a social group we are avoiding the issue of culture. It only re-emerges when one considers how identities are socially constructed. On the other hand, if we conceive of culture as the ideological forces sustained by a single society, that society being bounded by the social and territorial configurations of the state, then we must consider the relationship between institutional structures and cultural reproduction. However, if the agents of a minority language group are subject to the same institutional organizations as are the agents of the dominant language group, then the best that can be argued for the relationship between language and culture is that minority language groups may have a distinctive subculture. But if we conceive of culture as the manner in which meaning is constructed, a view that is entirely compatible with the discursivist stance of post-structuralism, where subjects and objects derive from the form of discourse, or from the relationship between linguistic form and the act of enunciation, then it becomes possible to conceive of distinctive cultures for each language group. Culture, ideology and discourse are interlinked. Evidently, the conception of culture bears a direct relationship to the problematic. It is such issues that Bourdieu does not address, and yet it is the very point with which intellectuals such as O'Riagain are obliged to come to terms. Unfortunately, the sociolinguists or sociologists of language who address such issues are few and far between.

It is here that we must return to Bourdieu's market analogy. The market analogy is, of course, highly familiar today because of the prevalence of neo-liberalism and the way in which it displaces the social with the idea of individuals operating on the basis of a market rationality in all spheres of life. We discuss this in detail in chapters 8 and 9. Despite paying lip service to the intricacies of the relationships between linguistic form, discourse and social constructivism, Bourdieu's argument is fairly simple. In contrast to Hechter (1975), who merely treats culture as a marker of the social group, he does seek to integrate the social and the cultural, arguing that value accrues to different social classes on the basis of how class varieties segment social reward. Thus each social class has a speech variety which is of value in the social world. It is this emphasis upon value that is responsible for the centrality of the market analogy in his

work. This value is conditioned by the sanctions and censorships of
the ideological process. While the link between social class and the
speech variety is explicit, the precise relationship between the
economic order, speech varieties and ideological process is less clear,
perhaps because the theory of economic order is not explicit, being
confined to analogies concerning markets and capital. The problem of
neo-classical economics and the conception of markets which operate
on the assumption of shared rationality of maximization is not
confronted, and is avoided by the role of the social in generating
normative order. It is also easy to recognize that there is the danger
that the linguistic becomes merely a correlate of social class, and that
placing the relevance of speech in the economic order is impossible in
any other terms. On the other hand, considering the same argument
by reference to distinctive languages and language groups, which
constitute status groups in being composed of cross-class membership, does allow for a clear link between economic and social
parameters. It is this that our own work has sought to achieve through
the concept of language prestige which it distinguishes from
Bourdieu's concern with status, and a consideration of labour market
segmentation. It is the kind of possibility opened up by the introduction of the cultural division of labour concept. This is largely
because the parameters of 'languages' are far more clearly defined
than are those of class varieties of a language. They can therefore be
made the explicit basis of employment credentials in an open way. It
is this that draws the issue of language out of the ideological and into
the socio-economic in a way that Bourdieu's discussion precludes.

It is also interesting to note that whereas Bourdieu has a firm rationalist stance to his work in the sense that he focuses upon the
pragmatic, rationalist actor as the basis of his argument, he does so
without very much conception of flexibility in the pragmatic use of
speech. In this respect his work contrasts with that of the speech prag-
matists and the interactionism of the anthropological linguists or of the
ethnolinguistic vitality school, who constantly emphasize the way in
which social position and social context lead the rational actor to
manipulate speech in the drive to seek out social advantage. It is easy
to see why this is so. If speech varieties are inextricably linked to
social class as class varieties, then it is difficult to conceive how the
single actor can have access to more than one class variety. Similarly,
it would only be the irrational who would not deploy speech in
order to facilitate social mobility. That is, social mobility would be

determined not by the economic order, but by the pragmatism of the individual. It is such points that lead many linguists to claim that Bourdieu simply does not understand language and linguistics! More important, perhaps, is how different problematics pertain to the relationship between the individual and political philosophy, Marxism treating the individual as constrained by structure, as opposed to the freedom of the individual to determine his or her own destiny within the liberal behaviourist philosophies that sustain pragmatic linguistics. The only rider to this is Bourdieu's observation that groups and individuals pragmatically strive to retain their advantage and thereby thwart general mobility, but even this flies in the face of evidence concerning upward and downward social mobility. Thus, it is far more likely that mobility will derive from the general process of economic restructuring than from the devices of the enterprising individual.

Bourdieu discusses the relationship between the process of artistic and intellectual production and the structures which limit the selection, legitimation and consumption of cultural goods. An 'intellectual field' involving systems of related cultural agents (artists, scientists, intellectuals) and agencies (theatres, research laboratories, universities) are related in an apparently autonomous and politically neutral cohesive structure. Separated by the ideology of artistic and intellectual freedom from the economic, political and religious forces, the authorities which govern the selection and legitimization of specific cultural works proliferate. Art is given a superior reality and is reified, being viewed as the independent creation of the artist, divorced from social context. The direct claim is that art for art's sake is an illusion.

Both the intellectual field, involving the structure in which the individual cultural agents work, and the cultural field, which involves the set of themes and problems taken up by cultural producers, are characterized by internal oppositions, conflict and competition. Thus, for example, in the intellectual field authorities compete for the right to select and consecrate culture and, in so doing, compete for power and legitimacy. In the cultural field, themes and problems compete for dominance. Thus universities, for example, become the basis for reinforcing those social groups which support and sanction their choice. Education is seen as the focus for the conservation of culture and for its reproduction, providing for the continuity and consensus within cultural goods. The individual unconsciously acquires a whole system of categories of perception and thought – a *habitus*. This is another way of expressing the importance of normativity and social order, and is not too far removed from the concept of institutionalization. Also there is a functionalist bent to the argument in that the link between education and the needs of state-level labour markets is conditioned by the ideological order. Common culture is seen as a source of social integration. On the other hand, the segregation of schooling creates a cultural rift between social classes, with the academic curriculum of the higher classes allowing them to understand and apply the cultural code. Within this essentially functionalist argument, culture therefore becomes a mechanism for class reproduction. However, culture does not merely classify knowledge, it classifies the classifiers by creating a distinction between those who have the monopoly of the instruments of legitimate culture and those who are deprived of them. Legitimacy of the symbolic order thereby assumes a symbolic form, a form that is hidden. Meanings are imposed through categories and concepts in thought and communication, allowing social classes to assert their power. By making legitimate only those cultural forms which are their own, the dominant classes are able to ensure the reproduction of their particular subculture and the 'master patterns' which underlie it. Schooling does not transmit a collective culture, but rather the subculture of the dominant classes. Also, for the dominant classes there is an overlap between family subculture and school subculture, simultaneously denigrating the family subculture of the subordinate classes.

Clearly we witness an analogy between economic capital and cultural capital, an analogy that links to expectations about the future, criteria for success, dispositions towards dominant values, codes that decipher the message of the dominant culture, good taste and so on. For those who do not acquire such capital, the school is the only link with the dominant subculture. The rift between school and home life, academic and everyday knowledge, become the sources of class differentiation and reproduction. The family becomes the source of inequality (see Fig. 1).

Bourdieu states in referring to Austin's performative problem:

> la question naïve du pouvoir des mots est logiquement impliquée dans la suppression initiale de la question des usages du langage, donc des conditions sociales d'utilisation des mots. (Bourdieu, 1982: 103)

> (the naïve question of the power of words is logically implicated in the

initial suppression of the question of language use, and therefore in the
question of the social conditions of the use of words.)

Such a statement carries an explicitly instrumentalist view of
language. Language is treated as a tool to be used by the rationalist
human subject. In this respect it is a theory of the material efficacy of
material practice, entirely consistent with the Marxist problematic.
He proceeds to claim that to seek the principles of logic and the efficacy of institutional language is to ignore the authority vested from
outside of language.

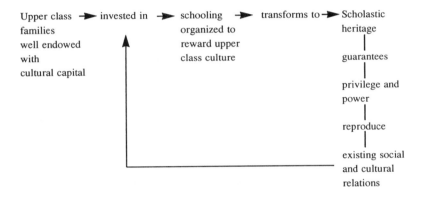

Fig. 1. **Schematic representation of Bourdieu's conception of social**
reproduction

In many respects the model which Bourdieu builds appears to be
little more than an overlay of the reasoning of market economy by
reference to certain aspects of language. As we have already noted,
these aspects usually pertain to class varieties which are analysed as
symbolic manifestations of class inequality viewed from a Marxist
perspective. What O'Riagain has sought to do is to extend these principles to encompass minority language groups as social groups. In
this respect, it is a significant departure from the consensus orientation of orthodox sociology of language. The claim is made that
cultural capital leads to profit within a market place which is an
expression of a certain form of justice. The converse is that there
exist cultural handicaps which, presumably, carry negative capital
and which will not lead to profit. These elements are the effects of

groups which contrast with the performative feature of institutional statements which are of the order of a structure. Bourdieu proceeds to claim: 'Cette autorité, le langage tout au plus la représente, il la manifeste, il la symbolise' (1982: 105). (That authority which language represents, manifests and symbolizes.) This implies that the authority which a person invests is exercised across the manifestation of language, and represents speech, where the symbolic effect does not have any practical effect other than as the conditions of social practice where that effect assumes meaning. In this respect it is not the effect of a consensus except under certain circumstances because of a unique circulation. That is, for any statement to have effect, it must carry an a priori legitimacy – it is subject to the conditions of circulation. Bourdieu's work systematically lacks any theory of how a preconceived symbolic effect achieves its effect in social practice. Language is relegated to a sign or symbol of power rather being seen as the exercise of power. Furthermore, despite being seen as power, power exists outside of language!

In many respects his work shares the deficiencies of orthodox sociology which post-structuralists have criticized:

- the social efficacy or a discourse derives from its representation of the real;
- this real possesses a latent 'objective' classification;
- thought lies outside of that 'real';
- only true thought can be effective in the last instance;
- the truth of thought is the adequacy of the latent 'objective' classification of the real;
- in social terms the application of the preceding involves a classification of individuals as groups – it is a sociology that derives its hypotheses from social psychology without distinguishing the places of the persons that it locates.

Some of these problems derive from the conspiratorial nature of the Marxist model and its link to the concept of ideology as a conspiratorial process rather than as the effects of discourse on social practice. 'Thought' is taken to be at the level of representation, where all representation assumes a referential frame which cannot be taken as pre-existing.

In many ways, it could be claimed that what Bourdieu is addressing are the linked concepts of social order and normativity. In this respect he sees the order as a series of laws associated with the transmission of capital, and it is here that we witness the reproduction analogy. Language is conceived of as a feature of culture rather than as culture writ large. As a consequence, the laws of transmission of linguistic capital are a particular case of the laws of transmission of cultural capital from one generation to the next. It is also linked to the educational system. Thus we have the family and education as central concepts. This is the inevitability of the Gramscian model and of the emphasis upon social and cultural reproduction.

What also seems to be clear is that the authority that is vested in language or language varieties derives from outside of language. The educational system is one of the forces that influences that authority. That is, language and authority are seen as separate but related entities. Yet there is recourse to the idea of discourse, conceptualized within the same terms of reference. This only becomes possible within the orthodox context of the separation of mind as reason and language as representation or expression. This is conversant with the orthodox position of the sociology of language, but directly opposed to the post-structuralist position which denies the rationality of modernism. The core of the modernist position is the social efficacy of discourse deriving from its correspondence with a 'real' categorization. This leads to the analysis of discourse being merely a sociological analysis, or really a psycho-sociological analysis of language productions. Bourdieu's discourse analysis involves a sociology of language which separates the internal articulation of the efficacy due to the external force. Thus he is able to isolate words and also to make them function as social symbols with their content being entirely superfluous. This betrays a lack of relevance of linguistic form and its relationship to meaning. It leads to the kind of discourse analysis where marks are allocated separately from content, these marks being symptomatic of a profound function linked to the prestige or status of the speaker. It is an insufficient position by reference to discourse analysis, the creation of positions, and meaning.

Despite the tendency to relate Bourdieu's work to Marxism, a tendency that is evident in Bourdieu's own claim while also being manifested in the political contradiction between Althusser and Balibar on the one hand and Bourdieu on the other, there is a sense in which it is possible to claim a Durkheimean thrust to his work. This is evident in the manner in which one is left with the impression that it is culture rather than economy that is the driving force that generates inequality. It continues with the emphasis upon the family and socialization as determining factors. In placing the 'blame' for failure on the family, he would appear to view failure as the result of environmental rather than educational forces. The school becomes the place of the imposition of normativity of the upper class, thereby reinforcing his claim for the nature of schooling. He would appear merely to have displaced the spontaneous explanation given by the school as it relates to the 'inequality of gifts' only to relocate it in the family as the basis of inequality. His theory of educational selection seems to be little more than a theory of cultural deprivation, even though cultural differences come to be defined within the school as cultural deprivation.

The Durkheimean problematic invariably generates problems by reference to social change and class conflict. As we have already indicated, socialization seems to be the determining, all-encompassing, explanatory force. Power is exerted on the individual through the school experience and the possibility of social change through the creation of a radical consciousness is denied. The individual is seen as a social product of the structure rather being an active creator of reality. However, that structure is a preordained structure rather than the structure of discourse as form.

We begin to recognize a mix of structuralism in terms of the influence of Saussureanism and Lévi Strauss, Marxism and Durkheimeanism. This mix appears to derive from an attempt to avoid a crude Marxism by resorting to the insights of structuralism in which symbolic systems are seen only to be able to perform political functions because they possess an inner logic and structure of their own. However, his insistence upon the predominance of the Marxist paradigm limits the extent to which he is able to pursue these insights through the emergence of the post-structuralist problematic. On the other hand this Marxist orthodoxy does not extend to dealing with social class by reference to the relations of production, rather, he resorts to a discussion of class as a hierarchy of occupations. He also sees class struggle as operating in the market place, over the allocation of economic products in the form of goods or income. A Marxist orientation would tend to place this within the context of the organization of production and in this respect Bourdieu's position would appear to be neo-Ricardian or even Weberian.

Such criticisms extend to Bourdieu's conceptualization of reproduction which is restricted to the reproduction of social class relationships. Marxism should involve a reference of reproduction in terms of:

- the production of capital goods to replace those consumed in the course of production, and the consumer goods required in order to reconstitute labour power;
- the creation of purchasing power capable of realizing the value of the capital and consumer goods;
- the distribution of purchasing power in such a way that there is a balance of supply and demand.

This involves the central understanding of the dynamics of the circulation of capital. In this respect the state is central but, once again, we find that the state is defined by Bourdieu in Weberian terms.

From our standpoint, or that of socialist feminism, we should also refer to the prioritization of social class as the predominant dimension of inequality rather than viewing the different bases of inequality as riding in tandem, each of them capable of generating disparate bases of identity formation or subject positions that may exist in harmony or in contradiction. There is a need to recognize the relevance of language as the basis of group formation, such groups being a central component of economic struggle. In this way, the same social actor will be a member of both a social class and a minority language group. The central issue involves the conditions under which class and language group conditions are activated.

We are obliged to ask what is the value of the market analogy for the comprehension of language groups as social groups? Certainly, we must understand the abstract nature of economic markets. This is not a banal issue since the same analogy is used from the right within the context of neo-liberalism. Thus we find the Welsh Language Board making constant reference to the marketing of the Welsh language, and expressing language planning in simplistic terms associated with raising the needs and expectations of speakers in order to create demand within the market of services. In Bourdieu's case, of course, it derives from a Marxist understanding of economic process, but yet seems to draw upon a Weberian understanding of social class as pertaining to the market place. What is inevitable is the need to consider how economics are conceptualized and the role that market forces play in that conceptualization.

To a large extent, Bourdieu's reference to historical materialism represents the same polemic in relation to Althusser and Balibar as that which was witnessed between Marx and Stirner and Feuerbach. That is, it is an internal debate, and much of what Bourdieu refers to must be placed in the context of Althusser's position on language and ideology and the manner in which this was taken up by Michel Pecheux and his team in developing a highly specific discourse analysis that linked ideology to the social construction of meaning (Williams, 1999b). The only rider is that where Marx developed a polemic position, Bourdieu develops an analytic position and it is by reference to that position that the value of his work must be judged.

The merits of Bourdieu's work link to his explicit sociology of language. Its weakness lies in the fact that the implicit postulates of sociology are not addressed, and the entire exercise, to a certain extent, is a tirade against the manner in which most linguists reify language in treating it as an object. He treats language as a subdomain of culture and the classic sociological models are applied to the 'sociology of whatever'. This is again reminiscent of our own work which claims that you do not need sociolinguistics or the sociology of language, and that the study of the sociology of minority language groups is no different from the study of any other social groups.

However, he appears to make the following claims which require careful attention:

1. There is a postulation of the 'objective' existence of a social structure outside of language based on the economic infrastructure and involving the relations of production. This must be looked at in relation to the customary techniques of Marxism and functionalism, as well as by reference to the role of ideology in social reproduction.
2. In relation to that social structure, language becomes sociologizable as a reflection, as ideology or as a false consciousness. Language use is then analysed as a mark, as an afterthought, seen as a mask. The social world is objective, speech is external to the reality of process, the notion of 'reproduction' carries a finalist and functionalist interpretation. The existence of socio-historic subjects is inconceivable other than as locked in 'power'.

Thus the social exercise of language is no more than a regional activity of social life. It rejects the idea that all social activity, including sociology as a social activity, is discursive.

3. The Production and Reproduction of Minority Language Groups

In pursuing our own attempts to come to terms with the study of minority language groups, we drew heavily on the Gramscian orientation towards social and cultural reproduction. To this we added some insights from the Latin American *dependistas* and the ongoing work on economic restructuring and the structure and dynamics of labour-market organization. In emphasizing the importance of treating the issue at hand by reference to language groups as social groups, we were trying to avoid the tendency to reify language and to disassociate language from social action. We also wished to make the social the focus of our work rather than resorting to culturist or rationalist explanations that derive from the modernist tendency to treat minority language groups as a deviance from the normative. This thrust tends to involve explaining the behaviour or absence of a particular behaviour in terms of difference, thereby making the dominant language group behaviour normative and that of the minority group deviant by comparison. This proceeds to the point where the deviance is explained by reference to the diacritica of difference between the respective groups. Resorting to evidence simply on the basis of, for example, the relationship between language competence and sectorial involvement, implies a causal relationship without establishing the specifics of this relationship. A causal relationship is established *post facto*. Thus the work of Menter a Busnes, an economic development agency devoted to promoting entrepreneurialism among Welsh speakers, has consistently made the claim for their lack of entrepreneurialism, which the agency attempts to justify by drawing upon a correlation between the low incidence of Welsh speakers within private-sector economic activity in comparison with non-Welsh speakers. The under-representation of minority language speakers does not necessarily imply the absence of entrepreneurialism, however defined, and numerous other arguments can be drawn upon to 'explain' the correlation. It is this kind of work that leads those such as Coulmas (1992) to advocate the exclusion of minority languages from economic activity.

In emphasizing the importance of the reproduction analogy, we focused upon how a social group is reproduced or not reproduced. That is, we were interested in the dynamics of social change and how it influenced language groups as social groups. This is an area conventionally discussed by referring to the static concepts of language maintenance and language shift, which also tend to reify language. Rather, we chose to consider the relationship between reproduction or the inter-generational transmission of language competence, language production (the inter-generational gaining of a language) and non-production (where inter-generational transmission is missing). One of our central concerns was the dynamics of the relationship between these three processes. The variables we chose to focus on are schematically represented in Figure 2.

The value of such concepts is that they allow us to consider the relevance of different agencies for these two processes. Some of these agencies are unique to one process rather than the other, whereas other agencies serve both functions. Thus it is not inconceivable that the most obvious agency of reproduction, the family, despite the universal competence of nuclear family members, plays no role in reproduction, but that other agencies such as education are capable of ensuring that reproduction takes place. We also sought to relate these processes to the more general processes of social and cultural reproduction. This was achieved by recognizing that a language group is only one among several social groups which overlap in relation to membership. Furthermore, each social group has the capacity to serve as the basis of social identity, individuals being interpolated as subjects by reference to the various social groups, either as individual components, or as overlapping components. In this respect, culture is conceived of as the means whereby meaning is structured, symbolic constitution relying upon such structuration. It evidently has considerable relevance for the reflexive process associated with language use.

This orientation links with the relationship between the general process of economic restructuring that pertains to the wider processes of economic change, including the contemporary process of globalization. Between this higher order process that determines social change, there exists the policy framework. This is conceived of in a much broader context than that which usually pertains to language planning. Indeed our approach recognizes that there is a grave danger in isolating language planning from more general social-policy prerogatives and processes, an issue to which we return in the concluding chapter. This is because we recognize that language groups fit into the more general processes of social change which language planning rarely addresses. As we shall discuss below, this involves the manner in which the current discourse on social policy derives from

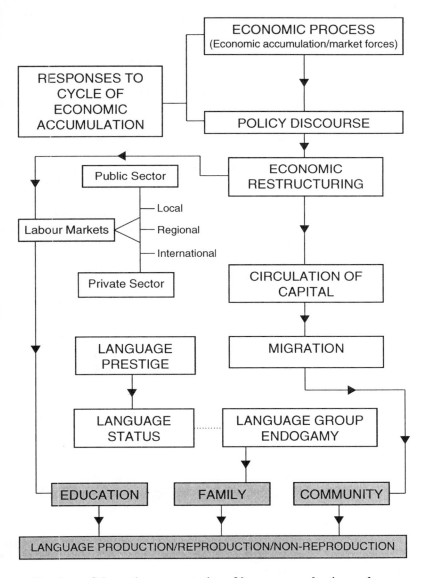

Fig. 2.   Schematic representation of language production and non-reproduction

neo-liberal principles, and it is this discourse which structures the means whereby subjects and objects, including language and speakers as members of language groups, are socially constructed. This allowed us to link language group structuration to the more general process of economic restructuring. Given the influence of the Single Market upon the ability of states to regulate the economy, it is clear that the relationship between the state and the economy within its borders must be realigned. It is no longer permissible to think of 'regional' development by reference to state regulation, nor to think of a labour market as pertaining to a single state. Rather it becomes possible and necessary to conceptualize labour markets in relation to local and regional configurations. Within this reconfiguration, one of the central dynamic factors involves the relationship between the public and the private sector, a dynamism that has particular significance for minority language groups as a consequence of the way in which language planning is conceived of as a feature of social policy.

Having conceptualized the process of language group constitution within a context that links the economy, social policy, politics, language and culture, we were able to consider the more precise details of the relationship between language and economy. We introduced the concept of language prestige to designate the value of a language for social mobility. This we conceptualized as a key variable in that we felt that it was the primary motivating force for those interested in language production as well as reproduction. Our reasoning derived from the way in which modernist discourse created a powerful link between rationality and economic order. Thus it became possible to link language and the labour markets by using this concept of language prestige. It made it clear that different languages held different relevances for different labour markets, English being of primary importance for the international labour market, the state language for regional labour markets, with the possibility of minority languages having a significance for the local and regional labour markets. What is missing is the conception of a state-level labour market, largely as a consequence of the advent of the Single Market.

In many ways, we adopted a similarly critical position by reference to economics. We felt that neo-classical economics and macro-economics were of limited value in understanding the relationship between language and economics, or the role which language plays in economic behaviour. That is, we sought to return to a form of economic anthropology which places a much greater emphasis upon the social subject than the more orthodox neo-classical economic approach which experiences great difficulty with accommodating the human subject into its concerns. Indeed, we felt that when this was attempted within the discourse of economics it was overly imbued with modernist rationalism to the extent that its normative focus predetermined its evaluation of groups such as minority language groups which lay on the margins or outside of the normative. This departure from the main thrust of orthodox economics, which, like sociology, is heavily influenced by a modernist statism, allowed us to focus upon local and regional labour markets rather than on the more customary state labour market.

However, we were also interested in the relations of production and their relationship to language use and language group membership. This is hardly surprising given the relevance of the concept of cultural division of labour for our work. The work on economic restructuring indicated that the emphasis on the spatial division of labour in relation to ownership that derives from the dependency framework, at least in the private sector, meant the tendency for firms from outside of Wales to seek labour within Wales, and the associated tendency for managerial positions to assume a strong tendency towards spiralism, would have implications for the relations of production and for the role of language in these relations. The entry of the use of Welsh into the relations of production is by no means uniform.

There is an evident link between education and the labour markets in that the function of education has always been to inculcate both a sense of normativity associated with state nationalism and an adequacy in relation to the economic needs of the state. Thus the entry of minority languages into the labour market is paralleled by their entry into formal education. Therefore, viewing education as a primary agency of language production and reproduction was also a means whereby a direct link with economic process was achieved within our schema.

An appreciation of the economic order leads to an awareness of the relationship between the circulation of capital and the more general process of the circulation of people, or migration. It is but a small step to recognize that the profound influence which in-migration of non-speakers into the autochthonous territories of minority language groups has upon language group reproduction really derives from cycles of economic change. Such in-migration influences language group endogamy and, in turn, the ability of the family to serve as an agency of language reproduction. It also has a profound influence upon the relevance of community as agency of both production and reproduction.

It would appear facile to claim that the family is the main agency of language group reproduction. However, the family, its structure and its relationships, both to the reproduction of competence and our central concern of language use, is complicated. The data presented in the Introduction and in Chapter 2 suggest that many families do not reproduce the minority language even when this is possible. Whether this is because of the negative identity, or because of the prevalence of arguments deriving from the official discourse and the normative order, or from other factors, is difficult to ascertain. In other cases, language group exogamy similarly influences the reproduction process and again we have presented aggregate-level data which indicate the extent to which this occurs in Wales.

We have also indicated how community was, and perhaps in some cases remains, a major agency of both the production and reproduction of the minority language group. The normative context of language use and its institutionalization in community activities would guarantee that the children of in-migrants who did not speak Welsh would learn it through community interaction. On the other hand, there are considerable differences in the demographic, institutional and language-competence structures across the communities in Wales. The way in which these structures relate to the other agencies, especially the family and education, is of considerable importance in understanding the processes of production and reproduction.

The third prominent agency of production and reproduction within our schema is education. Almost all Welsh-medium schools have shown their ability to produce a relatively high level of competence even when almost all of the pupils are drawn from families where Welsh is not spoken, and from communities where the language does not function. However, there is again a range of different contexts for the learning of Welsh in the schools of Wales. Again we would emphasize the need to consider the interrelationship between this agency and those of the family and community.

4. Language Use as Social Action

These agencies, together with the media, we conceived of as the main forces which determined the ability of a language group to produce or reproduce itself. That is, the focus here was very much on the process of generating 'ability' or competence. The relationship between ability and use was of a different order. Of course, we recognize that much of sociolinguistic theory, such as it is, focuses upon the issue of motivation and use, rather than on the structuring of language groups as social groups which we have addressed. As we mention below, this is the main issue facing many minority language groups today. We sought to conceptualize this relationship by reference to two key variables – institutionalization and legitimation.

Legitimation is a concept which incorporates both constitutional and social-policy aspects. Thus it could extend beyond language laws to encompass a variety of social policies which operate at different political levels. This is particularly relevant given the shift towards 'enabling' principles rather than the rights-based emphasis of legislation, a process that has emerged through the adoption of neo-liberal principles across Europe. It is also evident in the different educational policies that exist across the local authorities in Wales, and for the differing extent of the legitimation of language use in the public sector where the policies of the different authorities play such a significant role.

Institutionalization refers to repeated behaviour which the social actor takes for granted. That is, it is non-reflexive behaviour. It is a concept commonly used by reference to institutionalized racism or institutionalized sexism, where the speaker is unaware of his or her use of sexist or racist statements or behaviour. It is in this context that we think of language use as the taken-for-granted use of one language rather than the other within a bilingual setting. We refer to language use by using 'institutionalization' rather than the more customary concept of 'domain' because it extends beyond the relationship between context and use to encompass both interactional capacity and the manner in which the stabilization of discourses leads to language use becoming institutionalized to the extent that language use practices became 'taken for granted'. The tendency for domain to be yet another typological rather than analytic concept is also important. This also allows us to move away from the tendency to view action as conditioned by the centred human subject, and to consider the way in which social practice is located at the point where the human subject is constituted in and through discourse.

Thus, while the structuration of minority language groups does have considerable significance, and language prestige becomes a central feature of motivation, it is the relationship between institution-alization and legitimation that plays the main role in transforming structure, ability and motivation into actual language practice as stabilized practices. This is particularly important in that it allows us to distinguish between the rational motivation of economic orientation and the equally rational motivation that derives from the means in which non-economic discourses are stabilized.

In referring to institutionalization, we are obliged to consider how behaviour tends to be taken for granted as part of the common sense of life within the community. Language plays a central role in this respect and itself becomes a feature of institutionalized behaviour. Social change pertains to the manner in which this taken-for-granted is destabilized and the associated symbolic elements are reorganized. However, it would be erroneous to think of this as merely a reflection process where whatever happens at the behavioural level is merely a manifestation of some reified process referred to as social change. In this respect institutionalization is not only manifested in language use, it is also stabilized in language. That is, language is so complex that it is impossible for any individual to be reflexive about every word stated, how it is said and when it is said. Thus there are recurrent pieces of discourse which bear a direct relationship to social practice. These often rely upon prior discourse, stabilized in current language practice as traces of prior practice in relation to prior social contexts. In the same way, the use of different languages does not relate to a reflexive code-switching premised upon rational action, or upon such static concepts as domain or diglossia, but rather is linked to institu-tionalized behaviour associated with discursive structures. In this respect it relates to the social and institutional context, not as a reflec-tion or manifestation of that context, but rather as part of that context. Language is social behaviour. The respective use of one language or another depends not merely on the ability of the protagonists *vis-à-vis* the respective languages, but also on the manner in which language use is institutionalized or stabilized as language practice. Of course there are limitations determined by language ability, but there is also the issue of institutionalization among the bilingual population.

The other issue that must be considered here is that of normativity. It is a mistake to equate institutionalization with normativity as if social norms were somehow automatic processes associated with consensus between rational actors. The work of Foucault suggests that normativity is ingrained with power. It is also evident that there are different processes and struggles over normativity. At the local level, it is quite different from the manner in which there is a link between the state and normativity. Thus the concept of normalization with reference to language planning must be qualified if it is to be of any value. This means that language use within the community must be referenced in terms of the manner in which meaning is socially constructed as institutional behaviour, and how social change undermines the social and institutional contexts which support the associated stabilization. That is, there is a symbolic component to language which signifies meaning within social practice. Within bilingual contexts the use of one language rather than another becomes part of that signification.

In discourse terms, institutionalization refers to the stabilization of discourse by reference to the relationship between the social construction of subjects in relation to different objects. In this sense, it places institutionalization within a social constructivist view of social reality rather than the passive, perceptual models of subject–object relationships of positivism. It involves reference to the preconstructed or the taken-for-granted in discourse. Thus, for example, it is axiomatic that a region is part of some larger geographical or political entity. Until recently, mention of 'the regions' would have been understood by many as 'the regions of the UK', where the UK is the preconstructed that does not require stating. The overlap between state and society closes the space within which the difference between the inclusive 'us' and the excluded 'them' is established. The recent upsurge in importance of Europe leads many now to ask themselves if 'the regions' pertains to the UK, or to Europe. The meaning of the preconstructed is destabilized. Such things are an essential part of resolving the inherent ambiguity of meaning. The destabilization of the preconstructed leads to its deconstruction and to a realignment of the relationships between subjects and objects. Evidently there is a close link between stabilization and normativity. There is also a link between the context of reflexivity and the stabilization of discourse. The destabilization to which we have referred here also has implications for subject positions *vis-à-vis* the objects 'UK' and 'Europe'. There are many discursive contexts in which England is coterminous with the UK and the subject positions 'English' and 'British' are interchangeable. The link between a single state and a single society defined as normative is responsible for this overlap. It means that 'English' is the normative within 'Britain', the collectivity 'English' never being called 'ethnic' or deviant from the normative. The 'us' of English is coterminous with the 'us' of British, and contrasts with the 'them' of all those who are not 'British', the 'us' of identity links with the political 'we'. The normative of the English subspace is the same normative as the larger British space, whereas for the Welsh or the Scottish this co-determination does not exist, the situation being resolved by retaining the universal normativity and relegating the other to the position of non-normative, deviant or ethnic. This is achieved by strictly defining the cultural that links with the faithfulness that is required by the state as normative. The normative group is simultaneously defined by reference to language, culture and reason. The tendency to 'mean' 'British' when referring to 'English', and vice versa, leaves no space for 'Welsh' or 'Scottish' – they are accommodated in the general 'us' of 'British'. The destabilization of 'the regions' means that it is no longer possible to construct 'England' in the same way as previously in that the centrality of 'Europe' destabilizes that relationship between 'England' and 'the UK' which made them coterminous. Similarly the subject identities also shift and involves 'the break up of England'.

This has profound implications for subject places. It means that 'regions' may pertain to 'England' in a way that hitherto was not possible. The existence of several 'European regions' within 'England' breaks up the homogeneity of 'England' and the associated uniform subject position by the generation of 'regions' which pertain to a European rather than 'English' or 'UK/British' order. The 'us' of English is now fragmented into the 'us' of different regions of 'England' which are also European regions. This means that the associated subject positions which were previously homogeneous are multiplied and, in certain discursive contexts, are in opposition. That is, English identity is no longer as clear and stable as it once was. In some contexts the 'us' of the English region, which is also a European region, is pitted against the 'them' of a similar different region of 'England', which, being drawn into the same political 'we', is discursively no different from any other 'European region'. By the same token the overlap between 'European region', 'UK region' and 'Scotland' or 'Wales' means that the effect of the relationship between subject positions and these objects is different.

It is in this respect that we understand the institutionalization of language use as activity that is structured in and through language by the manner in which different subject positions in relation to different objects produce specific meanings of which 'Welsh' or 'language' is one. Thus it conditions the use of language as stabilized discourse but always with the possibility of destabilization of the relationship between subject positions and language as an object among other objects.

5. Conclusion

Most of what we have said above about the production and reproduction of minority language groups pertains not so much to language use as to the production of competence. This is a problem in the sense that it becomes clear that any focus upon language use requires some form or other of social-action theory, and we have sought to include this in our discussion. The question arises of the relationship between the structure held responsible for the generation of competence and the use of that competence in social life. This is an inherent problem of a sociology which sets store upon both elaborating the social as patterned behaviour which transcends face-to-face interaction and the actual implementation of the same behaviour between social actors. We have sought to resolve this issue by outlining how competence is generated within society before elaborating how individuals become social actors through the resolution of the ambiguity of meaning in interaction. Such a resolution is not a rational process in the modernist sense, but rather is itself structured by language. Thus the generation of competence and the conversion of the individual into a social being are both inherently linked to language. What such an orientation requires is to link the decentred approach of our social-action theory with a structural approach that is equally decentred (Boutet, 1994).

Furthermore, the contents of this chapter also point to the limited scope of our own study in that much of the data which we analyse below can do little more than describe the context of language use rather than language use itself. That is, it allows us to demonstrate where use is possible and where it is not. It might allow us to make tentative suggestions concerning the link between that possibility and the tendency to use Welsh, at least as it is reported by those using the language. That is, in discussing self-report data on language use, there is the recurrent problem of the normative effect, or the manner in which people report that which they feel they should say. We did try to control for this by asking individuals to report on what happened in concrete situations. What our analysis cannot do is to explore the nature of the process of language use as it relates to the details of institutionalized behaviour and the constitution of the subject *vis-à-vis* the social construction of meaning, at least not in the detail that we would wish.

These observations merely underline the complexity of the issue at hand and the danger of resorting to simplistic conceptions of minority language use and the steps that must be taken to promote it.

2
Research into Language Use: A Methodology

1. Introduction

Having presented an outline of our theoretical orientation, it is now necessary to clarify the methodological procedures which were deployed in guiding the study. The link between theory and method involves the shift from the construction of concepts to their use as the basis for measurement. The empirical method allows these measurements to achieve meaning through the application of an analytical procedure that resorts back to the theoretical framework. In developing the conceptual framework in the preceding chapter we have made implicit, and sometimes explicit, reference to tentative hypotheses concerning the relationship between language, economy and society. It is these hypotheses, involving the relationship between variables, which are explored in the empirical study. However, before proceeding to such issues, we would like to consider the available information about Welsh-language competence. Our reason for so doing is twofold. First, it will contextualize what is to follow, not only in this chapter, but also in subsequent chapters. Second, it is this data which serves as the basis for our sampling frame.

2. Incidence of Competence

Our starting-point for a description of the social and spatial distribution of Welsh-language competence is the 1981 census since it was this census which led to the first attempt to go beyond the published information by soliciting specific cross-tabulations from the OPCS (Williams, 1987a). Given that the same resource was available in the 1991 census, it allows us to proceed to a comparative analysis of these tables which goes some way further than the published material allows. We do not intend this analysis to be exhaustive, there are numerous other sources which can supplement what we have to offer (for example, Aitchison and Carter, 1994). We also devote space to the Welsh Office survey of language use undertaken in 1992 (Welsh Office, 1995a): limited though it is, it remains the only comprehensive use survey other than that reported upon here. In our view these two sources of data are the most useful for an overview of issues pertaining to both competence and use.

We begin with a consideration of the social class and occupational configuration of Welsh speakers and a comparison with the other two social groups – the non-Welsh-born, and Welsh-born non-Welsh speakers.

Social class and occupational configuration

In our work on the 1981 census we argued in favour of distinguishing between local, regional and international labour markets. By now this conception is common currency but at that time economists tended to insist upon a unitary, state-regulated labour market as the basis for their conceptions. Our standpoint was the basis for claiming that the recruitment of the working class was highly localized, focusing as it does upon the local labour market. The higher the social class the greater the involvement of personnel recruited from the regional and international labour markets. In this respect there is a sense in which the regional and international labour markets are far more open than is the local labour market. This is a consequence of the manner in which recruitment practices vary both by occupational level and by economic sector. The penetration of local and regional economies by international and state-level private-sector enterprises, and the integration of local public-sector activities into the state administrative structure, promote a structured overlap of the various labour markets. The control of recruitment and selection by agencies and enterprises located outside of Wales, together with the tendency for many of these agencies and enterprises to deploy their own personnel to positions in Wales within a spiralist mobility context, contributes to the generation of a specific structure within the workforce. This, together with the consequences of economic restructuring and the circulation of capital, and thereby of labour, was largely responsible for generating the cultural division of labour that was identifiable from the 1981 census figures. In contrast, the use of Welsh in segmenting local and regional labour markets serves as a means of counteracting the limited penetration of Welsh personnel into these higher occupations.

The distribution of the various groups by socio-economic groups in 1981 is given in Table 2.1.

Table 2.1. Welsh speaking and non-Welsh-born by socio-economic group, 1981

	Welsh-speaking		Non-Welsh-born	
	No.	%	No.	%
Employers and managers (large establishments)	816	37.9	1339	62.1
Employers and managers (small establishments)	1513	32.1	3202	67.9
Professional (self-employed)	188	39.9	283	60.1
Professional (employees)	638	30.3	1467	69.7
Ancillary workers	3054	46.9	3456	53.1
Supervisors: non-manual	182	38.3	295	61.7
Junior non-manual	3748	41.4	5299	58.6
Personal services	1394	45.8	1649	54.2
Supervisors: manual	693	43.6	897	56.4
Skilled manual	4285	48.9	4474	51.1
Semi-skilled manual	3250	50.5	3186	49.5
Unskilled	1776	54.0	1513	46.0
Self-employed	1001	39.3	1549	60.7
Farmers: employers and managers	509	73.3	185	26.7
Farmers: self-employed	1382	79.7	353	20.3
Agricultural workers	543	65.1	291	34.9
Armed forces	51	11.6	390	88.4
Unemployed/no job in last 10 yrs	4600	52.3	4200	47.7
Total	29623	46.5	34028	53.5

The 1981 figures indicate that the non-Welsh-born were proportionally over-represented in professional and managerial categories as well as in the supervisory categories. In contrast Welsh speakers are over-represented in the unskilled, semi-skilled and agricultural categories. Even when we make allowance for the slight disparity between the size of the respective groups this observation holds true. This distinction was even more marked in Cardiff where the preponderance of non-Welsh-born managers and professionals was particularly high. This was a consequence of the location of branch offices of companies with head offices located in England and of administrative centres such as the Welsh Office within the capital.

A central feature of the distinction between the labour markets was the manner in which social mobility varied. In the local labour market burgher mobility prevailed, whereas in the other labour markets spiralism was a common occurrence. Individuals were involved in career structures in quite different ways. The data allowed us to make statements about local labour markets and to recognize that the prestige of Welsh was restricted to certain locations where public-sector employment linked to the language prevailed – the administrative centres of Cardiff and the various local authorities. Within the private sector the situation was reversed and later studies identified, for example, the fact that in Gwynedd, the part of Wales with the highest incidence of Welsh speakers, over 50 per cent of the managers were born outside of Wales (Jones and Jones, 1994).

Useful though this comparison was in outlining the reality of a cultural division of labour, it was also clear that the third group – the Welsh-born non-Welsh speakers – were those who experienced the greatest degree of exclusion from the higher socio-economic groups (SEGs). As we discuss below, this was the point pursued by Giggs and Pattie (1992). However, whereas they interpreted this structuration by reference to an elitist Welsh-speaking group, we choose to emphasize that it merely reinforces the cultural division of labour, and that Welsh speakers are successfully resisting the cultural division of labour by resorting to an insistence on the relevance of Welsh for employment.

Table 2.2 allows us to compare the situation in 1981 with that ten years later.

Between 1981 and 1991 there was an increase of 19 per cent in the number of the non-Welsh-born in the workforce, compared with a decrease of 3 per cent in the number of Welsh speakers in the workforce. The Welsh-language group lost ground in the working-class SEGs of skilled and semi-skilled manual workers and the unskilled category. There was also a decline in the number of Welsh speakers employed in agriculture. In contrast the group gained ground in both managerial and professional categories. The non-Welsh-born, on the other hand, grew in number across a range of SEGs, most notably those of managers, ancillary workers, junior non-manual workers, and the skilled manual groups. In some locations it was clear that the in-migrant, non-Welsh-born were penetrating the local labour market. There was also a substantial increase in the number of unemployed within both groups. Furthermore, it would appear that the cultural division of labour has intensified.

Table 2.2. Welsh speaking and non-Welsh-born by socio-economic group, 1991

	Welsh speaking		Non-Welsh-born	
	No.	%	No.	%
Employers and managers (large establishments)	584	28.0	1497	72.0
Employers and managers (small establishments)	1777	29.4	4276	70.6
Professional (self-employed)	163	30.1	379	69.9
Professional (employees)	681	27.7	1778	72.3
Ancillary workers	3740	43.0	4957	57.0
Supervisors: non-manual	163	35.4	298	64.6
Junior non-manual	3863	38.8	6086	61.2
Personal services	1021	38.1	1657	61.9
Supervisors: manual	449	39.2	697	60.8
Skilled manual	2592	43.3	3384	56.7
Semi-skilled manual	2284	41.5	3213	58.5
Unskilled	1328	46.3	1542	53.7
Self-employed	1337	34.2	2563	65.8
Farmers: employers and managers	388	73.1	143	26.9
Farmers: self-employed	1044	77.3	307	22.7
Agricultural workers	458	55.0	374	45.0
Armed forces	56	10.0	504	90.0
Unemployed/no job in last 10 yrs	6768	44.9	8315	55.1
Total	28696	40.6	41970	59.4

Using 1991 census data we can summarize how Welsh speakers and non-Welsh speakers are situated within the overall occupational structure (Table 2.3).

Given that Welsh speakers constitute 16 per cent of the total working population it is clear that they are over-represented in the higher occupational categories and in agriculture, but tend to be under-represented in sales and the industrial occupations. This in turn leads to a consideration of the distribution of the population by reference to economic sectors (Table 2.4).

Hughes and Sherwood (1995: 22) comment that, since manufacturing activity in Wales is located in the industrial areas of south Wales, where the density of Welsh speakers is comparatively low, it is not surprising that it is dominated by the non-Welsh-speaking workforce. Furthermore, many of the rural locations have a high density of Welsh speakers, but even in those rural areas where the Welsh-speaking population has diminished, the agricultural sector is still mainly in the hands of Welsh speakers. However, it could be argued that this is far too simplistic an explanation and it should be recognized that the majority of Welsh speakers are to be found in industrial areas, even though they constitute a lower proportion of the total population in such areas. Other employment sectors within which Welsh speakers are prominent are the energy and water-supply industries, and the construction industry, together with banking and financial activities, and education and cultural services (Jones, 1992).

Table 2.3. **Welsh speakers and non-Welsh speakers, by occupation, Wales, 1991**

Occupation	Welsh speakers		Non-Welsh speakers		Total (100%)
	No.	%	No.	%	
Managers	3229	20	13270	80	16499
Professionals	2169	25	6608	75	8777
Associate professionals	1613	19	6946	81	8559
Clerical	2306	15	12706	85	15012
Skilled	2384	15	13714	85	16098
Personal Service	1788	17	8774	83	10562
Sales	1097	14	6826	86	7923
Industrial operators	1782	13	11635	87	13417
Agriculture	401	42	557	58	958
Other elementary occupations	1386	14	8362	86	9748

Source: OPCS, 10 per cent sample, 1994.

The Welsh-born non-Welsh speakers are overshadowed by both Welsh speakers and non-Welsh-born personnel in the higher occupational categories, and this is reflected in the social class structure (Tables 2.5 and 2.6).

The main disparity between Welsh-speaking and non-Welsh-speaking men occurs at the top of the class structure. Welsh-born non-Welsh speakers are under-represented among the middle and upper classes in general while being over-represented among the working classes. This also holds by reference to women (Table 2.6). The figures evidently demonstrate that the prestige of the Welsh language, or its value for social mobility, is such that it is clearly manifested in the class structure. It is this structuration that constitutes the statistical representation of the motivational inducement for non-Welsh speakers to ensure that their children learn the language.

Table 2.4. Welsh speakers and non-Welsh speakers, by top twelve industrial classes, Wales, 1991

Ranking according to number of Welsh speakers in each industry	Numbers of Welsh speakers employed	Ranking according to number of non-Welsh speakers employed	Total persons employed
1 Education	21460	5	77950
2 Agriculture	17290	16	35560
3 Retail distribution	16190	1	116510
4 Medical and health services	15700	4	81270
5 Public administration	15190	3	85400
6 Construction	15100	2	88470
7 Other services	8240	8	43810
8 Hotels and catering	8170	6	58650
9 Business services	6470	7	47210
10 Wholesale distribution	4900	10	30710
11 Recreational services	4840	14	24680
12 Banking and finance	3790	18	18940

Source: OPCS, quoted in Hughes and Sherwood, 1995: 12.

Table 2.5. Social class by language group of men, Wales, 1991

Social class	Welsh speaking %	Non-Welsh-born %	Non-Welsh speaking Welsh-born %
I	6	10	4
II	33	32	22
IIIa	10	11	10
IIIb	31	28	37
IV	15	14	18
V	6	4	8
Total no.	12406	18823	43771

Source: OPCS, 1991 census, 10% sample: unpublished.

Table 2.6. Social class by language group of women, Wales, 1991

Social class	Welsh speaking	Non-Welsh-born	Non-Welsh speaking Welsh-born
	%	%	%
I	2	3	1
II	36	35	23
IIIa	32	35	37
IIIb	7	6	8
IV	17	16	21
V	7	6	10
Total no.	9466	14228	32393

Source: OPCS, 1991 census, 10% sample: unpublished.

Tables 2.5 and 2.6 also clearly indicate the gendering of the labour market. We can expand on this observation. The vast majority of Welsh-speaking professional women are teachers (83 per cent), whereas professional Welsh-speaking men work in science and engineering (17 per cent), health (10 per cent), teaching (51 per cent) and other professional occupations (22 per cent). Educational experience is an important influence on how individuals are guided towards specific careers and occupations, and feminist economists have drawn attention to the fact that so-called 'gendered work preferences' which see women clustered in administrative and caring occupations, are linked to pre-market factors, partly involving education, but also associated with the wider familial and social experiences of women and men (Humphries and Rubery, 1995: 6–7). As we discuss in Chapter 5, the tendency for females to be channelled towards the arts and males towards the sciences sometimes overlaps with the provision of Welsh-medium and English-medium education in the associated subjects. Thus Welsh tends to be restricted to the teaching of the arts whereas English transcends both the arts and the sciences. This, in turn, relates to the prevailing discursive construction of the arts as emotional and the sciences as rational. That is, we encounter the central point of Enlightenment thought – the prioritization of the rule of reason as the basis for overcoming the indiscriminate danger of behaviour guided by emotion. Thus Welsh is emotional, the language of poetry and singing, while English is rational, the language of mathematics and science, in the same way as women are emotional and men are rational (Williams, 1987a). Language is constructed as an object in different ways in relation to different subject constructions.

Language group endogamy

We argued that the circulation of capital associated with the cyclical processes of economic restructuring led to a circulation of personnel and an associated in-migration to Wales. This, together with the effect of the negative identity on Welsh language reproduction, inevitably leads to an intensification of language group exogamy, and a decline in the ability of the family to serve as an agency of minority language reproduction. By 1981 there were almost as many families where only one partner spoke Welsh as there were where both could speak the language. This was reiterated in 1991, with 39,820 families having one Welsh-speaking parent and 42,870 families where both parents spoke Welsh (OPCS, 1994: table 6).

We have previously demonstrated that the Welsh language is more likely to be reproduced where both parents speak the language, but that the likelihood is considerably reduced when one of the parents is non-Welsh-speaking (Williams, 1987a). The 1981 census of population indicates that only 58 per cent of families with one Welsh-speaking parent reproduce the language, but when both parents speak Welsh, the rate of reproduction is considerably higher at 93 per cent. Figures from the 1991 census confirm that in families where the mother only speaks Welsh the language is more likely to be reproduced in the home than it is when the father only speaks Welsh, and it also appears that daughters are more likely to learn to speak Welsh than sons. When the mother only speaks Welsh, 58 per cent of daughters and 48 per cent of sons learn Welsh, and a not dissimilar pattern when the father is the only Welsh speaker, with 55 per cent of daughters and 43 per cent of sons able to speak Welsh (Baker, 1997). Table 2.7 shows patterns of language group endogamy and exogamy, and the subsequent patterns of Welsh language reproduction among the children of such families in 1981 and 1991.

There has been a substantial increase in language group exogamy over the decade, which points to the family being increasingly being weakened as an agency of language reproduction. However, the data also shows that there has been an increase in the rate of language reproduction within those families where only one partner has a Welsh-language competence. Where the father only speaks Welsh, there has been an increase of 13.4 per cent in the rate of Welsh language reproduction compared with a figure of 16.8 per cent when only the mother speaks Welsh. What we do not know of course is the context of this reproduction, whether it derives from family use or from involvement with the other agencies of reproduction. Nor do we know the extent of competence that is reproduced. Where both parents are Welsh speakers, there has been a further increase in the already high rate of language reproduction, from 91.2 per cent in 1981 to 92.8 per cent in 1991. Almost half of the families with only one parent having a Welsh-language competence do not reproduce the language.

Table 2.7. Household composition and language, 1981 and 1991: children in families

	1981 No.	%	1991 No.	%
Both parents speak Welsh:				
Children do not speak Welsh	287	8.8	285	7.2
One or more children speak Welsh	2978	91.2	3655	92.8
Father only speaks Welsh:				
Children do not speak Welsh	840	63.8	965	50.4
One or more children speak Welsh	476	36.2	951	49.6
Mother only speaks Welsh:				
Children do not speak Welsh	725	58.0	848	41.2
One or more children speak Welsh	525	42.0	1210	58.8
Neither parent speaks Welsh:				
Children do not speak Welsh	20558	92.8	25997	87.2
One or more children speak Welsh	1600	7.2	3805	12.8

Source: 1991 census, 10% sample: table 6.

The community

The in-migration to which we have referred above, together with other aspects of social change, also undermined the community's capacity for language production and reproduction. This is an issue which the geographers have analysed in detail (Aitchison and Carter, 1994). Most of the data that supports the claims made derive from the decennial census. The picture that emerges is of a rapidly declining density of speakers across most locations. Whereas the pattern of absolute number of Welsh speakers is similar for both the 1981 and 1991 census, the density has declined uniformly. The main change is to be found in rural areas with both the absolute numbers and densities being highest in dominantly urban and suburban areas. While much of what is presented by geographers describes the spatial changes over time they also suggest that there are social changes that are related. Thus they point to the tendency for the rural Welsh-speaking population to be older. Conversely they imply that for some reason the society in urban areas finds it more difficult to 'maintain their fluency and pass it on to their children' (Aitchison and Carter, 1994: 116). What is implied is that the interaction of the various agencies of reproduction has tended to focus upon the very areas where density is in decline.

Education

The localized nature of production and reproduction resources was also noted by reference to education. We will discuss the legislative context of provision in Chapter 5. Suffice to note that at the time of the 1981 census there were considerable gaps in the provision of Welsh-medium education. It was this provision which largely determined the rate of language production (see Figs. 3 and 4).

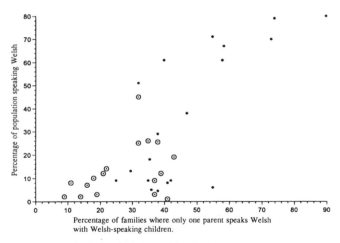

⊙ Districts with limited provision of Welsh-medium education.

Fig. 3. Language group exogamy and Welsh language reproduction, 1981

Aitchison and Carter (1994: 117) have indicated that, despite the extent to which there has been an extension of Welsh into educational practice, this tends to be misleading. They emphasize that even ten years ago Welsh was entirely absent from most schools, and far from universal in the others. Only about 10 per cent of pupils were taught Welsh as a first language and a further 39 per cent as a second language. It remains to be seen whether the introduction of Welsh into the national curriculum will have any bearing upon language use. We have our doubts. It is also relevant to note the tendency claimed for families where only one parent spoke Welsh to use Welsh-medium education as a compensation for the absence of the language in the family (Roberts, 1985, 1987). Thus it would appear that there is a tendency for the different agencies to function as an interrelated system.

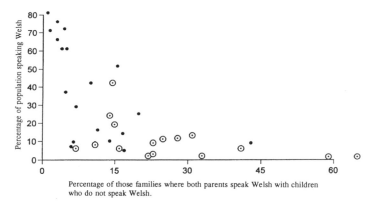

Percentage of those families where both parents speak Welsh with children who do not speak Welsh.

⊖ Districts with limited provision of Welsh-medium education.

Fig. 4. Non-reproduction of Welsh

3. 1992 Welsh Office Social Survey

We now proceed to a consideration of a survey undertaken as part of the Welsh Housing Condition Survey in 1992, under the direction of Howell M. Jones at the Welsh Office. This survey is important for two reasons. First of all, it interviewed almost 28,000 individuals on a carefully controlled sampling base. Second, it took the first steps towards a language use survey in asking some questions about the use of Welsh by the respondents. It was not a survey which claimed anything more than the gathering of what was seen to be valuable data about language use. In this respect, it was not conditioned by any particular theoretical orientation. This is characteristic of government surveys which, for one reason or another, seek to shy away from the political implications of theoretical problematics. Of course, even this discourse of denial retains a political position. The questions asked in the survey were conditioned not so much by an attempt to come to terms with the dynamics of change in language use, but rather by the information which civil servants at the time deemed necessary to collect so that social-policy objectives could be pursued.

The first important point made in the report pertains to what is meant by a 'Welsh speaker'. Despite the careful attention to randomness the survey found that 21.5 per cent of the respondents were Welsh speakers – 22.1 per cent of females and 20.9 per cent of males. This compares with a figure of 18.7 per cent in the 1991 census. This is the kind of discrepancy which we have discovered in various national surveys and which has been reported by others (Balsom, 1985). The implication is that the Welsh Office survey is the more accurate of the two evaluations. One of the reasons for the underestimation of the census data involves the manner in which the data were collected. The census data are collected for all household residents from the head of household. It is possible that those respondents who did not themselves speak Welsh, or who never used the language with other members of the household, may have been reluctant to record information about others about which they had little knowledge. The Welsh Office survey on the other hand asked the same question as that asked in the census of the head of household about every member of the household, but subsequently asked each individual aged over sixteen the same question about themselves. The comparison of the three estimates is given in Table 2.8.

A number of things stand out from the comparison. First, the social survey consistently gives higher estimates across all age groups than does the census. Second, the self-report affords higher estimates than does the head-of-household information. The highest discrepancy is for the youngest age group which is the group for which both sources used the head of household. Similar discrepancies were apparent with literacy levels. A slight difference in the question asked may account for the difference between a figure in the census of 16.3 per cent of

the population able to read Welsh and that of 22.5 per cent in the
1992 Welsh social survey.

**Table 2.8. Comparison of language competence by age (1991 census and
1992 Welsh Office social survey) (%)**

Age of person (years)	1991 census	1992 social survey informant	
		Head of household	Individual
3–15	24.3	27.9	32.4
16–29	15.9	16.9	17.6
30–44	14.8	16.1	16.7
45–64	17.4	18.4	18.7
65+	22.6	24.1	24.2
Total	18.7	20.4	21.5

The Welsh Office survey proceeds to break down those who spoke
Welsh into different ability categories on the basis of self-assessment.
Respondents were also asked if they spoke more Welsh than English
at home as a child, this being the basis for ascertaining whether or not
the respondent was a 'mother-tongue' speaker of Welsh. The incidence of the responses are given in Table 2.9, together with the
language ability of the respondent's parents. Evidently on a

Table 2.9. Distribution of Welsh speakers by self-assessed competence

Ability self-assessment	% of speakers			Mother-tongue speakers as % of all Welsh speakers	Population (no.)
	Male	Female	Total		
Cannot speak Welsh and never have	0.0	0.0	0.0	0	1706900
Cannot speak Welsh but could once	0.0	0.0	0.0	0	107800
Speak only a little Welsh	31.3	30.0	30.6	6.0	467300
Speak a fair amount of Welsh	89.3	89.9	89.6	27.8	94900
Fluent but never/hardly ever speak it	69.7	77.7	74.5	44.0	16500
Fluent but speak only occasionally	98.2	97.3	97.7	59.1	44200
Fluent and speak it half the time	100.0	100.0	100.0	63.6	78200
Fluent and speak it most of the time	100.0	100.0	100.0	93.2	229100
Total	20.9	22.1	21.5	55.3	2751400

Source: Welsh Office 1992 social survey, table 1.

self-report basis, 368,000 of 590,800 Welsh speakers (62.3 per cent) are fluent Welsh speakers. Furthermore, 326,600 or 55.3 per cent are 'mother-tongue' speakers. However, as the table indicates, they are not always the same people. The problem here pertains to self-reporting on an ill-defined criterion. It is quite likely that the 'mother-tongue' speakers who claim to 'speak a fair amount of Welsh' are indeed fluent by the criterion which those who recorded themselves as fluent have employed. It also appears that by these measures over a million people or 38 per cent of the population speak or spoke some Welsh.

This information is qualified by an attempt undertaken in the 1992 Welsh Office social survey to establish some kind of measure of competence which guarantees comparability across all cases. Those respondents who did not claim fluency were filtered and asked to respond to a range of descriptions as in Table 2.10. This does shed

Table 2.10. Understanding of Welsh by non-Welsh speakers and non-fluent speakers (%)

	Cannot understand any spoken Welsh	Can understand simple phrases of spoken Welsh	Can understand general conversation in Welsh	Can understand Welsh language TV news programmes	Total population no.
Cannot speak Welsh and never have	81.7	18.3	0.0	0.0	1706900
Cannot speak Welsh but could once	28.4	64.4	4.6	2.6	107800
Can only speak a little Welsh	4.2	78.5	12.3	5.1	467300
Can speak fair amount of Welsh	0.3	12.8	45.3	41.6	94900
Total	60.8	32.0	4.4	2.8	2374400

Source: Welsh Office 1992 social survey, table 4.

light on ability and it is clear from the above table that over three-quarters of those who claimed to speak 'only a little Welsh' could not understand enough to participate in a general conversation. On the other hand, among those who claimed to 'speak a fair amount of

Welsh', almost half could participate in a general conversation. What is unclear is the extent to which the respondents understood these measures as constituting a scale. This now suggests that the number who can at least participate in a general Welsh conversation is of the order of 536,000, a figure that is close to that obtained in the 1991 census. Of course, this does not mean that they involve the same categories of respondents. Information is also available about the language of the parents of those who claimed a Welsh-language competence (Table 2.11). We can also elaborate upon this relation (see Table 2.12). One of the interesting facts that emerges from this

Table 2.11. Parents' Welsh-language competence (%)

Parents' language:	Mother tongue as % of Welsh speakers	Total population	Welsh-born	Non-Welsh-born
Both parents Welsh-speaking	85.4	420000	98.2	1.8
Mother only Welsh-speaking	30.4	165700	94.3	5.7
Father only Welsh-speaking	16.0	155600	92.4	7.6
Neither parent Welsh-speaking	3.0	1990300	76.8	23.2
Total	55.3	2751400	82.0	18.0

Source: Welsh Office 1992 social survey.

Table 2.12. Respondents' ability by parental ability (%)

Ability self-assessment	Parents' Welsh-language ability (%)				
	Both	Mother only	Father only	Neither	Total no.
Cannot speak Welsh and never have	2.1	4.0	4.1	89.8	1706900
Cannot speak Welsh but could once	12.0	9.6	9.4	69.0	107800
Speak only a little Welsh	9.2	10.7	10.0	70.1	467300
Speak a fair amount of Welsh	35.2	12.1	13.2	39.6	94900
Fluent but never/hardly speak it	44.7	10.7	10.0	36.9	16500
Fluent but speak it only occasionally	65.3	10.0	10.1	14.7	44200
Fluent and speak it half the time	66.8	12.6	7.1	13.6	78200
Fluent and speak it most of the time	90.8	4.5	2.6	2.2	229100
Total	15.4	6.1	5.7	72.9	2751400

Source: Welsh Office 1992 social survey, table 5.

data is the comparison between those respondents both of whose parents are or were Welsh-speaking and those for whom neither parent speaks or spoke the language. Thus of the former there are 92,000 who currently speak little or no Welsh and of the latter there are 66,000 who now speak a fair bit of Welsh or more. That is, there is a net deficit of 26,000 between reproduction loss and reproduction gain. These figures make no reference to cases of language group exogamy, that is, to those cases where only one parent speaks or spoke Welsh.

Information pertaining to the relationship between age and parental competence sheds further light on the capacity of the society to sustain a reproduction context for the language (Table 2.13). This table clearly demonstrates that the percentage of the population within each age group with parents who both speak Welsh declines with age. That is, the capacity for resorting to the family as the basis for reproduction is declining rapidly, with only 9.3 per cent of children between three and sixteen years of age living in families where both parents speak the language. Even though 32.4 per cent of those within this age group speak Welsh, only 8.6 per cent of the population are 'mother-tongue' speakers in accordance with the definition of the 1992 Welsh Office social survey. Given what we have stated above about the tendency for some such parents not to use Welsh in the home, the value of the home as the agency of reproduction is even less than these figures suggest. This suggests that the focus upon the extent to which non-Welsh-speaking parents have sought to use different agencies for the production of the language for their children has tended to ignore the impact which this, together with language group exogamy, has upon reproduction rates. This also has implications for the corpus of the language.

Table 2.13. **Parents' language, by age group (%)**

Age of respondent	Parents' Welsh-speaking ability (%)			
	Both speak Welsh	Mother only	Father only	Neither
3–15	9.3	7.4	4.9	78.4
16–29	11.1	5.4	5.2	78.3
30–44	13.0	4.8	5.6	76.6
45–64	17.8	6.1	6.5	69.6
65 & over	25.2	6.8	6.1	61.9
Total	15.4	6.1	5.7	72.9

Source: Welsh Office 1992 social survey, table 3.

The survey also threw more light upon the relationship between in-migration and the ability to speak Welsh among in-migrants. This clearly bears relation to the difference which we have outlined between production and reproduction. Over a quarter of the population of some counties were raised outside of Wales, namely those of Clwyd, Gwynedd and Powys (as defined in the 1991 census, and before the 1997 restructuring of county boundaries). As we have suggested above, this bears a direct relationship to social class, with 38 per cent of professionals having been raised outside of Wales compared with only 13 per cent of the unskilled. However, only 5 per cent of Welsh speakers were raised outside of Wales, compared with 22 per cent of the non-Welsh speakers. Furthermore, less than 3 per cent of those fluent in Welsh were raised outside of the country. If we restrict the above analysis to those raised in Wales, the percentage of those with some competence in Welsh increases to a figure approaching 50 per cent. Evidently the figures of the decennial census hide a number of important facts, and it is possible to use the available figures to cover a range of interpretations – both positive and negative.

Finally, we would like to consider what the survey has to tell us about the relationship between language production and reproduction on the one hand, and the socio-economic structure on the other. We have already suggested that a refined analysis of the 1981 and 1991 census data indicates that there is a strong case to be made for the existence of a cultural division of labour, with non-Welsh speaking Welsh-born people being the most disadvantaged, followed by Welsh speakers, and with in-migrants being the most privileged. This is sustained in the evidence from the social survey (Tables 2.14, 2.15).

Table 2.14. Respondents' Welsh-language ability, by social class (%)

Social class	Welsh-language ability (%)			
	None	Little	Fair amount	Fluent
I Professional	68.6	17.7	2.0	11.8
II Managerial	62.1	17.3	3.8	16.8
IIIa Skilled non-manual	69.6	16.1	3.0	11.3
IIIb Skilled Manual	74.9	12.2	2.3	10.6
IV Semi-skilled	72.6	12.3	2.5	12.5
V Unskilled	76.7	10.9	2.8	9.6
Miscellaneous	74.4	15.9	1.0	8.8
Total	70.0	14.5	2.8	12.6

Source: Welsh Office 1992 social survey, table 3.

Table 2.15. Non-Welsh-born and Welsh-born respondents, by
social class (%)

Social class	Non-Welsh-born	Welsh-born Ability in Welsh		
		None	Some	Fluent
I Professional	8.4	1.8	4.9	4.0
II Managerial	36.3	22.1	31.3	34.4
IIIa Skilled non-manual	17.0	19.8	21.7	17.7
IIIb Skilled manual	18.0	25.2	18.6	18.8
IV Semi-skilled	13.7	21.0	16.1	18.8
V Unskilled	3.9	7.3	4.8	4.6
Miscellaneous	2.6	2.7	2.5	1.7
Total no.	2261	6125	2021	1467

Source: Welsh Office 1992 social survey, table 3.

Almost half of the non-Welsh-born fall into classes I and II, compared with only 31 per cent of those Welsh-born respondents who do not speak Welsh, and almost 40 per cent of those born in Wales who do speak Welsh. There is another interesting statistic here. It seems that 26.4 per cent of the self-employed speak Welsh compared with only 17.2 per cent of employees. This runs counter to the claim made by Menter a Busnes that Welsh speakers lack enterprise – as we have previously noted, this agency is dedicated to increasing entrepreneurialism among Welsh speakers. They have employed market researchers to undertake surveys to establish this claim, but have failed to produce an associated explanatory argument other than an assertion that relates values to culture. Undoubtedly, as the census data indicates, there is a skewing from the average by reference to the percentage of Welsh speakers in the different SEGs. However, we would argue that this may well be explained by considering how the language serves to segment the labour market within certain employment categories, most notably in the public sector, rather than needing some form of cultural explanation. This may well explain the discrepancy between males and females by reference to self-employed and employee occupational status (Table 2.16).

The tendency for females to predominate in clerical work in the public sector and the under-representation of both females and Welsh speakers within the managerial class in the private sector may go a long way towards explaining these differences (Morris, 1997). Given that one of the main factors in the promotion of entrepreneurialism is meant to be self-confidence, to be told that one is deficient because of one's language hardly benefits the cause of its promotion.

Table 2.16. Economic position of fluent Welsh-speaking males and females (%)

| | % of Welsh speakers | | |
	Male	Female	Total
Employees	16.0	18.4	17.2
Self-employed	27.2	24.2	26.4
Not in paid job	12.3	16.3	13.3
Total	17.5	18.7	18.0

Source: Welsh Office 1992 social survey, table 1.

4. *Social Structure and Social Process*

The preceding data allow us to develop a relationship between social structure and social process by reference to the theoretical framework which we outlined in Chapter 1. This gives an indication of how the nature of the language group is changing over time and of the factors that are influencing that change. However, as we have seen, the data are based on assumptions about the link between a single indicator of social action (the ability to speak Welsh) and indices of social structure. The present language use survey was undertaken in order to throw more light upon the detail of that social action – what people actually do with the Welsh which they can speak – and the various aspects of social structure. Thus the focus shifts from one of competence ('Can you . . .?') to one of action ('Do you . . .?').

Nonetheless, in order to contextualize language use, a tentative analysis of the preceding data is required. What we witness is the manner in which the continuous process of economic restructuring influences the ability of the language group to sustain itself. At times this restructuring process accelerates and complicates the manner in which the language group seeks to reinstitutionalize and relegitimize the context for its production and reproduction. Associated with this process is the ideological effect of institutionalization and the manner in which it influences motivational factors. This, in turn, is not disassociated from language prestige, or the value of the minority language for social mobility.

The data suggest that the entry of Welsh into the regional labour market, focusing primarily upon the public sector, has had the effect of a positive motivation for learning in certain locations. That is, language prestige is by no means uniform across the region. We noted this tendency on a local basis as early as the beginning of the 1970s (Williams, Roberts and Isaac, 1978). This generates demand for the production agencies, most specifically schooling, on the part of non-Welsh speakers. While this positive aspect of production is in process, the increased in-migration and the developing process of language group exogamy undermines the ability of the main agency of reproduction, the family, to operate. In a sense the increased language prestige has a motivational effect for both Welsh and non-Welsh speakers. This means that the negative identity associated with the denigrating effect of non-normativity and language group affiliation declines, but only simultaneously with the decline in the influence of the family as an agency of reproduction. This is a perilous situation in that, whereas an effective schooling system may well generate competence, without the other support agencies of production certain dialogical aspects of language which will be missing (Bakhtin, 1981). Not only does the corpus of the language change, but also the patterns of language use will be institutionalized differently from a context in which the language operates across a range of agencies and institutions.

This brief overview of the statistical data which tells us about the position of Welsh speakers in the economic structure, and their different degrees of language competence, serves as the basis for developing an adequate sampling frame for our study of language use. Evidently it would be inappropriate to extend a language use survey to accommodate those with limited competence and this was one of the first issues to be consulted in developing such a frame.

5. Methods

The interview schedule

It should be mentioned at the outset that we did not conceive of this particular study in isolation but sought to develop a comparative perspective, limited though this objective must remain. Thus we were eager to develop an interview schedule which asked similar questions

to the other main language use surveys previously undertaken in
Europe – Frisian, Basque, Galician and Irish. While wishing to
develop measures for our own theoretical perspective and the associated concepts, wherever possible we also attempted to incorporate
questions which would facilitate some basis for comparison.

Competence

The interview schedule derives from the need to develop measures by
reference to all of the concepts developed in our theoretical orientation. These covered a range of headings including use in relation to
the family, community, work and education. They extended to
accommodate measures of attitude and opinion in order to link up
with the interests of the main Language Planning agency in Wales,
the Welsh Language Board. All of these issues assume a certain
degree of competence that is not accommodated in the census questions concerning language ability, where the central question makes
no reference to any measure of competence nor to any context of use.
For this reason alone there is a need to pursue the issue via language
use surveys. Thus, for example, the 1991 census for Northern Ireland
indicates that 141,000 people claim an ability to speak Irish.
However, a language use survey in the area suggests that only about
10 per cent of these can sustain a conversation in Irish. Evidently
competence is one element that requires detailed attention. There
should be some means of establishing the relationship between
production and reproduction, language of domestic interaction, and
competence. On the other hand it is not practical to administer a
language test to the interviewee. To an extent, competence can be
established by conducting the interview through the medium of
Welsh. All of the interviewers working on this survey were fluent
Welsh speakers who initiated the contact with the potential interviewee in Welsh, and who proceeded with the interview mainly in
Welsh.

Clearly competence is a crucial aspect of language use. However,
it encompasses four competencies – speaking, understanding, reading
and writing (some would argue for the inclusion of a fifth, namely
thinking in a language). As mentioned previously, the census data do
give some information about reading and writing whereas speaking
and understanding are encompassed in a single question without
distinction so that a range of abilities pertain to these two elements.
This relates to the issue of proficiency. This has to be measured by

reference to self-report which is not ideal except that it can be compared with the interview experience where speaking and understanding are concerned. Furthermore, the goal of a language use survey is not to measure proficiency in relation to standard language, but rather by reference to competence in terms of the communicative aspects of language use. Competence thereby assumes a particular meaning within our survey.

Bilingualism is a tricky concept in that it sometimes implies equal competence in two languages – a balanced bilingualism – a situation which is strictly impossible to achieve. Thus we sought to develop a symmetry across the two languages – the minority and dominant languages, Welsh and English. This was incorporated, on a self-report basis, with questions concerning the four elements referred to above. Levels of competence were incorporated into the four questions on a range of 1–4. To this were added questions about the competence of others linked to the respondent – parents, partner, siblings, grandparents, children within the family and a range of other interlocutors in work and the community. The issue of the validity of data deriving from reporting somebody else's ability is even more complicated with these questions. In all of these supplementary questions, the competence about which we requested information pertained to speaking. We also felt that it was important to contextualize the learning experience for those who were not first-language speakers of Welsh. Thus questions were asked about the context of learning and the motivation.

Family
The issue of competence has already given the basis for establishing the language ability of different family members over four generations. Here we are concerned with the relationship between competence and use within the family, both within and across generations. In considering the use of language within families a range of dyadic and polyadic relationships and interactions are possible. The most obvious starting-point is the respondent. Thus questions were designed which sought to ascertain the nature and extent of language use between the respondent and members of the nuclear and extended family. Evidently this can lead to a vast network of kinship ties, and in this survey restrictions were placed on this extension by confining the universe to the nuclear family, both past and present, and the respondent's in-laws. To this were added questions about the

language use behaviour of the respondent's spouse. This had to be linked to information about geographical mobility, in that kinship networks tend to be limited in relation to access.

Two 'situations' questions were asked, one about answering the telephone and the other about the group activity of communal family meals. The first sought to link the family environment with the outside world, while the second sought to distinguish between communal and individual language use behaviour. All of the questions afforded the possibility of using one or both languages within the bilingual setting. It also had to accommodate the use of both languages. Additionally, scales were introduced in order to tap the extent of use of the respective languages within the universe of possibilities.

Education
With education, we move to a consideration of agencies which serve both a production and reproduction function, in which Welsh is taught as a second language to non-mother-tongue speakers, and also used as the medium of education of those whose mother tongue is Welsh. On the one hand we were particularly interested in the relationship between educational policy, accessibility and use of the available resources. On the other hand we were interested in the relationship between this use and its effect upon competence and use. The range of provision within Wales had to be accommodated, both by reference to the school and school subjects. Furthermore, it was essential to gather data about all levels of schooling.

Community
The community is considered in relation to both formal and informal social contexts. The formal involves institutions which exist within the community, whereas the informal focuses upon interpersonal relations with networks of neighbours and friends. In many respects we adopt a broad conception of community, since we include those institutions which provide a service in the day-to-day life of each member of a community, ranging from the newsagent to the dentist or solicitor. We also include the settings where people tend to gather. This breadth had to be accommodated in our interview schedule. Furthermore, we also wanted to conceive of this agency by reference to more than the respondent by considering the use made by any dependent children, as the activities in which such children are involved are to a great extent subject to parental influence.

By reference to interpersonal interaction it was not conceivable that any developed form of social network analysis could be incorporated into the formal questionnaire. Yet we were eager to know the extent to which Welsh was incorporated into such networks. We asked two types of questions, the first pertaining to a subjective assessment of the competence of those with whom they interact, and the other the actual language used in interaction, both with these same interlocutors and within the various settings within which they interact. This information has a value beyond the language use context in that it portrays the nature and extent of social interaction within communities and how this varies in relation to the social characteristics of the individual.

By considering the settings of the informal daily activities with which most people are involved, we wished to know the extent to which it was *possible* to use Welsh before establishing whether or not Welsh was actually used. There was a delicate issue of wording here in that 'ability' in both Welsh and English conveys meanings equivalent to having the linguistic competence oneself and the interlocutor having the requisite competence. Thus this distinction had to be made clear in the interviewing process.

The formal institutions had to be accommodated by listing all of the institutions that are of relevance to community and broader life for young people and adults. The information gathered here involved degree of involvement and language used. An attempt was made to gather a subjective evaluation of how the use of Welsh had changed during the respondent's life within these settings by choosing four broad categories – the shop, conversation in the street, church or chapel and other clubs or societies.

Work

Clearly, the use of Welsh at work is of central importance to our understanding of the extent to which the language is produced or reproduced. Thus it was important for us to establish the relationship between the competencies which people carry into work and the use which they make of them in work. We were particularly interested in the extent to which hierarchical work structures are either a facilitator or a barrier in the use of Welsh at work. Similarly we wanted to know the extent to which employers are proactive in promoting the use of Welsh in work. This is partly in order to ascertain whether the claim for language prestige as a motivational aspect of language production translates into use, or whether it is merely an ideological concept. Inevitably a survey such as this one which seeks to cover a range of topics cannot expect to accommodate the detail which is necessary to pursue the contextualization of language use to the extent that would otherwise be possible. Thus we have not been able to differentiate between the use of Welsh in work from the use of Welsh at work to the extent that we would like, nor have we managed to pursue the difference in relation to public- and private-sector employment. These remain topics for further research.

Attitudes

We have reservations about the value of using attitudinal scales within language use surveys, or indeed any form of survey. The link between the measures on these scales and behaviour is at best tenuous. Furthermore, the relationship between attitudes and identity is contestable and depends upon the manner in which subjective identity is theorized and conceptualized. Nonetheless, we recognize that they have become institutionalized within language use surveys, and for the basis of comparison we decided to include them without wishing to put too much weight upon what they claim to reveal. The main reason for including the attitude scales relates to the claims made by the Welsh Language Board that attitudinal change is the main precursor for extending the use of language. Our focus on institutionalization contradicts this claim and we wished to examine the validity of our own claims as well as those of the Welsh Language Board.

Formal cultural activities

Here we refer to two sets of information. First the various form of media productions including print and audiovisual media, and second the cultural activities which tend to focus upon the use of the Welsh language – *eisteddfod*, theatre, *cerdd dant*, *Urdd*, and so on. These are important in that they are held to be the core activities around which membership of the language group is evaluated. That is, such activities tend to link to a range of other Welsh-language activities.

Sampling

As with most surveys, the language use survey seeks to generalize from a relatively small group to the larger population of which that group is a part. It also seeks to establish the basis for developing an analysis by reference to subgroups within the sample. In our case, we are seeking to make general statements about fluent Welsh speakers living in Wales, which extend beyond the limited range of information that is available form the decennial census. It involved interviewing a small fraction of the general universe on a range of issues concerning all of the variables which we developed in our discussion of theoretical issues.

While we do not wish to enter into the general debate about sampling procedures, we will simply note that the basic varieties of probability sampling include random sampling, stratified sampling and cluster sampling. The quality of the sample is a critical issue in survey research. In this respect the size of the sample is important as is its representativity *vis-à-vis* the general population universe. Evidently the size of the sample is partly determined by the resources available to undertake the work. Whether or not a sample is representative is generally measured against characteristics of the population known from other sources such as the decennial census which has asked the entire universe about its characteristics including language ability. As we noted at the beginning of this chapter, there is a problem here with reference to Welsh. The census asks whether or not persons can speak, and/or read and/or write Welsh (OPCS, 1994: 3). The 1992 Welsh Office social survey indicates how this question is, in itself, inadequate. For this reason, we chose to use the same Welsh Office survey as the basis for developing a representative sample of fluent Welsh speakers.

Beyond the questions about reading and writing in the census survey, no attempt is made to probe the extent and nature of competence. Furthermore, in relation to dependent children, the questions tend to be answered by their parents who may not themselves have any knowledge of Welsh. The self-report nature of the exercise means that the 'meaning' of the questions is a matter of interpretation about each question, giving a range of different 'meanings'. This has been noted by a number of investigators who have found discrepancies between the census figures and those deriving from independent surveys. The general trend with adults is that the census tends to underestimate the number of Welsh speakers, but the situation may well be reversed in the case of children.

In many language use surveys, the tendency is to use a random sample from some data base containing information about the overall population in order to discover the sample of speakers of whichever language is of relevance. For example, within the comparative study of language use surveys of minority language groups within the European Union (O'Riagain, 1994), the Irish language use survey used electoral registers in order to establish a probability sample of names for interviewing. In the Basque survey, census data were used to develop a random, stratified and multi-staged cluster sample as a basis for selecting the sections where the survey was to be conducted. The strata of each section were then subdivided into provinces which, in turn, were divided into sociolinguistic areas. The list of people to be interviewed in each section was randomly chosen from the census data base. In the Frisian case, on the other hand, where census data are not available, a general sample was established by using local government registrations, and the universe was stratified by reference to different municipalities.

We chose to employ a different strategy in trying to obtain an exact probability sample of 1,000 Welsh speakers. This was largely in order to reduce interview costs within a study which had access to limited resources. This does create certain sampling problems in that the issues of randomness and spatial distribution are brought into question. First of all, it does not seek to develop a representative sample by reference to the whole population, but only by reference to Welsh speakers with sufficient competence to use the language in interaction. Our goal was achieved by stratifying the sample by four social characteristics: age, gender, social class and location. Only those over sixteen years of age were included in this process. The first step involved taking the representative county-by-county distribution of fluent Welsh speakers as defined in the Welsh Office survey. Thus the 1,000 respondents were located by reference to their incidence within the overall population of Welsh speakers. We then knew the number of respondents required in each county. Within each county, the number of respondents was distributed by reference to age, gender and social class, in accordance with the overall configuration for all Welsh speakers in that county as determined by the data from the Welsh Office survey. This then gave us a proportional, representative distribution. The sample by location and gender is shown in Table 2.17.

Using the more detailed sampling frame it then became possible randomly to select informants by using quota sampling. Thus in each county, a number of sampling points was selected and the required respondents distributed across these sampling points. In Gwynedd and Dyfed, for example, there were five sampling points, while in Powys and South Glamorgan, there were two. Interviewers then operated within each sampling point, filling their respective quotas. While this approach is widely used by opinion researchers, it does create problems by reference to randomness and spatial distribution. It would have been possible to have used telephone interviewing on the entire population in selecting the interviewees on a random basis, but this gives rise to other problems associated with refusal and non-access to telephones, while expense also precluded this course of action.

Table 2.17. Sample distribution by county

County*	Male	Female	Total
Gwynedd	154	129	283
Clwyd	75	71	146
Powys	23	18	41
Dyfed	152	146	298
West Glamorgan	53	57	110
South Glamorgan	21	19	40
Mid-Glamorgan	35	35	70
Gwent	6	6	12
Total	519	481	1000

* As defined in the 1991 census.

It is here that we should make reference to the fact that, unlike the Welsh Office survey, and indeed most surveys undertaken in Wales, all of our interviewers were fluent Welsh speakers. This meant that they were able to commence the interview in Welsh rather than resorting to the customary practice of asking the interviewee in English whether or not they would prefer to be interviewed in Welsh, usually at a time and date to be arranged. As we have noted elsewhere (Williams and Morris, 1995), the response rate for interviews undertaken in Welsh varies considerably according to the language used to introduce the interview. More importantly in this instance, it allowed us to ascertain whether or not the person encountered was capable of using the Welsh language; and furthermore, having asked the same competence questions as those used by the Welsh Office survey, we were in a position to make a direct comparison with that survey and to aggregate from our own figures to those for the population as a whole.

Of the 1,000 respondents, 15 per cent had learnt English as their first language while a further 4 per cent claimed that they had learnt both languages simultaneously. Furthermore, 90 per cent claimed that their Welsh was 'very good', a further 8 per cent that it was 'quite good' and the remaining 2 per cent claiming competence but to a lesser degree; 7 per cent of the respondents had been born in England and one respondent was born in Scotland. Over a third of those who claimed the lowest degree of competence were drawn from among the non-Welsh-born. Neither location, age nor social class had any significant bearing upon level of competence.

Interview procedures

The interviews were conducted by fully trained, bilingual interviewers drawn from across Wales. They were all given a day's induction which involved the customary explanation of the survey, the sampling design and the interview schedule. They then undertook one-to-one practice interviews on each other. Each interviewer was given a quota of respondents for their particular sampling points which conformed with the demands of the sampling frame together with instructions concerning how to fulfil the quota. Refusals involved using replacements as necessary. A sample of interviewees was telephoned in order to ensure that the interviewing was successfully and adequately undertaken. Each interview schedule was fully checked prior to commencement of data entry. The data entry was undertaken by two inputters entering each schedule. This ensures cross-comparison and minimizes entry mistakes.

PART II

Language Use

3
Language Use in the Family

1. Introduction

The use of a particular language in the family is by no means an essential prerequisite of achieving fluency in that language. Many have learnt languages which their family members simply do not understand. Nonetheless, the family is one of the primary agencies of language reproduction, by which we mean the inter-generational transmission of the language. Not only is family socialization an important ingredient for the mastering of competence, but it is also in the family that many of the dialogic aspects of language associated with communicative competence are mastered. Some have argued that learning English as a second language (L2) gives a superior mastery of standard forms than is the case for many first language (L1) speakers (Griffith, 1976). The limited work undertaken on the relationship between linguistic form, competence and family language with reference to Welsh indicates that there are certain forms that would require the intensity of language interaction that tends to be restricted to the family (Williams and Thomas, 1986).

The family is also responsible for directing much of our non-family activities as children, and in this respect it is a mistake to separate a discussion of the family from other language use contexts. Not only is it the parents who guide the language used in the home, but it is also they who encourage or insist upon involvement in activities outside of the home. This influence often extends to encompass the relationship between language and such activities. Many community activities are family-based and are part of the socialization process whereby children are integrated into language-related activities.

Much has been written about the negative identity and the decision of parents not to encourage their children to learn the language that is their own mother tongue. This is a process which we refer to as non-reproduction and is highly complex. Some claim that peer-group pressure plays a strong influence on the language of courtship, and that this, in turn, is the main determining factor associated with the absence of use of minority languages in the family. Such an argument suggests that by the time marriage or co-residence occurs, the use of one language or the other is already institutionalized for the partners. Others claim that the low status of the minority language results in a conscious, rational decision to avoid the language in the home for fear that the associated social stigma will be transferred with the language. Still others claim that the birth of the first child is a time when crucial decisions about the language of the home are taken. Evidently, according to these arguments, the manner in which Welsh is constructed as an object bears a direct relationship to the associated subjects. Furthermore, it suggests that this relationship changes during the life cycle.

Conversely, we have written extensively about the process whereby families who do not speak Welsh seek to ensure, for different reasons, that their children do learn the language (Williams, Roberts and Isaac, 1978). Whereas this is not the direct concern of this particular study, some of the respondents do fall into this category of Welsh speaker. Finally, there are those cases where only one partner speaks Welsh. We have already referred to the incidence of language group endogamy in the preceding chapter and the effect that it has upon the propensity to reproduce the language.

It is evident that the family is not the isolated, private institution that some claim it once was. Such a view ignores the fact that family members are also individuals operating within society at large. Nonetheless, it is also clear that the manner in which the media penetrates the family opens it to new influences. This also, of course, means that it is possible to influence the family and its language use practices in ways that are counter to the prevailing tendency of state hegemony and its relationship to linguistic uniformity. These were the issues which we sought to investigate in our language use survey. They are by no means the only situations and we did expect to encounter cases where parents do not use Welsh in the family, but rely upon agencies other than the family to reproduce the language, even though they themselves may well be fluent in the language. What the survey does not encounter is those cases where non-reproduction has taken place.

2. Language Use in the Respondent's Original Family

As indicated in the preceding chapter, there was a significant proportion of the respondents deriving from families where neither parent spoke Welsh. These were people who had acquired Welsh through the agencies of language production. As Table 3.1 indicates, a further 3–4 per cent were people with one or both parents with only a rudimentary knowledge of the language. Almost 9 per cent had only one parent who spoke Welsh, and a similar number had parents neither of whom spoke Welsh. However, the vast majority of respondents were mother-tongue speakers.

Table 3.1. Language ability of respondent's original family (%)

	Very good	Quite good	Some	None
Welsh				
Father	81	5	4	10
Mother	84	4	3	9
Brother/s	81	6	3	10
Sister/s	81	5	3	10
Maternal grandparents	85	3	2	10
Paternal grandparents	81	4	2	13
English				
Father	82	14	4	0
Mother	81	15	4	0
Brother/s	93	7	0	0
Sister/s	93	6	1	0
Maternal grandparents	44	31	20	5
Paternal grandparents	45	30	18	7

Note: In this and subsequent tables, % totals may not always = 100 due to rounding up/down of decimals.

English-language competence was even higher, this partly being accounted for by the inclusion of the parents of those who had learnt Welsh outside of the family context. However, there is an indication that for many families this is a relatively recent phenomenon, and when the grandparental generation is taken into account a small percentage had little or no knowledge of English, and fewer than half of them were fluent in the language. These were people raised in communities where Welsh was institutionalized as normative practice, and English was only encountered in the formal context of schooling.

Well over three-quarters of the respondents came from families where both parents spoke some Welsh. Of these, the majority (76 per cent) were families where both parents had a very high level of Welsh-language competence. A further 6 per cent were families where only one parent spoke the language, and the remaining 7 per cent were families where neither parent spoke Welsh (Table 3.2); 9 per cent of the respondents derived from families where parental Welsh-language ability was either nil or very limited. The inter-generational incidence of ability is fairly consistent, with the majority of the respondents coming from a background where a knowledge of Welsh was long-standing.

Table 3.2. Parental Welsh-language ability (%)

Father's Welsh-language ability	Mother's Welsh-language ability				
	Very good	Quite good	Some	None	Total N
Very good	94	2	2	2	808
Quite good	55	34	4	6	47
Some	59	10	24	7	41
None	23	4	7	66	104

The respondents themselves had different levels of ability in understanding, speaking, reading and writing Welsh, with the proportions of the sample able to understand and speak the language 'very well' being considerably higher than those who were able to read and write in Welsh to a similarly high level. By comparison, the ability of the respondents to understand, speak, read and write English was more consistent. This largely reflects the relatively recent expansion of Welsh-medium education. As we shall see in Chapter 5, the schooling experience of many of the respondents was such that the only exposure to Welsh was as a subject and in religious instruction. Until recently this was the experience of many, even in areas of high Welsh-language density, and led many to express surprise when, as adults, they learnt that their schoolteachers were fluent Welsh speakers. The family's contribution to the transmission of the Welsh language appears to be mainly an oral one. On the other hand, for some, the chapel and Sunday school were the main sources of exposure to the literary Welsh standard. The services were conducted in a formalized discourse and many of the Sunday school activities involved learning to read and write in Welsh. As a consequence of this context, there is often a high discrepancy between oral and written abilities. This is evident from Table 3.3. This is not true of

Table 3.3. Respondent's ability levels in Welsh and English (%)

	Very good	Quite good	Some	None
Welsh				
Understanding	91	7	2	0
Speaking	87	10	3	0
Reading	77	17	5	1
Writing	70	21	7	2
English				
Understanding	97	3	0	0
Speaking	95	5	0	0
Reading	95	5	0	0
Writing	91	9	0	0

English, where competence is more likely to transcend the different abilities, this being a function of the role of schooling in transmitting the formal registers of standard English.

Whereas the Welsh-language ability of the sample was high, one of the main aims of the survey was to investigate actual language use, and to consider the relationship between competence and use within the family. Table 3.4 indicates that the actual use of Welsh is somewhat lower than the ability levels would permit, with approximately one out of every ten of the respondents having used English with other family members even when they could speak Welsh. In some cases, this discrepancy between ability and use is linked to the inability, or limited ability, of one parent to speak Welsh, and obviously, one pertinent factor in the Welsh language use patterns within families is the use made of Welsh between the parents themselves. Most respondents who had two Welsh-speaking parents reported that Welsh was the actual medium of communication between them. For 80 per cent of the respondents, the father's Welsh-language ability was 'very good' and, of these, 93 per cent spoke only Welsh with the father. Of the remainder, about a half spoke only English with their fathers while a minority used both Welsh and English, and some only Welsh with their father. The figures for the mothers are not dissimilar. Of the respondents, 83 per cent claimed that their mother had a 'very good' level of Welsh-language competence. Of these, 91 per cent spoke only Welsh with their mother, 5 per cent spoke both languages and 4 per cent spoke only English. Evidently, in these cases there is little indication of seeking to avoid the use of Welsh when competence is high. A further 9 per cent had a mother who spoke no Welsh. Of the remaining 8 per cent, over half spoke only English with their mother. When Welsh was the exclusive language of communication with the mother but the father had limited ability, almost one in four of the respondents spoke some Welsh with the father. Conversely, when English only is used with the mother, about one in seven use some Welsh with the father, this largely depending upon the father's Welsh-language competence.

Table 3.4. Possible and actual use of Welsh within the respondents' original families (%)

Language used with:	Welsh		Difference
	possible use	actual use	
Father	86	76	–10
Mother	88	77	–11
Brother/s	87	76	–11
Sister/s	86	79	–7
Maternal grandparents	88	82	–3
Paternal grandparents	85	79	–6

The figures which we have been obtaining from the census data concerning the reproduction of Welsh within families where only one parent speaks the language now assume a greater degree of detail. In the experience of the respondents, when English was the only language used with one parent or another, it was only when there was a very high level of Welsh-language competence that Welsh was used with that parent. However, since, even in these circumstances, there are more cases where English only is used with the Welsh-speaking parent, it is obvious that there are other factors which play a role in the tendency to use at least some Welsh in these families.

Given the relationship between language density and the incidence of language group endogamy, the Welsh-speaking ability of parents was largely determined by location. Gwynedd and Dyfed displayed the highest incidence of cases where the parents of both respondents spoke Welsh. This is consistent with what we know about the history of language density. Many of the respondents were raised during a time when density in these locations was very high, and where marriages tended to be locally endogamous. The lowest incidence of language group endogamy was encountered in Gwent, Mid Glamorgan and South Glamorgan. Again these are locations where density has been relatively low for more than one generation. Respondents living in these areas were also the ones most likely to have been brought up in mixed-language households, with only one parent having an ability to speak Welsh, or to have two non-Welsh-speaking parents. This is partly indicative of those locations where language prestige is high and where the possibility of learning Welsh outside of the home exists (Table 3.5). The counties with high language density have a greater tendency to produce a high degree of language group endogamy, but it is also important to recognize the locational variation in the ability of the different agencies to produce the language.

Table 3.5. Parents' ability to speak Welsh, by respondent's county of birth (%)

| | Welsh-speaking parents | | |
	Both	Only one	Neither
Gwynedd	91	8	1
Clwyd	84	9	7
Powys	74	17	9
Dyfed	94	5	1
West Glamorgan	88	8	4
South Glamorgan	38	24	38
Mid Glamorgan	66	24	10
Gwent	50	33	17

Note: Welsh speaking = very good or quite good competence.

Turning to inter-generational parental language use (Table 3.6) we find that 8 per cent of the respondents were born outside of Wales and that, of these, almost 70 per cent came from homes where English was the parental language of interaction. Most of these are adult in-migrants who have learnt Welsh. The data for the industrialized counties with low Welsh-language density indicates that there is a greater tendency for the respondent's parents to have used far less

Welsh than in those counties where such density is high. This is partly a measure of the variable status of the language within the normative structures. However, it is also important to recognize that the sampling process derived proportionally more respondents from mixed language ability families from the counties with low Welsh-language density.

Table 3.6. Parental language use by birthplace of respondent (%)

Birthplace	Welsh	More Welsh than English	More English than Welsh	English only	Other language	Total no.
Gwynedd	86	2	1	11	0	316
Clwyd	70	7	7	16	0	99
Dyfed	88	1	4	7	0	306
Powys	61	0	0	39	0	23
Mid Glamorgan	34	7	12	47	0	74
South Glamorgan	19	13	6	63	0	17
West Glamorgan	66	13	6	14	0	80
Gwent	0	0	20	80	0	5
England	21	1	10	68	0	71
Scotland/N.Ireland	0	0	0	100	0	1
Outside UK	13	0	0	75	13	8
Total no.	722	36	45	197	1	1000

Table 3.7. Parents' ability to speak Welsh, by age group of respondents (%)

	Welsh-speaking parents		
	Both	Only one	Neither
19 yrs and younger	62	34	4
20–24 yrs	79	16	5
25–29 yrs	68	24	8
30–39 yrs	69	20	11
40–49 yrs	69	17	13
50–64 yrs	78	17	5
65+ yrs	90	8	2

Note: Welsh speaking = very good or quite good competence.

Most of the parents of the respondents who were born in South Glamorgan, Mid Glamorgan and Gwent usually spoke English with each other all or most of the time. The proportions are, respectively, 69, 59, and 100 per cent. Table 3.7 also suggests that the incidence of families where both parents speak Welsh has been declining over time as a consequence of the relationship between the general process of economic restructuring and language group exogamy.

3. Present Household Language Use

Table 3.8 indicates the level and patterns of language use within the respondents' present families. It suggests that the use of Welsh between respondents and their partners is less than between the respondents' own parents. In almost a third of the cases, English only, or a mixture of English and Welsh, is used in the home. There is

Table 3.8. Respondents' present household language use (%)

Language used:	Welsh	Welsh and English	English	Total N
At mealtimes	69	13	18	694
With father	78	2	20	411
With mother	76	6	18	470
With partner	64	9	28	647
With children	71	16	13	595
With in-laws	62	8	30	584

a consistency across these figures and the associated interactive contexts. The high use of English with the partner and in-laws is a consequence of the inability of some of these interlocutors to speak Welsh. In contrast, use of Welsh with the respondent's own parents is higher. The same factor is responsible for the mix of languages at mealtimes and with children. There is also a suggestion that, even when the partner has a limited Welsh-language competence, interaction with children by the respondent will involve the use of Welsh. We can now proceed to a more detailed analysis of this general trend.

Table 3.9 reinforces these observations, indicating that the language competence of the partner has an effect upon the language used at mealtimes. However, there are those cases when both partners are fluent Welsh speakers where English is introduced at mealtimes, and conversely there are those where Welsh is introduced even when one partner speaks no Welsh. This tendency is repeated within the more general language use between partners (Table 3.10). However, it is clear that this pattern differs somewhat from that indicated by reference to mealtimes. The introduction of other interlocutors, such as children and in-laws, results in a greater propensity to use Welsh at this particular setting.

Table 3.9. Language ability of partner by language used at mealtimes (%)

Welsh language ability of partner	Language used at mealtimes				Total no.
	Welsh	Welsh and English	English	Other	
Very good	90	6	4	0	479
Quite good	28	26	46	0	72
Some	7	44	48	1	85
None	10	16	74	0	58

Table 3.10. Welsh-language ability of respondent's partner by language used between partners (%)

Welsh language ability of partner	Language use between partners				Total no.
	Welsh	Welsh and English	English	Other	
Very good	90	6	4	0	446
Quite good	18	32	50	0	68
Some	3	9	89	0	81
None	0	2	98	0	51

Table 3.11 shows the relationship between the Welsh-language competence of the partner and the language used by the respondent with the children. Even when both parents have a high Welsh-language competence, 7 per cent use some English with the children. Conversely, when the partner speaks no Welsh, 9 per cent of the respondents use Welsh exclusively with the children and 40 per cent use both languages with them. This suggests that language group exogamy is not necessarily accompanied by non-reproduction. However, it is also clear that the language competence of the partner is an influential factor in the extent of Welsh language use by the fluent Welsh speaker with his or her children. Neither age nor social class are significant contributory factors in the patterns of Welsh/English language use within the family, with all age groups

and all social classes showing similar patterns in day-to-day use, family mealtimes, answering the telephone and so on. Mothers are not any more or less likely to use Welsh with their children than are fathers.

Table 3.11. Language ability of partner by language used with children (%)

Welsh language ability of partner	Language use with children				
	Welsh	Welsh and English	English	Other	Total no.
Very good	89	8	4	0	420
Quite good	46	27	27	0	63
Some	29	37	34	0	75
None	8	41	52	0	37

Table 3.12 shows the language use patterns in the home with partners and with children, by social class. This data indicates that the highest tendency to use English with partners is found at the extremes of the class structure. However, the highest incidence of the use of English with children was found among the managerial class. There are, of course, other variables which will intervene in this pattern.

Table 3.12. Home language use patterns with partners and children, by social class (%)

	Welsh	Welsh and English	English	No.
With partners				
Managerial	53	9	38	40
Professional	65	9	26	167
Skilled non-manual	67	10	23	168
Skilled manual	69	9	29	116
Semi-skilled	69	6	25	59
Unskilled	57	4	40	58
With children				
Managerial	60	28	13	47
Professional	74	16	10	196
Skilled non-manual	70	16	14	176
Skilled manual	71	16	13	129
Semi-skilled	68	14	19	65
Unskilled	78	10	10	53

When we consider the relationship between the language used with the partner and children respectively (Table 3.13) we find that almost two-thirds of the respondents use Welsh exclusively as the home language. Of the others, 30 per cent use only English in the home, 10 per cent use both languages with partners and children and 38 per cent use either Welsh or both languages with the children and English exclusively with the partner. The tendency to use more Welsh with the partner than with the children is limited. The main variable here is the Welsh-language ability of the partner. Where this is limited, 38 per cent of the respondents will use only English in the family, 35 per cent will use both languages with the children and English with the partner and 20 per cent will use only Welsh with the children and only English with the partner. The higher incidence of the use of Welsh and bilingual use patterns with children than with partners is an indication of the desire to ensure that Welsh is transmitted inter-generationally, even if the pattern with the partner does not ensure such a transmission.

Table 3.13. Language use of respondent with partner and with children (%)

Language use with partner	Language use with children			
	Welsh	Welsh and English	English	Total no.
Welsh	95	5	0	351
Welsh and English	38	45	17	47
English	22	33	45	141
Total no.	381	87	71	539

Finally, we turn to the relationship between the language used with children by the respondents and the language which the children use together (Table 3.14). Evidently, in the majority of cases where parents use only Welsh with their children, this also becomes the only medium of interaction between the children. The percentage that drastically deviates from this pattern by using either only English or mainly English together is small. Experience indicates that this has much to do with the relationship between identity changes associated with adolescence, specific formation of social networks and a negative identity vis-à-vis Welsh. On the other hand, once both languages are used with the children, the probability of those children favouring English in their interaction increases considerably. If parents use only

English with the children the likelihood that the children will use Welsh as the main basis for interaction between them, even when competence is high, is remote.

Table 3.14. Language used with children, by language children use together (%)

Language used with children	Language children use together					Total no.
	Welsh only	Mostly Welsh	Welsh and English	Mostly English	English only	
Welsh	89	5	3	2	1	362
Welsh and English	13	10	28	29	21	80
English	3	2	3	33	59	58
Total no.	333	27	36	49	55	500

In considering the use of language by children, there are a number of other variables that should be considered. These extend to include the language of interaction in the school, the local vitality of the language and the social networks of which the children are a part. Evidently our data does not permit us to consider such details. What is possible is a superficial consideration of the relationship between language density and language use among children (Table 3.15). Where language density is high there is a greater tendency for the children to use Welsh together. The converse would also appear to be true. However, we hasten to add that there is a range of other factors

Table 3.15. Language children use with each other, by locality (%)

	Language used by children			Total no.
	Welsh	Welsh and English	English	
Gwynedd	88	3	8	154
Clwyd	68	2	30	81
Powys	59	0	41	17
Dyfed	77	9	14	161
West Glamorgan	61	7	32	71
South Glamorgan	53	26	21	19
Mid Glamorgan	31	17	52	42
Gwent	20	40	40	5

that should be considered in interpreting this simple correlation. The language competence of the respondent's partner appears to be one crucial factor. When both the parents can speak Welsh, the language use among children is high – however, there is a substantial reduction in the proportions of children speaking Welsh together in mixed-language households (Table 3.16). When both parents have a high Welsh-language competence, in 71 per cent of the cases interaction within the household is entirely through the medium of Welsh. At the other extreme is the 5 per cent of these homogeneous cases where English is the only medium of interaction. The remaining households consist of 8 per cent where Welsh remains the dominant language of interaction, 7 per cent where English is the dominant language and 9 per cent where it is not easy to indicate priority. The picture changes markedly when the partner's Welsh-language ability declines. Clearly Welsh is no longer the predominant language of the home, but this does not mean that Welsh is not the focus of interaction between the one Welsh-speaking parent and the children. This was certainly the case for 25 per cent of such households, but in another 25 per cent of households English was the exclusive language of the home.

Table 3.16. **Language children use with each other by parents' language ability (%)**

Language used by children	Both parents Welsh speaking	One parent only Welsh speaking
Welsh always	77	21
Most often Welsh	5	4
Equal Welsh and English	5	16
Most often English	6	27
Always English	7	32
Total no. of respondents	447 (100%)	98 (100%)

Finally, we can consider the relationship between the language used with the partner and the language used by the children (Table 3.17). The data confirm the pattern already discussed in Chapter 2, section 4 – that is, when the parents speak English to each other, the children are more likely to replicate this pattern. It also shows that when parents speak both languages with each other, half of the children use English only together, a third use Welsh only and the rest reflect their parents' bilingual pattern. When parents speak Welsh together, their children are most likely also to use Welsh with each other. Amalgamating these figures, it would appear that in 65 per cent of households Welsh is the only or predominant language used, and in a further 20 per cent English is either the only or the predominant language used.

Table 3.17. Language children use with each other, by parents' language use (%)

Language of children with each other	Language use with partner			Total no.
	Welsh	Welsh and English	English	
Welsh always	89	4	8	311
Most often Welsh	68	16	16	25
Equal Welsh and English	31	19	50	36
Most often English	15	17	67	46
Always English	0	24	76	55

4. Media in the Family

The other agency which contributes to the production and reproduction of Welsh is the extent of use of the Welsh-language media within the family. The advent of mass media and their penetration of family leisure time mean that they can have a distinctive influence upon both competence and use. In contrast to some other minority language groups, Welsh speakers have a wide range of media possibilities, and this range extends to cover a range of language abilities. Thus the 1992 Welsh Office social survey to which we referred in Chapter 2 used the ability to follow Welsh-language television as one of its benchmarking criteria by reference to use. The figures of the media industry indicate that there is a considerable number of people with limited Welsh-language ability who follow Welsh-language programmes. However, an analysis of media activities is by no means a simple process. The vast literature on media use and influence takes us beyond what our limited data can offer. Here we merely refer to the incidence of the use of the Welsh- and English-language print and broadcasting media among the respondents.

Before proceeding to a consideration of the data it is useful to consider the nature of Welsh-language media provision. There is no Welsh-language daily newspaper and only one weekly. In addition there are magazines devoted to current affairs and literary production which appear on a weekly or monthly basis. Most widely read are the local community newspapers or *papurau bro*, which between them have a readership in excess of 200,000 (Williams and Williams, 1991). Book production is funded by the Arts Council and the Welsh Book Council distributes the end product. Today approximately 650 books are published annually in Welsh. About a third of these are for children and schools. Welsh-language radio broadcasting dates to the 1930s when a regional section of the BBC was created for Wales. In 1953 this was linked to a Broadcasting Council and Radio Cymru was established in 1979. In 1998, around ninety hours of radio were broadcast weekly in Welsh. There is also some Welsh-language radio broadcasting on the independent channels. Television broadcasting followed the same pattern. S4C was established in 1982 as a commissioning agency. In 1998 there were about thirty hours of Welsh-language television programmes broadcast weekly, while the introduction of the digital service at the end of 1998 led to a substantial increase in the number of hours of Welsh-language broadcasting (at the time of writing, this service is not yet widely available in Wales). The main problem involves having to satisfy on one channel tastes that vary by age, gender and social class. By and large, the viewing patterns follow the same trends as for English-language broadcasting.

The extent of readership among the respondents was established by asking about the extent of current and past readership. The data are presented in Table 3.18. There is an obvious difference between readership patterns in the respective languages. This has less to do with non-literacy in Welsh than with the institutionalization of readership behaviour. There is a tendency for the older population to read more books in both languages, and the higher the social class the greater the tendency to read books. It is also the older population and the middle classes that are most likely to read Welsh-language newspapers.

Table 3.18. Readership patterns by language (%)

| Frequency | Welsh | | English | |
	Books	Papers	Books	Papers
Regularly	19	37	41	79
Sometimes	29	19	30	14
Seldom	21	15	15	3
Never	31	30	14	4

The comparable figures for radio and television are presented in Table 3.19. Whereas most people do watch Welsh-language television, they do not listen to the radio programmes. This has been of concern to the main broadcasting outlet, the BBC, which has constantly tried to mix and experiment with different formats. On the other hand, the same is true of English-language radio broadcasting. Indeed, the figures for the two languages by reference to radio programmes are remarkably similar. The figures for listening by reference to age, gender and social class reflect the same distribution as described for reading. However, there is a greater tendency to watch English-language programmes, this being a measure of the manner in which choice is managed on the different channels by reference to age, gender and social class. Thus, within the channel-switching patterns, Welsh-language television is merely another option of which the respondents take charge.

Table 3.19. Broadcasting exposure by language (%)

Number of hours per day	Welsh		English	
	Radio	TV	Radio	TV
0	38	10	42	4
1	36	54	33	33
2	11	25	12	31
More than 2	15	11	13	32

Having established the general patterns of exposure to the Welsh-language media, we would briefly like to consider the relationship between this pattern and the incidence of Welsh-language use within the family. Since programme choice, despite the increasing tendency to have more than one receiver within each household, is largely a family affair, it might be expected that where only one partner speaks Welsh the tendency would be to use less of the Welsh-language media.

Resorting to the language used at mealtimes in the home as a measure of language use in the home, we are able to ascertain the relationship between home language and the use of the media. We begin with a consideration of broadcasting (Table 3.20), which shows the number of respondents who listen to radio or watch television for 0 hours, 1 hour, 2 hours, or more than 2 hours daily. In one sense the pattern is the same for both media – the more Welsh that is used in the home, the greater the tendency to use Welsh-language radio and tele-vision. However, the degree of difference varies significantly across the two media. Whereas 29 per cent of those who use only Welsh in the home do not listen to Welsh-language radio, the figure increases to half when both languages are used in the home and to 68 per cent when English is the language of the home. This contrasts with figures of 7, 10 and 21 per cent respectively for television. This is only partly accounted for by the tendency to use radio less than television. Rather, it indicates that Welsh-language television is much more likely to pene-trate the lives of the respondents, and that the language used in the home does not have the same impact upon the tendency to watch Welsh-language programmes as it does for radio programmes. This is reflected in other surveys and the audience-reach figures of the broad-casters which do indicate a very high level of involvement with Welsh-language television. However, the Welsh-language competence of the partner and the language used with the partner does a play a role, even with television. Where the partner has no Welsh-language ability as many as 22 per cent of the respondents watch no Welsh-language television; when English is the only language used between partners the figure is 16 per cent; when English is the only language used by the respondent with the children the figure is 26 per cent; and when the children use only English together it increases to 29 per cent. This compares with 10 per cent of the entire sample who do not watch Welsh-language television. What is interesting about these figures is that they suggest that, for a minority, watching Welsh-language televi-sion is one of the few Welsh-language activities in the home.

Table 3.20. Home language and daily Welsh-language broadcasting exposure (%)

Home language	Radio				No.	Television				No.
	0 hrs	1hr	2hrs	>2 hrs		0 hrs	1hr	2hrs	>2 hrs	
Welsh	29	40	13	18	614	7	50	30	14	614
Welsh and										
English	50	32	9	9	114	11	66	19	4	114
English	68	25	2	4	165	21	64	8	8	165

Turning to the print media we undertake a similar exercise (Table 3.21). Again we recognize the same trend as with the broadcasting media. There is a difference between book and newspaper reading, and the amount of Welsh used in the home does have an impact upon consumption. The main difference in both book and newspaper readership occurs in the transition from the exclusive use of Welsh in the home to the introduction of English.

Table 3.21. Language of the home and use of Welsh-language print media (%)

Home language	Books				No.	Newspapers				No.
	Reg.	Occas.	Seldom	Never		Reg.	Occas.	Seldom	Never	
Welsh	24	29	21	26	614	45	21	13	21	614
Welsh and English	9	38	19	34	114	24	13	20	43	114
English	9	22	19	49	165	21	16	15	48	165

5. Conclusion

This chapter has focused upon the language background of the respondents themselves, the Welsh-language competence of the interlocutors within the nuclear family of the respondent, and the language use between the different interlocutors. What it achieves is a clearer picture of the data presented in the aggregate data of the census and the 1992 Welsh Office social survey. It suggests that among those with a high Welsh-language competence, there is a correspondingly high tendency to use Welsh within the household and that by and large this is sustained inter-generationally.

Most of the respondents came from a family background where Welsh was the main medium of interaction. The high level of use is sustained where the partner also has a high level of Welsh-language ability. Where this is not the case, it affects the language used with the children within the family. Yet there is also a tendency to compensate for the inability to speak only Welsh in the home by using the language more with the children than with the partner who has limited competence in Welsh. This suggests a commitment to using the family in order to sustain the language inter-generationally.

We have touched upon the relationship between the use of Welsh in the family and the density of language within the region. The latter topic involves the extent and nature of language use within the community, and this is the topic of the next chapter.

4

The Use of Welsh in the Community

1. Introduction

Community is conceptualized as an aspect of civil society and in this respect refers to institutionalized behaviour that tends to be separate from the activities of the state. This institutionalized behaviour pertains to the establishment of formal institutions which structure the activities around which such behaviour is organized. It may relate to highly localized behaviour focusing upon voluntary associations, or can refer to a different level of spatial and social aggregation, and in that sense it becomes structured. However, it also relates to the stabilization of social relations within social networks. In this context, we refer to the collective subject drawing upon the past but constantly compromising the present as individual subjects.

In referring to institutionalization, we are obliged to consider how behaviour tends to be taken for granted as part of the common sense of life within the community. However, such institutionalized behaviour becomes normativized and thereby transcends local contexts. Language plays a central role in this respect, and itself becomes a feature of institutionalized behaviour. Social change relates to the manner in which this taken-for-granted is destabilized and the associated symbolic elements are reorganized. However, it would be erroneous to think of this as merely a reflection process, where whatever happens at the behavioural level is merely a manifestation of some reified process referred to as social change. In this respect institutionalization is not only manifested in language use, it is also embedded in language.

This leads to a consideration of normativity. Institutionalization does not equate with normativity since social norms do not involve a consensus between rational actors as some manifestation of pre-existing social norms. The link between normativity and power is clearly central to the work of Foucault. There are also struggles over normativity, these involving different processes. The relationship between the manner in which the collective subject asserts and manipulates the nature of normativity at the local level is not the same as the link between the state and normativity. While each community is unique, there are also processes which contribute to a collective consciousness that transcend each community but which remain part of civil society. Thus the concept of normalization with reference to language planning (LP) must be qualified if it is to be of any value. There is a tendency to conceive of what is referred to as 'normalization' simply as the process of making some action normal, without considering the intricate relationship between the different processes of institutionalization and normativity.

This means that language use within the community must be referenced in terms of the manner in which meaning is socially constructed as institutional behaviour, and how social change undermines the social and institutional contexts which support the associated stabilization. That is, there is a symbolic component to language which signifies meaning within social practice. Within bilingual contexts, the use of one language rather than another becomes part of that signification. It is this understanding that leads us to preface our consideration of language use at the community level with a brief overview of the nature of social change in Wales. Language use is institutionalized by the signification of objects that are central to social institutions, and by the dyadic relationship and associated subject positions that are associated with these objects. Thus, for example, religious life may revolve around the chapel, which is constructed as a specific kind of object with a particular historical context. The chapel relates to subject positions for the individual and the interlocutor. Language pertains to the significations associated with these subjects and objects. Clearly, as social change influences the salience of institutions within the community, the stabilization of the relationship between subjects and objects is loosened and new significations that bear a relevance to language use begin to be stabilized. Some significations may be negative and others positive for different individuals as they relate to the different subject places of the associated discourse. Thus, it is important to come to terms, not only with signification processes *vis-à-vis* historical institutions, but also with the nature and incidence of social change within the community.

Community is currently seen as the salvation of states confronted with low levels of political participation, the fiscal crisis and an economy that fails to generate the desired level of productivity. Thus we encounter calls for the elimination of civil society/political society/state distinction and the inclusion of voluntary activity within civil society as a kind of political engagement. Sceptics would claim that this is merely a reaction to the low levels of political participation within a representative democracy that limits participation to periodic voting exercises. The focus on human capital that is currently the cornerstone of the socio-economics that drives the regional development perspective also relies heavily upon the concept of community. Thus community is seen as constituting an energy that is more than the sum of its component parts.

It is this mystic ingredient that must be unlocked for development to be promoted. Evidently, current thinking seeks simultaneously to articulate political, social and economic activity, all of which are activated via 'community'. Responsibility and accountability are no longer the prerogative of the state, but of the community. It is the responsibility of local government to play a role in community leadership in order to strengthen local identity and accountability. Yet the voluntary sector is also seen as the replacement for public-sector action, much of which resides in the local authorities. The voluntary sector covers all sorts of activities and is claimed to involve half the adult population of Wales on a weekly basis, these activities being 'worth' £2 billion annually.

The community developers' task is to work on a range of human limitations within the community – lack of confidence, isolation, limited skills and so on. These deficiencies, it is argued, can be reversed, community energy 'activated' and economic activity stimulated within a 'third sector' that pertains to neither the public nor the private sector. The danger of a dual labour market is ignored in the scramble to discover an acceptable solution to exclusion.

This sense of community departs significantly from Rousseau's conception of community as the basis of normativity and social order. The advent of industrialization led to the argument that society was so complex that responsibility for social order should reside with the state. This change led to the state being seen as the sum of all communities within its territory and the impossibility of an opposition between state and community (Williams, 1992a). What we are currently witnessing would appear to be the antithesis of this process.

Community institutions

We have already referred in the introduction to the local hegemony held by religion in many aspects of community life in Wales during the nineteenth century, and how this hegemony was challenged by the trade-union movement in some locations at the beginning of the twentieth century. The importance of religion in rural Wales was well documented in the various community studies undertaken during the 1950s (Rees, 1950; Rees and Davies, 1960; Jenkins, 1960). They all point to the extent to which normativity in a range of community activities was conditioned by the importance of the chapels and their officials. The various institutions within the communities shared the same leadership, and the life chances of the individual depended to a great extent upon conformity with the social behaviour determined by the normative order. The influence of the deaconry and the ministers extended beyond the individual chapel and the local community into the realm of political activity at the county level. Character references from such individuals were the *sine qua non* of individual progress for a population that was far less mobile than is the case today. Within some of the industrial communities the trade union came to play a similar role, but even here the religious institutions were not irrelevant to social life.

The language of many of the Nonconformist religious institutions was Welsh. However, some chapels changed to English as the language of their religious activities at key times during the nineteenth century, this being associated with the in-migration of non-Welsh speakers into those communities and the impact of the negative identity by reference to language. Within industrial Wales there are numerous examples from the second quarter of the twentieth century of families where the oldest children learnt Welsh through its use in the family and involvement in the local chapels, whereas these practices were abandoned by the time the younger family members were being socialized. There was also the Anglican Church in Wales which tended to be regarded differently from the Nonconformist sects in that it was popularly perceived to be thoroughly Anglicized, although this was probably more so the case within the higher echelons of the establishment than it was at the local community level.

By no means all of the population of rural Wales were members of the various religious organizations but there is no doubt that they were all heavily influenced by them. The difference between the secular and religious has been characterized by Dafydd Jenkins (1960) in terms of distinctive status groups which he called *Buchedd*. At a time when the majority of people in rural Wales were mother-tongue speakers of Welsh, membership of these status groups made little difference to language use. Welsh was institutionalized as the language of the community. On the other hand, it did serve to generate language varieties, based largely on vocabulary use *vis-à-vis* the literary standard. Of course, the picture was different in those communities where the extent of competence was less.

The process of secularization and the relationship between migration and the circulation of capital has changed this picture in recent years. The influence of religion upon normative practice has declined drastically over a relatively short period of time. Similarly, membership and participation in the religious institutions has also declined. The chapels are no longer able to assert the influence they once held on community behaviour. Some would argue that nothing has replaced this influence and that community is in decline, being replaced by individualized behaviour subject to normative structuring deriving from outside the community. Given that much of the standardization of Welsh was associated with the manner in which the religious institutions used the biblical standard, the secularization process does have an effect upon the corpus of the spoken language. More importantly for the topic of this chapter, it also has an influence upon the capacity of the community to play a role in the production and reproduction of Welsh.

Population movements

Migration is structurally determined by the circulation of capital associated with the dynamics of economic restructuring. Thus cycles of migration flows are related to the economic cycles of growth and stagnation. During the 1960s and early 1970s, Wales experienced an upsurge in in-migration. This followed a pronounced period of rural out-migration which coincided with the decline of the quarrying industry and the displacement of labour by machinery in the agricultural sector. The second half of the 1980s saw a return of the high rates of in-migration. In many respects these population movements were selective, with Wales attracting in-migrants from neighbouring industrial areas in the north-west of England and the English Midlands. Many of these in-migrants were retirees, especially as

more recent years have given the retired a longer life expectancy and
a degree of financial and other independence hitherto unknown. The
disparity in income level, and consequently in the cost of property,
between Wales and the south-east of England has afforded some in-
migrants a higher level of living through residence in rural areas
which are romanticized as desirable living locations which give
access to an ill-defined 'quality of life'. These population movements
have been the source of considerable debate and resentment, partly
because of the impact upon the cost of housing in relatively depressed
areas of Wales, and partly because of the impact of the incomers
upon local structure and the ability of local communities to play a
forceful role in the production and reproduction of Welsh. To a great
extent this issue pertains to the ability of the community to generate
and regenerate normative structures which conform with stabilized
social practice, and thereby to assimilate the in-migrating population,
rather than for the community itself to be subject to more universal
normativity patterns. Language becomes the clearest marker of this
polarization. Currently, almost a quarter of the population of Wales
was born outside of Wales, and some locations have a much higher
proportion of the population that is non-Welsh-born.

The in-migration of people, mainly older and non-Welsh-speaking,
has been matched by an out-migration of young people, many of them
Welsh speakers and often well-qualified. Yet this is not a static picture
but part of a social process which varies with time and with the changing nature of economic restructuring over time. Even though, to our
knowledge, the work that can demonstrate this assertion has yet to be
undertaken, there seems to have been a change from the situation of
the 1950s and 1960s when young people moved from Wales to London
and north-west England to one in which currently Cardiff plays a much
more significant role by reference to population movement. The emergence of the capital as a significant administrative and financial centre
has had an influence on various parts of Wales. Nonetheless, what is
clear from the decennial census is that parts of Wales which had over
75 per cent of its population reporting a Welsh-language competence
as recently as 1961 have experienced a drastic decline in that level of
competence (Aitchison and Carter, 1994). Of course, there are numerous reasons for this change but population movements have made a
significant contribution, either directly or indirectly.

Such aspects of demography have been associated by researchers
with the change in the incidence of Welsh-language competence in

order to determine the 'future of the language' (Baker, 1985; Aitchison and Carter, 1994). Sometimes this orientation has involved attempts to estimate the level of density of Welsh speakers needed in a community in order to facilitate the use of Welsh as a 'community language' (James, 1985). These aggregate studies dovetail with the spatial orientation to which we referred in the Introduction, but suffer from an inadequacy to accommodate structural analysis based on aggregate data about competence with social-action theory that incorporates a clear understanding of the process of institutionalization. We are not convinced that the approach we have taken, and the data which we offer, adds very much to this issue. On the other hand, community structure, in the sense of the existence of local institutions, their membership and language of practice, is more directly influenced by the in-migration of monoglots and the out-migration of bilinguals, especially where the support structures make learning the language that much more difficult or unnecessary. In many locations, there is a sense of social struggle constructed around community institutions in operation. Welsh speakers seek to conserve Welsh as the language of these institutions, exploring different means of ensuring that this is the case without excluding non-speakers. There results a delicate situation full of dangers. In other cases, parallel institutions develop in the same community, one conducting its activities through the medium of Welsh and the other through the medium of English. The third tendency one encounters is that whereby Welsh is used not through formal institutions but through individuals constructing social networks with other Welsh speakers. All these contexts have relevance for the language use data which we consider below.

Before moving to that data it is worth considering some recent studies of language and social networks. However, we hasten to add that such social-network studies do not tap the issue of structure, and that their focus is very much upon dyadic relationships. Furthermore, there is a difference between the concept of social network and the detailed analysis of such networks that is implicit in what is referred to as network analysis (Mitchell, 1969; Boissevain, 1974). The concept tends to be invoked in opposition to that of society, as the interactive behavioural patterns that are not necessarily conditioned by the social. Few of the following studies make explicit use of network analysis.

Aitchison, Carter and Rogers (1989) adopted the concept of social networks to study schoolchildren and their families in the Tregaron area, noting the use made of Welsh by children at home, in the school playground and in clubs and associations in their local communities, with the data being collected primarily by means of questionnaires and interviews. Beth Thomas's study (1988) of the mining community of Pontrhydyfen in south Wales also took up the concept of social networks, and showed that the majority of Welsh speakers in the community were older than fifty years of age, and that they belonged to large dense multiplex networks forged in the pre-war years.

Another study of a village community in Anglesey populated by a local-born group of Welsh speakers, Welsh-speaking in-migrants and non-Welsh in-migrants (Morris, 1989) found that the Welsh speakers had larger and denser networks than the non-Welsh-speaking in-migrants, and the networks were primarily structured by language. This work focused on the details of network analysis, and three important points emerged. First, that the size and density of the social networks varied by each of the three groups, with the local Welsh-born group drawing upon kinship networks not available to the other two groups, and the Welsh-speaking in-migrants using local institutions which exclusively used Welsh as a basis for networking. Second, that the networks of the non-Welsh-speaking in-migrants were far more dispersed, and focused upon a limited number of local institutions. Third, whereas there was an overlap in the composition of the networks of the two Welsh-speaking groups, this was not the case for the non-Welsh-speaking group. Welsh speakers and non-Welsh speakers had little contact on a daily basis, and their relationships therefore tended to be uniplex ones, based on a single social context or role, while those between the Welsh speakers themselves, both the locally born group and those who had in-migrated to the village, were multiplex relationships. Clearly, in this case, language plays an important role in structuring social networks.

Another study (Williams and Williams, 1998) involved young English in-migrants between eighteen and thirty years of age, all of whom had been through the bilingual primary school system in Gwynedd, and of whom half currently used Welsh while the other half did not. This study found that most belonged to social networks which included mother-tongue speakers and that they did use some Welsh in the associated interaction. However, the main indicators of current use were the networks established following language-related streaming at the secondary school, courtship or marriage with mother-tongue speakers and the extent of Welsh language use among fellow workers. That is, whereas all of the cohort had established a high degree of competence at the end of primary school, whether or not they drew on that competence as adults was very much a lottery. A recent study of three communities commissioned by the Welsh Language Board (C. H. Williams and Evas, 1998) is similar to the work of Thomas in Pontrhydyfen (1988) or Aitchison, Carter and Rogers in Tregaron (1989), in that it relies primarily upon survey data rather than participant observation or structured network analysis. There is constant reference to 'networks', but this is a general use of the term and there is no evidence that the survey data was accompanied by any formal network analysis. The survey data, in turn, is structured by the more orthodox maintenance/shift paradigm and a continuation of the modern/traditional dichotomy. Furthermore, it is limited by the size of sample in the respective communities, and by the difficulty of comparing data from a common questionnaire that was gathered by different means. The basis for comparison is thereby limited. Nonetheless, these communities were claimed to be representative by reference to differing language densities. In this respect, it is difficult to understand the value of a survey design that focuses upon specific communities when the qualitative data that pertains to the specifics of these communities is not drawn upon. We are not told how the respondents were selected, and it is difficult to see how it becomes possible to generalize from the surveys to the broader population.

The Report indicated a number of findings from the data-gathering exercise:

* second-language Welsh speakers lack confidence in using Welsh;
* the negative identity is rapidly receding;
* Welsh speakers are keen to discover more contexts for the use of Welsh;
* there are communities with high language group endogamy where reproduction is the norm and others where it is not;
* the link between school and family is crucial for reproduction in some locations;
* bilingual competence among community leaders is important for Welsh language use;
* there is indication that some communities are segmented by language.

There does not appear to be any coherent attempt to develop the comparative perspective as the basis for interpreting these findings, and the analysis tends to be descriptive rather than analytic. The generally positive attitude of Welsh speakers removes one explanation for restricted use, and there does not appear to be any alternative means of accounting for the relatively low correlation between competence and use that is revealed by the survey data. It is questionable whether these kinds of studies can be effectively integrated with data from large-scale surveys or from census data. However, they do serve to give an indication of how interaction is structured within localities and the factors which play a part in that structuration. These and other similar studies all have a contribution to make to the general understanding of the process of change, and some make constructive suggestions regarding language planning. In many respects they serve to indicate the variation that exists within the wider population that we have tapped at the aggregate level.

2. *Language Use in the Community*

The preceding description has suggested that there has been a fairly profound change in the context of the use of Welsh within most communities. In order to ascertain the extent to which this change was part of the perceived experience of the respondents, and the extent to which it actually was part of that experience, the respondents were asked to compare the use of Welsh in their home community when they were children with the current use of Welsh in their communities. They were asked about the use they made of Welsh in the street, in the shops, in chapel/church and in the social clubs and associations. In order to make a comparison of Welsh language use within communities over time, the data in Tables 4.1 and 4.2 are restricted to those who still reside within their original county boundaries, and therefore do not include the 80 respondents who were born outside Wales, nor the further 252 who had moved from the area where they were raised as children.

Table 4.1. Language use in the respondents' community as children (%)

	Often	Sometimes	Rarely	Never
Street	81	11	6	3
Shops	76	14	7	3
Chapel	92	4	1	3
Clubs	77	10	5	7

No. = 648.

Table 4.2. Language use in the respondents' present community (%)

	Often	Sometimes	Rarely	Never
Street	54	30	13	3
Shops	46	34	15	6
Chapel	81	8	2	10
Clubs	58	25	7	10

No. = 648.

Most claimed that Welsh was heard in all four social contexts when they were young and the figures for the present situation show a decline. Frequent use of Welsh in the street has reduced by 28 per cent, in the shops 30 per cent, clubs by 19 per cent and the chapel by 10 per cent, while the occasional use of the language has increased, although by a smaller proportion. The context within which the perceived decline in the use of Welsh was least was the chapel, but it is important to recognize that the relevance of the chapel/church for language production/reproduction pertains not so much to the use of Welsh in this context, but rather to the degree of involvement of the population in its activities.

Language use in daily community activities

In any study of language use within a bilingual context it is important to ascertain the extent to which the individual uses one language rather than another in his or her daily life. Often this has been analysed by reference to a process which is regarded as involving code-switching or the rational choice of one language or another, with the assumption that the use of both is possible. As we have maintained, this is one of the assumptions implicit in the concept of domains. In this survey we have rejected such concepts and have sought to ascertain the extent to which it is possible for the interlocutors to use both languages before establishing which language is used. Table 4.3 shows the patterns of Welsh language use in different social contexts in the community – first, where it is possible to use the language and where the respondents do so; second, where it is possible to use Welsh but the respondents choose to use English; and third, where it is not possible for them to use Welsh because the other agent does not speak the language. Not all the respondents are involved in all the contexts, as is indicated by the last column.

Table 4.3. Use of Welsh by context in the community

	I can and do		I can but don't		Not possible to speak Welsh		Not applicable
	%	(No.)	%	(No.)	%	(No.)	No.
Priest/minister	92	(820)	2	(20)	6	(50)	110
With child's teacher	83	(300)	9	(30)	8	(30)	640
Local councillor	76	(670)	2	(20)	22	(190)	120
Library	69	(520)	4	(30)	27	(200)	250
Solicitor	63	(500)	5	(40)	32	(250)	210
Car repairs	57	(440)	4	(40)	39	(300)	230
Bank manager	57	(430)	5	(40)	38	(290)	240
Police	56	(360)	8	(40)	36	(240)	360
In pub	55	(420)	5	(40)	40	(300)	240
Post office	52	(500)	3	(30)	45	(430)	40
Buy petrol	52	(420)	4	(30)	44	(360)	190
Buy newspaper	51	(450)	2	(30)	47	(420)	110
Tax office	49	(340)	5	(50)	46	(320)	300
Water Board	48	(320)	9	(60)	43	(290)	330
Social worker	47	(170)	9	(40)	44	(160)	640
Family doctor	46	(460)	9	(80)	45	(450)	10
Shopping	46	(430)	5	(50)	49	(460)	60
Hairdresser	46	(430)	4	(40)	50	(460)	70
Social Security	42	(230)	7	(40)	51	(280)	450
Dentist	41	(380)	6	(40)	53	(490)	80
Theatre	37	(280)	1	(30)	59	(440)	250
Optician	35	(280)	3	(30)	62	(500)	190
Call taxi	34	(240)	6	(40)	60	(420)	300
Electricity Board	33	(250)	7	(60)	60	(460)	230
Sports training	33	(100)	17	(40)	50	(150)	700
Restaurant	32	(270)	8	(70)	60	(500)	160
Telephone operator	30	(270)	8	(70)	62	(560)	100
Ask stranger time of day	30	(260)	6	(60)	64	(560)	130
Repair washing machine	30	(200)	5	(30)	65	(430)	340
Driving test	30	(140)	16	(70)	54	(250)	540
Buy hi-fi	26	(180)	6	(50)	68	(470)	310
Travel agent	25	(200)	4	(30)	71	(570)	200
Gas Board	22	(130)	9	(50)	69	(410)	410

What is disturbing about these figures is that in almost half of the contexts more than half of the respondents who associated with the contexts claimed that the possibility of using Welsh was absent. This is the kind of competence context that leads to uncertainty about the relevance of a language for use, something that has a distinct effect upon institutionalization. It can of course be resolved by seeking out contexts where competence is available, but this is not always practical, and, in any case, our activity patterns are never that stable.

Second, the data reveal that when the possibility of using Welsh is available, the vast majority of respondents will use the language. This implies that the main issue associated with translating competence into use is not attitude, but competence availability. There are two exceptions where more than 10 per cent of the respondents claimed that they would not use Welsh when it was possible. First is the driving test, where a third of those who claim that they can use Welsh choose not to do so. This may well be explained by the availability of the test in Welsh, the inconvenience of requesting a test in Welsh, the language used in the learning context, and the desire not to generate a negative reaction in a situation of power imbalance. Second is 'sports training'. This tends to be a group activity which often involves non-Welsh speakers. By and large this would appear to be a complete refutation of the relevance of the domain concept and the associated implication that it is context that structures and conditions language use. This is not to imply that there are not some contexts where this might be the case and which we have not explored in this survey.

In considering the incidence of the possibility of using Welsh, there is a considerable range from a low of 22 per cent who claimed that it was possible to speak Welsh with the employees of the Gas Board to 92 per cent who claimed that it was possible with the local minister or vicar. Finding a pattern from among these universal figures is difficult. The utilities display a range from this figure for the Gas Board to figures of 30, 33, 48, 49 and 52 per cent for the telephone operator, Electricity Board, Water Board, tax office and the post office. Figures for the service and retail sectors tend to vary, ranging from 25 to 34 per cent for the travel agent, hi-fi purchase, washing machine repair, restaurant and taxi service, but increasing to between 46 and 57 per cent for hairdressing, newsagents, buying petrol, the pub and the local garage. We find the same range of variation for professionals, from a low of 35 per cent for the optician to a high of 63 per cent for the solicitor. The highest figures pertain to local authority services where 76 per cent claim they can and do use Welsh with their local councillor, 83 per cent with their child's teacher, 69 per cent at the local library and 56 per cent with the police. However, there are also low figures here as well, with only 37 per cent claiming they can and do use Welsh at the local theatre, 33 per cent at the local sports training facilities, 42 per cent at the social security office and 47 per cent with the social worker. Among the other categories, 57 per cent claim to be able to use and to use Welsh with their bank manager and 92 per cent, the highest incidence, with their minister or vicar.

As we have indicated, in general the health service does not do well in facilitating the use of Welsh. A recent survey commissioned by the Consumers' Association (Williams and Harris, 1993) indicated that the democratization of the health service associated with the new political order was far from effective in respect of both language-related and gender-related services. The system then in operation was simply not in a position to meet the needs and expectations of consumers who wished to have the services of a Welsh speaker or a female attending to their needs. This deficiency is currently being pursued by the Consumers' Association in another study that considers language. Similarly, despite the efforts of recent attempts by CCETSW to insist on the provision of the Welsh language in the Social Services, 44 per cent of the relevant respondents claimed that it was not possible to use Welsh with their social worker.

Considering these contexts by reference to language density should suggest the extent to which Welsh speakers seek out other Welsh speakers by reference to at least some of these activities. In South Glamorgan, Welsh speakers constitute just 7 per cent of the population (see Table 4.4). While the figures in Table 4.4 are universally lower than the general figures, given the low percentage of Welsh speakers in the area it would appear that there is a degree of selectivity involved with at least some of these activities. In a sense this is inevitable, since within a context which has such a low density it is inevitable that language-based activities will operate by reference to social networks rather than community. Thus individuals will integrate with specific social networks that relate to other Welsh speakers around certain institutional contexts such as work, the pub, the choir and so on. In other contexts which apply to the wider population, the use of the minority language will not be possible. However, even here there is some indication that there are some contexts in which the use of Welsh is selective in the sense that it exceeds the statistical expectation. This is a manifestation of the high prestige and status of Welsh in South Glamorgan and the increasing tendency for service providers and the private sector to recruit Welsh speakers for functions that pertain to their public profile.

Table 4.4. Welsh language use in selection of contexts, South Glamorgan

	I can and do		I can but don't		Not possible to speak Welsh		Not applicable
	%	(No.)	%	(No.)	%	(No.)	(No.)
Teacher	87	(13)	13	(2)	0		25
Priest/minister	75	(24)	0		25	(8)	8
Dentist	32	(12)	3	(1)	65	(24)	3
Tax office	32	(10)	0		68	(22)	8
In pub	29	(10)	0		71	(25)	5
Restaurant	26	(10)	0		74	(28)	2
Buy theatre tickets	26	(9)	3	(1)	71	(24)	6
Councillor	26	(7)	0		74	(20)	13
Library	21	(7)	3	(1)	76	(26)	6
Family doctor	20	(8)	3	(1)	77	(31)	0
Post office	15	(6)	5	(2)	80	(32)	0
Sports training	11	(2)	11	(2)	78	(14)	22
Paper shop	6	(2)	0		94	(31)	7
Taxi firm	5	(2)	0		95	(36)	2
Buy petrol	3	(1)	0		97	(33)	6

No. = 40.

It is also significant that, while there is some variation in the propensity to use Welsh with the different interlocutors by different age groups and social classes, the tendencies are always in the same direction, and the degree of difference is not such that it has a high level of significance. This, of course, is what would be expected of a highly motivated population and the institutionalization of language use. It could be claimed that where this variation is greatest, the lower is the stabilization of language use by reference to any particular context. This is what we find when we encounter the uncertainty associated with contexts which twenty years ago would have been highly stabilized by reference to the use of Welsh, but which by now retain a level of uncertainty. It is this that we witness in the data in Table 4.4 where the use of social networks gives a stabilization that is not available in the more general community context. Of course, there are also those contexts such as language use with the school where the reverse is the case. The process of relegitimization and reinstitutionalization of language use by context is an ongoing process.

3. *Social Contacts and Language Use*

The general picture of the use of Welsh and English with different interlocutors within the respondents' daily activities was supplemented by information concerning the capacity of those with whom they were in contact in different contexts to be able to speak Welsh and to use the language. Our intention here was to shift the analysis from the level of dyadic relationships to the broader issue of social networks. We did not seek to develop this data along the lines of any formal network analysis. Nonetheless, it does give an indication of the density of the contacts made by the respondents in different contexts and settings (see Tables 4.5, 4.6, 4.7).

The data indicate that social networks are largely constructed along language lines: a high proportion of the respondents' friends and neighbours are Welsh-speaking, and it is also apparent that Welsh is the language used in these contacts. The majority of respondents who had experience of the contexts indicated that more than half of their neighbourhood interaction was with Welsh speakers, the same being true of those whom they met in social contexts. The figure was even higher in respect of cultural activities, but lower by reference to shopping and sports activities. The similarity between the figures for competence and those for use we interpret as indicating that most respondents will use Welsh in these settings if they know that the interlocutor speaks the language. That is, there is no evidence of any

Table 4.5. Welsh-language ability of contacts, by social contexts (%)

	All or most	More than half	Half	Less than half	None	Not applicable (no.)
Friends in pub	37	27	16	12	9	245
Neighbours	32	21	17	14	16	14
Shop workers	17	17	19	16	30	40
Sports clubs	19	23	18	14	26	618
Cultural activities	50	20	12	7	10	374

reticence to use Welsh. There is also some indication that these settings are where the respondents seek out other Welsh speakers, since only 7 per cent claimed that they never used Welsh in the pub, and only 9 per cent in cultural activities. The incidence of the use of Welsh is lower for interaction with shop workers and sports clubs. As might be expected these patterns are subject to considerable spatial variation, a variation that corresponds with language density.

Table 4.6. Use of Welsh language with contacts, by social contexts (%)

	Always Welsh	More Welsh than English	Both Welsh and English	More English than Welsh	Always English	Not applicable (no.)
Friends in pub	38	26	17	13	7	258
Neighbours	33	22	18	15	12	35
Shop workers	18	17	20	20	28	81
Sports clubs	19	20	22	15	25	631
Cultural activities	51	19	13	9	9	385

Table 4.7. Language used with neighbours, by locality (%)

	Always Welsh	More Welsh than English	Both Welsh and English	More English than Welsh	Always English	Not applicable (no.)
Gwynedd	51	28	11	8	2	3
Clwyd	12	10	21	35	22	12
Powys	15	24	27	12	20	1
Dyfed	32	30	23	10	5	2
West Glamorgan	25	14	26	18	15	4
South Glamorgan	29	3	10	15	40	2
Mid Glamorgan	29	10	12	14	36	11
Gwent	42	8	0	8	42	0

4. Welsh-Language Cultural Activities

Beyond the range of formal community activities, such as those relating to the organization of community life (the community council, the school governors and so on which may or may not function through the medium of Welsh), there are a number of voluntary activities which focus exclusively on the use of Welsh. Many of these focus upon a particular conception of culture involving literary and musical activities which are deemed to derive from the past. In this respect they play a prominent role in the conception of Welsh culture and Welshness. Indeed, in some discourses they are the measuring stick of such conceptions, linking with an associated subject identity and with the signification of that to which preservation pertains. In this respect, as with all bilingual societies, it is exclusive and inclusive in that it excludes the non-Welsh speaker from this inclusion but suggests that it is something to which they should, nonetheless, aspire through learning the language. Some of these activities are specific to the particular community while others transcend community, thereby becoming the signification of national culture. Where the activities are specific to a community, they nonetheless carry a specific format and structure that gives a sense of uniformity so that anyone from another community will be familiar with these activities in any particular community. At the turn of the century, such activities were in a sense the ritual activities which confirmed community membership, and where the use of Welsh was taken for granted, or non-marked. By today the reverse is true, they confer a certain Welsh national membership at one level, but the use of Welsh is also symbolic and highly marked. The national activities are sometimes peripatetic, moving annually from one location to another. Local committees are established to raise funds in the following year's venue. These activities often become the focus of community-based Welsh-language activity during that year, and it is hoped that the energy and activities that are generated will persist beyond the event. These were the activities which we sought to identify in this part of the questionnaire.

The cultural activities which are directly linked with the Welsh language are comparatively well attended and supported. In the case of the present survey, the respondents were asked about their attendance at cultural activities currently, or in the past, and therefore the information gathered does not necessarily relate to contemporary practices. Many of the older respondents did not now follow these activities, although they may have done so in the past, while 'gigs' (rock or pop concerts) were a new concept to some and therefore outside their experience, either past or present. Ninety-five per cent of respondents aged fifty or over had never attended a Welsh rock or pop concert.

The eisteddfodau are the most popular Welsh-language cultural activity frequented by the respondents, particularly the Eisteddfod yr Urdd which involves mainly children and young people under the age of twenty-five. The Urdd, or Welsh League of Youth, is a very popular out-of-school activity in many localities, and the Urdd National Eisteddfod held in May each year is strongly supported by schools throughout Wales. The organization of the Urdd eisteddfodau is such that many local 'heats' are held prior to the national event, which means that many thousands of children and parents throughout Wales become involved at some stage. It is important not to confuse the Urdd National Eisteddfod and the Royal National Eisteddfod. The latter is a week-long event of cultural competition for adults, and includes a range of fringe events involving concerts, pop events and theatre. The peripatetic nature of the National Eisteddfod affords most people the opportunity of attending in their area. However, more than half the sample had never, or rarely, taken part in any of the activities, and it is apparent that the interest in a number of them, including the traditional singing and poetry meetings, are restricted to a very small minority (Table 4.8).

Table 4.8. Past and/or present attendance at Welsh cultural activities (%)

	Regularly	Occasionally	Rarely	Never
Urdd National Eisteddfod	20	27	13	41
National Eisteddfod	19	30	12	39
Welsh theatre	15	34	15	36
Rock concerts	8	14	10	68
Urdd youth camps	7	16	9	68
Cerdd Dant Festival	5	9	9	77
Talwrn y Beirdd	3	6	6	86

People from managerial and professional-class backgrounds are more likely to attend eisteddfodau than respondents from other social classes – 25 per cent and 29 per cent respectively attend, or used to attend, the National Eisteddfod regularly, compared with just 7 per cent of manual-class respondents. Overall, it is the professional classes who are most likely to attend these events, while between 50 and 60 per cent of the unskilled and semi-skilled have never been to an eisteddfod in their lives. Age and gender make little difference to patterns of attendance at the National Eisteddfod, but women and young people are more likely to attend the Urdd National. This to a large extent reflects the nature of the competitions which involve children and young people, and the predominant gender pattern of childcare, where it is mothers rather than fathers who are most likely to accompany their offspring to such events. Theatre-going is another activity associated with the higher social classes. Members of the professional class are the ones most likely to attend regularly, while people living in Clwyd, South and Mid-Glamorgan and Gwent are also more likely to go to the theatre than people in Gwynedd (where 55 per cent had never attended a Welsh-language drama). Women on the whole are more likely than men to be regular or occasional attenders, and the most regular attenders of Welsh-language theatre are professional women who are first-language speakers, and aged fifty years and over.

5. Other Social and Community Activities

While the 'cultural' activities referred to above may signify 'Welshness' in a particular sense, they are by no means the only community-based activities in Wales. It is here, where the language of involvement is not so closely linked to the activities, and where language use is contested and relatively stable, that one encounters the struggle over language. In many communities, Welsh remains the language of such activity and this is claimed to be a major incentive for non-Welsh speakers to learn the language. Elsewhere attempts are made not to exclude non-Welsh speakers while simultaneously retaining the principle of Welsh language use. This demands certain skills and commitment on the part of the chairperson chairing the meeting or event. In this respect one encounters two related tendencies. On the one hand, a tendency for those who feel strongly about using Welsh to feel 'obliged' to accommodate specific leadership positions in the community, and on the other, the seeking out of specific individuals who can play the brokering role between the two language groups for such positions. It is here more than anywhere else that there is a crucial need to discover and foster the means of best practice, and the use of appropriate cost-effective technologies that can allow community activities to proceed bilingually without exclusion.

One of the agencies which serves as the information base that integrates local communities is the *papur bro*. These are local news sheets prepared and distributed by volunteers which contain information about individuals, community activities and discussion sections.

There are fifty-two of these throughout Wales and a recent survey (Williams and Williams, 1991) indicates that the readership is close to 240,000. It is both the cheapest and most widely used Welsh-language medium in Wales. What stands out from Table 4.9 is the low level of activity, with only five of the twenty-nine activities attracting the majority of the respondents. Furthermore, of these only one, religion, involved behaviour structured around a formal organization. This is not necessarily surprising in that it is a tendency encountered across Europe (Williams, Strubell and Nelde, 1996). Furthermore, many of the activities listed are age or gender specific while others pertain to specialist interests. Again we encounter the formal institutions that are language specific – Merched y Wawr, Urdd, chapel and voluntary activities that are equally language specific – the *papur bro* and the local eisteddfod, where Welsh is almost the only language used. There are other activities, most notably the choir, Young Farmers' Clubs, amateur dramatics and folk dancing, where the use of English is limited. Still other activities seek to accommodate the non-Welsh speaker and language use is more mixed. Most notable here is the Mudiad Ysgolion Meithrin or Welsh nursery group where many of the children come from non-Welsh-speaking families. Local politics, charity work and the Parent–Teachers Association are somewhat similar in that there is a greater tendency to use both languages than merely to resort to English, this reflecting the attempt to accommodate while retaining Welsh. This may also apply to some of the listed activities which do not attract much activity from among the respondents. Finally, we consider the individual activities such as theatre attendance, sports activities and keep fit. The language used may well be dictated by availability within the locality, and people may, for example, attend theatre productions in either Welsh or English.

The only activity that is predominantly carried out in Welsh only is going to chapel or church. In Wales, the Nonconformist chapels have been a mainstay of the Welsh language for almost two centuries, and the recent process of secularization is part of the problem in reproducing the Welsh language effectively. In the present sample, 38 per cent note that they attend church or chapel regularly, 22 per cent sometimes, and 41 per cent seldom or never. The data shows that L1 speakers are almost twice as likely to attend a place of worship regularly as L2 speakers, and that a higher proportion of L2 speakers never attend church or chapel (Table 4.10). The most regular

Table 4.9. **Community activities of the respondents and the language used (%)**

	Only/mainly Welsh	Both Welsh and English	Only/mainly English	Not applicable
Chapel/church	59	7	4	30
Visiting friends	45	35	10	9
Pub	28	25	10	37
Eating out	24	33	19	25
Local eisteddfod	23	1	0	76
Community paper	21	0	1	78
Theatre	15	25	11	49
Charity work	12	12	6	71
Choir	10	3	1	86
Merched y Wawr	10	0	0	90
Urdd Club	10	0	0	90
Local Politics	9	5	2	84
Independent sports	8	8	7	77
Parent–Teachers Assn.	8	8	3	82
Young Farmers' Club	8	2	0	90
Sports Clubs	7	12	9	72
Welsh nursery group	7	2	1	91
Drama group	7	2	1	90
Other activities	6	3	2	89
Folk dancing	4	1	0	95
Keep fit	3	6	10	81
Fishing club	2	2	1	95
Environmental group	1	3	1	95
British Legion	1	2	2	95
Women's Institute	1	1	2	95
Freemasons	0	1	1	98
Round Table	0	0	1	99
Rotary Club	0	0	1	99
Lions Club	0	0	0	100

attenders of places of worship among the present sample are the older generation, aged sixty-five years and over – 68 per cent said they attend church or chapel regularly, compared with just 6 per cent of those aged between twenty and twenty-four – and women participate on a more regular basis than do men. Between a third and half of the younger people never attend a place of worship. Social class is not a distinctive factor in religious attendance.

Table 4.10. Attendance at church/chapel, by first language of
respondents (%)

| First language | Attend church/chapel | | | | No. |
	Regularly	Occasionally	Seldom	Never	
Welsh	41	23	15	21	805
English	25	14	19	42	155
Bilingual	33	20	15	33	40

Table 4.11. Attendance at place of worship, by locality (%)

| Locality | Attend church/chapel | | | | No. |
	Regularly	Occasionally	Seldom	Never	
Gwynedd	25	24	19	31	283
Clwyd	45	24	14	18	146
Powys	32	22	17	29	41
Dyfed	44	23	15	18	298
West Glamorgan	49	19	16	16	110
South Glamorgan	23	13	13	53	40
Mid Glamorgan	43	14	7	38	70
Gwent	33	25	17	25	12

What is evident from these data is that while religious attendance
and memberships may well reach significant levels, the degree of
influence on the lives of community members is far from being sufficient for it to operate as a normativizing institution and the basis of
social order and social control in the way that it once did. This does
not mean that it does not have some significance for those who are
involved, nor that the leaders of the religious institutions do not play
significant leadership roles, both in the local community and in the
more general political processes on a more dispersed geographical
basis. Rather, what is implied is that its influence in the daily lives of
community members has changed significantly.

Language of children's community activities

The data given so far pertain to the community activity of adults.
However, 649 of the respondents were also parents, and the data in
Table 4.12 refer to the activities in which their children were involved

and the language used in these activities. Clearly, there are a limited number of activities which stand out as involving a significant number of these children – religious activities, cultural institutions and activities and sports. Some of these overlap, and may not directly involve the parents. Thus, for example, many of the branches of the Urdd are run by the primary schools rather than by the local community. While it remains a voluntary activity the link with schooling means that there is a greater tendency to participate than might otherwise be the case. For some parents it functions as an after-school play group. The link to the local eisteddfod means there is a tendency for the same pieces learnt for the Urdd eisteddfod to become those set in the local eisteddfod, with teachers and some parents supporting the local eisteddfod by ensuring that children participate. Both the Urdd and local eisteddfod can appeal to a broad church in that the competitions

Table 4.12. Language of children's activities (%)

	Welsh	Welsh and English	English	Not applicable
Sunday school	40	4	4	53
Urdd Eisteddfod	39	1	0	60
Local eisteddfod	32	3	0	66
Aelwyd yr Urdd	31	1	1	68
Music lessons	12	4	11	72
Football	10	5	6	79
Swimming lessons	9	4	17	70
Drama group	9	1	2	88
Sports training	8	6	8	79
Rugby	8	5	5	88
Traditional singing	8	0	0	92
Orchestra	4	2	5	88
Gymnastics	3	2	6	89
Fishing Club	3	2	3	92
Horse riding	3	1	4	92
Cycling Club	2	1	1	96
Girl Guides	1	1	9	89
Boy Scouts	1	1	5	93
Cadets	1	1	2	96
Bird watching	0	0	2	98

No. = 649.

are not restricted to activities that demand fluency in Welsh, but involve artistic skills and musical accomplishment, as well choral and similar group activities. In this respect it is a useful forum for the integration of the L2 speaker. Nonetheless, there is a need to distinguish between the majority of participants and the few *aficionados* of the eisteddfod who diligently train their children in the requisite skills, and move from one local *eisteddfod* to another to compete.

In contrast to these activities which are almost exclusively conducted through the medium of Welsh, the sports activities are much more varied by language use. Many of these activities are arranged by the local council at the local sports centres or by local sports clubs. This often leads to complaints by some parents that such activities which, in contrast to the cultural activities, tend to appeal to the children are being offered through the medium of English only, thereby polarizing Welsh- and English-language activities. They argue that, if the local authorities provide education through the medium of Welsh, there should be continuity, and that the same choice should apply to leisure activities in order to avoid the ghetto-ization of the language in a limited range of activities.

The remaining activities are very much minority activities. Some of them such as the Girl Guides are institutionalized as English-language activities linked with the language of the broader Guide movement. This often results in the leader being a Welsh speaker who in other contexts may well use Welsh exclusively with the children, but English only in these activities.

6. Conclusion

The preceding data suggest a number of conclusions. First, it would appear that the extent of Welsh-language competence and the linking of this competence to use as institutionalized behaviour in most of Wales has declined to the point where there is a profound uncertainty concerning the possibility of using Welsh in a range of contexts where a generation ago this possibility would not have been questioned. It is this kind of situation that undermines the stabilization of institutionalized behaviour. It tends to be explained in different ways – by reference, for example, to the lack of confidence in situations of uncertainty which leads to the use of the normativized language that is common to all, in this case English. On the other hand, there are some activities where Welsh is used where it might not have been a generation ago.

What this indicates is that normative structures are constantly being stabilized and destabilized. It is here that it is useful to consider the relationship between institutionalization and legitimization. As we mentioned in the Introduction, we conceive of legitimation, not merely by reference to the 1993 Welsh Language Act and its consequences, but also by reference to social policy. In this respect the consequences of the Act in the form of the activities of the Welsh Language Board become features of social policy. By the same token, policy developed by statutory bodies that refer to language also become part of social policy. Thus legitimation enters into the realm of social practice and discursive statements, be they policy statements or legal statements, are transformed into social practice where they have an effect by reference to the construction of meaning. Such practices invariably carry a status which is implicit in the discourse and reinforce social practice. In this sense they become important aspects of the institutionalizing process, but they are only the prerequisite of some institutionalized practices.

This leads us to a consideration of the Welsh Language Act and its consequences. It is an issue with which we deal in greater detail in Chapter 8. The central thrust of the 1993 Welsh Language Act involved developing the basis whereby Welsh speakers can be enabled to use Welsh in the public sector. The activities of the agency responsible for implementing the Act – the Welsh Language Board – have focused mainly on supervising and overseeing the preparation of effective plans by public-sector bodies that lead to the implementation of this enabling goal. The only point we wish to make here is that the preceding evidence clearly demonstrates the need for such developments, but that they should also be accompanied by procedures that will ensure the integration of enablement with institutionalization.

While such developments do influence the language use of the individual there is also the need to consider community behaviour in relation to the voluntary activities linked to civil society, and how these relate to other activities that are central to the daily behaviour of individuals. In this respect there is a need to relate the activities of language promotion at the community level with the management of human capital that is implicit in community development. The various single-community studies to which we have referred above, despite their reliance on survey methods rather than participant observation, do suggest that the range of situations within Wales is complex. These studies should be considered side by side with the aggregate data which we have presented above.

5
Language Use in Education

1. Introduction

Education has been the site of struggle over Welsh for over a century. The introduction of compulsory universal education in the nineteenth century, and the state's goal of using it as means of promoting a normative order premised upon the unity of the United Kingdom and linguistic homogeneity, had a profound impact upon the linguistic competence of Welsh people. While there were periods when the exclusion of Welsh and its replacement by English as the language of reason appeared to be a formal policy, it is by no means clear that this was a prolonged objective, nor that it was universally applied and promoted. Although parents were encouraged to ensure that their children learnt English, and in some cases were informed that this involved changing the language of the home, by and large the separation between the home as a private domain and the public education was respected.

Much of the education in Wales prior to the 1870 Education Act had been in the hands of religious bodies, who delivered an uneven provision, being mainly concerned with teaching children to read the Bible and other religious texts in Welsh. In the eighteenth century, a system of Circulating Schools set up by Griffith Jones of Llanddowror taught some 150,000 children and adults in over 3,000 schools, and the success of this early venture encouraged the leaders of the new Methodist religious revival to set up their own schools to foster reading skills in Welsh. One of the early leaders of this movement, Thomas Charles, set up Sunday schools, which were open to all pupils, regardless of age or creed, who could demonstrate a 'desire to learn'. In time, the Methodist revival led to an expansion in Welsh-language publishing. In addition to the hymns and sermons of the new religious leaders, texts concerned with history, poetry and antiquarian interests began to appear. Although the Methodist church in Wales operated at all levels through the medium of Welsh, its leaders were not particularly concerned with fostering the Welsh language *per se*. Rather, they recognized that to save the souls of the great majority of the population who were monoglot Welsh, they had to nurture the language. In this respect, they appeared to differ from the established Anglican Church, which was also active in promoting its own schools, but teaching mainly through the medium of English to monoglot Welsh pupils (Davies, 1993). Increasingly, from the beginning of the nineteenth century, more strenuous attempts were made to teach English to children in schools in order that they could reap the economic benefits of an English education and integrate more fully into British society (Webster, 1982; Baker, 1985; Williams, H. G., 1999).

It is apparent that the religious bodies could only achieve so much in the field of education, their main aspirations lying elsewhere, and after 1833 the state began to take a more active role in educational provision. Probably the most significant development during this period was the publication of the *Report of the Commissioners of Inquiry into the State of Education in Wales* which appeared in 1847. The Report, commonly referred to as the 'Blue Books', gave a damning picture of Welsh society, forcefully condemning the Welsh language as a vast drawback which kept the Welsh people in a state of poverty, immorality and degradation. There was a considerable public reaction to the report, with churchmen and other public figures vigorously denouncing its claims. Despite their protestations and refutation of the contents, for almost a century thereafter the report served to destroy the confidence of Welsh educators and the public alike in the use of Welsh in the education system. By the end of the nineteenth century, the voluntary Welsh-medium system of popular education had been undermined by a state-sponsored English-medium system (J. L. Williams, 1973: 94).

In the years following the 1889 Welsh Intermediate Education Act, Welsh was considered by headteachers to be 'an inferior language and certainly an unnecessary one; it was of no help in "getting on"' (G. E. Jones, 1982: 18). Its low status and perceived irrelevance led to the exclusion of Welsh from almost all formal education, and it was not until 1927 that some changes were seen in this pattern. A report on *Welsh in Education and Life* attempted to encourage the use of Welsh in education, partly in order to stimulate the growth of a Welsh middle class; as it argued,

Welsh Wales will be unable to develop a middle class because the members of that class will necessarily become Anglicized as they rise in the social scale, unless some immediate provision is made for their children in those areas in which economic conditions have forced the parents to settle. (Davies, 1993: 62)

The report recommended increased resources to be allocated to training teachers and for the preparation of appropriate teaching materials through the medium of Welsh. At the time, not one of the 135 secondary schools surveyed used Welsh as an everyday language in school.

By the mid-1940s, Welsh had become the main teaching medium in schools in the more Welsh-speaking areas, and attempts were made to teach some Welsh to monoglot English speakers in the more Anglicized areas (Baker, 1985: 42). One key development for Welsh-language policy in schools was the report of the Central Advisory Council for Education (Wales) in 1967, a document usually referred to as the Gittins Report. It argued that Welsh should be introduced to learners at an early age, and that it should also be used as a medium of instruction in schools, with the objective of achieving an effective bilingualism by the end of the primary school stage. The recommendations of the Gittins Report formed the basis of what was to become a substantial transformation in the place of Welsh in the school curriculum in the 1970s. Another significant development was the transfer of control over primary and secondary education in Wales to the Secretary of State for Wales in 1970. The setting up of designated bilingual schools – at primary level in 1939 and secondary level in 1956 – was a key development which mushroomed between the 1960s and 1980s. The subsequent growth in Welsh-language education boosted the status of Welsh and the burgeoning class of Welsh-speaking education professionals.

In the UK the application of state policy in schooling is the responsibility of the local authorities who are free to develop their own version of these policies, and this accounts for the regional variations in provision and practice referred to above. From the passing of the 1944 Education Act until the mid-1970s, the emphasis was on developing the kind of partnership between the central and local state that is implicit in the concept of a 'national policy, locally administered'. During the 1980s education policy was increasingly centralized. The national curriculum after the 1988 Education Reform Act has led to a

centralized policy on first-language (L1) and second-language (L2)
Welsh lessons being universally imposed on almost all schools in
Wales. As a consequence, there is plethora of approaches to the role
of Welsh in the schooling process, the variety of which cannot be
explained simply by language demographics – the difference in
language policies between Clwyd and West Glamorgan, for example,
cannot be accounted for by language densities within their respective
populations, as Baker argues (1995: 156). Rather, much if not all of
the associated policy is politically motivated. Local authorities have
responded to parental pressure and have occasionally adopted a
proactive stance. The result is that in the primary schools in north-
west Wales all, or almost all, of the curriculum is delivered through
the medium of Welsh, while at the other end of the language dimension, schools in areas such as Gwent, Pembroke and the border areas
with England deliver the curriculum mainly in English, but teach
Welsh for half an hour or so a day (Baker, 1995: 156). One of the
most developed and detailed policies derives from Gwynedd County
Council, where the percentage of first-language Welsh speakers is the
highest in Wales. On the other hand in South Glamorgan, where the
incidence of Welsh speakers is among the lowest in Wales, constant
pressure by well-organized, politically aware parents has led to a
comparatively favourable Welsh-language provision in schools. This
is also the location where Welsh-language prestige is highest. Dyfed,
the area of Wales with the second highest density of Welsh speakers,
also has a detailed language education policy, with established catego-
rizations of bilingual schools: those where Welsh is the dominant
language of the curriculum; bilingual schools where the use of Welsh
and English vary according to demand and resources; and schools
where English is the main language of instruction and where Welsh is
taught as a second language. Other local education authorities in
Wales provide a variety of bilingual education policies and practices
within their schools.

   There is also a need to consider the influence of teacher autonomy.
In many cases the implementation of local authority policy in the
teaching of Welsh was left to the head teacher. This in itself generates
a range of contextualization. Even where an authority may have a
blanket policy by reference to the provision of Welsh-medium teaching it is possible to encounter opt-out cases where the same authority
ignores practice that provides limited provision. The recent introduction of parental choice in school selection means that this variation in

provision becomes a crucial element in the associated decision making. It may lead to 'Welsh dodging' or the opposite. It has led activists to insist upon effective monitoring practices that will ensure effective Welsh-language provision where policy dictates. This, in turn, links to a dissatisfaction with the current monitoring of achievement in schools where it is increasingly evident that different standards are applied to English and Welsh, with children achieving qualifications in Welsh when they are incapable of using the language. The Welsh Language Board requires local authorities to generate language plans for the provision of Welsh in schools throughout all LEAs in Wales. This in itself can generate tension between some local authorities and the Board. However, even if fully implemented, it is unlikely that it will lead to the desired level of monitoring since the Board places a great deal of importance on self-monitoring, although it monitors some aspects itself. For some the answer to a situation which they regard as entirely inappropriate to promoting Welsh as a national language is to establish an independent education system on a par with that in Scotland. The body responsible for this system would give priority to a provision within which Welsh achieves parity with English.

Much of what has been gained by reference to Welsh-medium education has been the consequence of 'parent power'. Where the local authorities have not adopted a proactive approach to introducing Welsh into its schools there have been a series of local protests by parents insisting upon Welsh-medium provision for their children. Such protests have multiplied as the prestige of Welsh has increased. The emergence of Cardiff, first as a capital and subsequently as a major administrative and financial centre within the UK, was paralleled by the industrial decline of the south Wales Valleys. The demise of coal production and the steel industry led to large-scale unemployment and deprivation, and these locations increasingly became dormitory areas for the south Wales coastal belt. Simultaneously, the restructuring of that coastal belt involved the growth of a number of institutions which used Welsh in their daily activities. As early as the 1970s (Williams, Roberts and Isaac, 1978) it was noticed that these parallel developments were generating a reassessment of the relevance and prestige of Welsh among parents in locations where the stigmatic effect of hegemonic principles had been most effective. Working-class parents, who did not see their children's future in terms of a link between social and geographic mobility and yet sought social mobility for their children, recognized the value of Welsh for certain occupations. This served as the motivation for demanding the means whereby their children would have access to the language. Many of these parents were the children of those who themselves spoke Welsh but who had ensured that their children did not learn it, often in the belief that it was detrimental to their ability to master English and to 'get on in the world'.

This process has been replicated elsewhere but not on a uniform basis. The focus is often on the local administration centres, largely for two reasons. First, the geographical mobility of professionals within Wales focuses upon these centres and ensures a confident Welsh-language leadership in these localities. Second, it is in the public rather than the private sector that the prestige of Welsh has been established and consolidated, often involving these same 'quiet activists'. This also means that the social profiles of the schools where Welsh has been introduced vary considerably. In some locations, mainly in the declining industrial areas, the vast majority of the children come from homes where neither parent speaks Welsh. In low-density areas many of the children come from homes where only one parent speaks Welsh and where the language is rarely used, leading one analyst to claim that there is a conscious tendency for these parents to resort to schooling as the basis for reproducing the language (Roberts, 1985, 1987).

One response to the 'parent power' that motivated the extension of Welsh-medium schooling has been a corresponding 'parent power' movement resisting such developments. This contributes to the uneven curricular development within such schools, although it must be acknowledged that the situation has improved considerably from the situation of the 1950s where 'Welsh and Religious Instruction' were the only contexts in which Welsh was heard in most Welsh secondary schools. A number of Welsh-medium schools and educators have been reluctant to extend the use of Welsh to the teaching of science subjects. This is an extension of the modernist discourse and how it distinguishes between reason and emotion (Williams, 1987a). Science is viewed as the epitomy of reason whereas the arts – poetry, music, and so on – pertain to the world of emotion. It is this object construction and the associated social construction of a patriarchal society that contributes to the tendency to direct males towards the sciences and women towards the arts. This was replicated in the tendency to teach science through the medium of English and the arts through the medium of Welsh. That is, males were rational and females emotional, and by the same token English was the language of reason while Welsh pertained to the emotional.

In this work we treat schooling as a primary agency of language production and reproduction. It should be evident from the above that the cases in which it is the main agency of language production are increasing. This has been a cause of concern for some. The fear revolves around the awareness that even in 1981 there were almost as many homes with Welsh speakers where both heads of household did not speak the language as there were those where both household heads did speak Welsh. This means that unless the kinds of language use trends we report upon here can be reversed Wales is close to the point where the majority of the speakers of Welsh will have learnt the language through production rather than reproduction. This suggestion is supported by an awareness that extending the use of Welsh in the transition from school to work is far from being a common occurrence (Williams and Williams, 1998). There are others who adopt a language purity stance, claiming that those who learn the language through production fail to master the linguistic competencies of the standard form. However, we suspect that this focus upon the struggle in language rather than on the struggle over language is rapidly receding.

2. *Language of Respondents' Education*

Given what we have indicated above about the relatively recent increase in the provision of Welsh-medium teaching it is not surprising that fewer than half the respondents obtained all of their primary education through the medium of Welsh. On the other hand about three-quarters of them had received some of their primary education in the language. In this respect it should be recognized that some 12 per cent of the respondents had learnt Welsh as adults (Table 5.1).

It appears that to an extent Welsh is structured into the experiences of the informants as a means of achieving competence rather than as an academic medium of instruction. We suggest this because of the decreasing tendency among the respondents to have received Welsh-medium tuition at the higher-education levels. Only 15 per cent of the respondents had received their entire secondary-level schooling through the medium of Welsh. This is partly accounted for by the age of the respondents and the availability of Welsh-medium teaching in their localities.

Table 5.1. Language of respondents' education (%)

Level of education	Welsh only	Welsh and English	English only	Other language	Not applicable
Primary	45	32	23	0	0
Secondary	15	43	38	0.3	4
Further	4	9	27	0.2	60
Higher	5	9	19	0.3	67

The younger respondents are more likely to have received all or part of their education in Welsh. Approximately 14 per cent of the respondents were born after 1971, when Welsh-medium education became more widely available, 28 per cent were born between 1956 and 1970, 34 per cent between 1931 and 1955, and 24 per cent before 1930. Bearing in mind this age distribution, it is perhaps not surprising to see that less than half the sample received all their primary education in Welsh, although in total about three-quarters had obtained some Welsh-medium instruction at that level (Table 5.2). The data in this table certainly oversimplify the context of such factors as the respective use of Welsh and English in education. Nonetheless, the influence of the increase in Welsh-medium and bilingual education over time is evident. This trend has not extended to

Table 5.2. Language of respondents' education by age (%)

Age	PRIMARY			SECONDARY		
	Welsh	Welsh/ English	English	Welsh	Welsh/ English	English
> 19	72	28	0	51	45	4
20–24	64	28	8	26	65	9
25–29	55	35	10	28	55	17
30–39	51	32	17	18	51	31
40–49	42	34	24	11	44	45
50–64	40	29	31	7	34	59
65+	30	34	35	6	29	65

encompass further and higher education where Welsh-medium provision remains rudimentary. The bulk of Welsh-medium teaching at the tertiary level in Wales is concentrated mainly at the university colleges of Bangor and Aberystwyth, although smaller numbers are taught at Wales's other university colleges. At the two main centres, however, Welsh-medium students represent only 6 per cent of the total student population, and the lack of Welsh-medium development at the higher-education level is a topical issue (D. G. Jones, 1998, 1999). The laggardly development of vocational Welsh-medium education in further education colleges has also been the subject of some discussion in recent years, and the situation is currently being reviewed by the Welsh Language Board (1999).

3. Language of Children's Education

Given the increasing exposure to Welsh-medium or bilingual education since the early 1970s, and the suggestion that where it is available it will be used, it is interesting to turn to the language of education of the respondent's children (Table 5.3). There is a far higher tendency for the children to receive their education through the medium of Welsh at all levels than was the case by reference to their parents. Given that in Gwynedd all public education at the primary level is through the medium of Welsh but with English introduced gradually until there is parity of instruction by the age of eleven, although the day-to-day language of the school remains Welsh, some of this increase is not necessarily a consequence of parental choice. It should also be recognized that the data cover a considerable time span.

Table 5.3. Language of children's education (%)

Level of education	Welsh only	Welsh and English	English only	Not applicable
Primary	72	16	12	0
Secondary	40	46	14	10
Further	31	40	29	33
Higher	14	14	33	40

Table 5.4. Language of children's education, by age of respondents (%)

Age	PRIMARY				SECONDARY			
	Welsh	W/E	English	N/A	Welsh	W/E	English	N/A
> 19	0	0	0	100	0	0	0	100
20–24	2	2	0	96	0	0	0	100
25–29	18	2	0	80	1	7	0	92
30–39	46	10	5	39	16	19	3	62
40–49	64	12	7	17	42	34	4	20
50–64	60	14	9	17	39	40	6	15
65+	50	11	15	24	20	35	22	23

The pattern shown in Table 5.4 is the same as for the respondents themselves. However, if anything, the tendency for opting for Welsh-medium or bilingual education is even more pronounced. As provision becomes more widespread and more accessible fluent Welsh speakers take maximum advantage of this provision.

What is suggested here is that the choice for the older respondents, if indeed it was a choice, involved either Welsh-medium or English-medium education for their children at the primary level. For the younger age groups this extends to include bilingual education at secondary level. For those under the age of thirty there is a rejection of English-medium education. This is a manifestation of the changing policies over time and its impact upon choice and provision.

The data appear to imply that the change is in the direction of 'Welsh-only' education at the primary level whereas at the secondary level there has been a parallel shift away from monolingual English-language education; however, the data do not allow us to determine the extent to which this is in the direction of monolingual Welsh-medium education or bilingual education. Undoubtedly this depends upon the policy of the respective local authorities and the availability of one form or other of education. The increase in Welsh-medium education at the tertiary level is also striking even if it does not reach the level of that in the primary and secondary levels.

The matter of language choice was approached by directly asking the respondents about their preferences of language for their children's education and the availability of that preference (Table 5.5). Evidently, the majority opted for a Welsh-medium preference while a substantial number indicated that there was an absence of choice. Of those who claimed that no choice was available at the primary level, 29 per cent were in Gwynedd. Given that the local authority in Gwynedd has a bilingual educational policy this could mean several things. The respondents may be located where the local school has been allowed to deviate from the official policy or where it has not been implemented by the head teacher and the school governors. On the other hand it could be a claim that either Welsh-medium or English-medium options were not available. Of the remainder within this category, 43 per cent were in Dyfed, 4 per cent in Powys, 10 per cent in both West Glamorgan and Clwyd, and the remainder divided between Gwent and Mid Glamorgan. It is significant that, if this is a measure of effective provision, the most positive locations are those with the lowest density of Welsh speakers – South Glamorgan, Mid Glamorgan and Gwent. Of those who claimed an absence of choice at the secondary level, again Dyfed stands out, with 38 per cent making such a claim compared with 31 per cent in Gwynedd. Of the remainder, 12 per cent were in West Glamorgan, 10 per cent in Clwyd and the remainder divided among the other counties. This speaks for itself by reference to public perception of choice within existing policy.

Table 5.5. Availability of language choice in education (%)

Language choice	Primary	Secondary
Welsh	60	58
No choice available	31	28
No preference	5	7
English	4	7

Where there is a choice of language as a medium of education, this has to be within reasonable travelling distance. The development of Welsh-medium provision has reached the point where the majority of parents in Wales are within reach of such a provision. However, this does not mean that there are no gaps in the provision, nor that an element of sacrifice might not be involved, with children having to spend far more time being bussed to Welsh-medium schools than would be the case if they chose the nearest English-medium school. That is, with limited exceptions, Welsh-medium education remains an 'opt-in' additional component of universal English-medium provision rather than being a normative entity. Of the respondents, 86 per cent claimed to be able to obtain primary education for their children in the language of their choice within their own catchment area, and 76 per cent at secondary level. The difference between these figures and those pertaining to 'no choice available' in Table 5.5 is partly accounted for by the increase in provision between today and the time referred to by those parents whose children have already been through the system. Thus 68 per cent of those who claimed that there was an absence of choice at the primary level and 84 per cent of those who made the same claim by reference to secondary education were over fifty-five years of age.

Eleven per cent of primary school pupils and 19 per cent of secondary school pupils have to travel outside their own catchment area to receive education in their chosen language, and a small minority, between 3 and 5 per cent note that there is no choice available. The majority of those who claimed to have to travel outside of the normal catchment area at the primary level were from West Glamorgan (33 per cent), Mid Glamorgan (23 per cent), South Glamorgan (16 per cent) and Dyfed (12 per cent). This is partly a manifestation of the differences in the size of catchment areas in rural and urban areas. The only difference by reference to secondary education was the lower percentage located in Dyfed and South Glamorgan.

Table 5.6 indicates the spatial distribution of parental choice at the primary level. The absence of choice is most prevalent in the three counties with the strongest Welsh-medium educational policies, that is, where Welsh-medium education most closely approximates the normative. Thus in Gwynedd most public primary education is through the medium of Welsh. The exceptions are located in specific urban centres. The option for most of those parents seeking to avoid such education for their children is to resort to provision in the private sector, and a large number of parents who can afford it seek this option. In Dyfed and Powys, and to a lesser extent in Clwyd 'no choice available' involves an unwillingness or inability to have children travel to schools where the parental choice, be it Welsh or English, is available. Elsewhere the spectrum changes and Welsh-medium provision tends, at least thus far, to be the exception rather than the rule. What emerges from these data is that parents have a clear conception of choice and that for the respondents this, almost exclusively, was expressed in terms of a preference for Welsh-medium education.

Table 5.6. Choice of language of primary education, by locality (%)

	Welsh	No choice available	No preference	English	No.
South Glamorgan	91	0	4	4	23
Gwent	83	17	0	0	6
Mid Glamorgan	81	11	0	8	53
Clwyd	72	22	0	6	92
West Glamorgan	66	23	6	5	86
Powys	59	36	0	5	22
Gwynedd	52	35	10	3	162
Dyfed	49	46	4	2	182

The issue of school choice is complicated. It is further complicated by the addition of Welsh-medium education into the equation. Parents tend to cite a range of reasons for selecting Welsh-medium education for their children. Among them is the belief that Welsh-medium schools have a greater degree of discipline, that the commitment of the teachers to promoting the language leads to a more positive approach to education in general, and that Welsh-language cultural activities give a wider range of presentation skills while also promoting a sense of community (Williams, Roberts and Isaac, 1978; Williams and Roberts, 1983). Such reasons are additional to the possibility that a knowledge of Welsh affords additional life chances within the regional labour market. Furthermore, such reasons are by no means universal across Wales but partly rely on the prestige of Welsh within local labour markets. In those areas where Welsh-medium education is universal, some parents may choose between one Welsh-medium school and another Welsh-medium school, the reasons given for selection being unrelated to language provision. Furthermore, where provision makes it possible, there does tend to be continuity between attendance in Welsh-medium education at the primary level and such education at the secondary level. That is, the decision concerning the language of education is made at an early stage in the child's educational career. Thus the number who begin Welsh-medium education at the secondary level is limited. Where choice is available some Welsh-medium secondary schools may even discourage parents from selecting the school for children who have not attended Welsh-medium primary schools. Consequently, generalizing from the data is difficult.

The figures at the secondary-school level (Table 5.7) are not significantly different from those for the primary level, indicating a high degree of continuity between the two levels. A higher proportion of parents in South Glamorgan, West Glamorgan, Dyfed and Gwynedd choose English-medium education for their children, although the proportions who take this option are still fairly small. In all probability, one of the reasons for this is associated with the situation in which parents reside within an area where they are part of the catchment area of a Welsh-medium primary school and an English-medium secondary school. Inevitably there will be a range of other factors in operation. Their decision may involve the perceived quality of the respective primary and secondary schools in the localities, or perhaps these parents are happy for their children to receive a grounding in Welsh without it necessarily being their choice as a medium for all their education. However, it appears that there is a substantial through-put of Welsh-medium pupils in these areas, with a high proportion of Welsh speakers in the southern counties of Wales choosing a Welsh-medium secondary education for their children.

Table 5.7. Choice of language of secondary education, by locality (%)

	Welsh	No choice available	No preference	English	No.
South Glamorgan	84	0	5	11	19
Gwent	83	17	0	0	6
Mid Glamorgan	75	16	2	8	51
Clwyd	73	20	0	7	82
Powys	68	26	0	5	19
West Glamorgan	56	25	8	11	73
Dyfed	52	37	4	6	161
Gwynedd	46	34	15	5	146

The analysis of parental choice of language of children's primary school education by the social class of their parents (Table 5.8) indicates that the higher the social class the higher the percentage of children receiving Welsh-medium education. However, it is also significant that this discrepancy is not reflected in the alternative option of English-medium education. Nor are the figures for those expressing 'no preference' high. The variation in the percentages is therefore accounted for by the higher incidence of those among the lower social classes who claimed that no choice was available. As we have indicated, this will mean different things in different locations. In a limited number of locations it will mean that English-medium education is not available. In other locations it will mean the converse. The difficult thing to explain is why this response should vary by social class rather than by location. We have already indicated that the claim that choice is not available has dwindled across the age span of the respondents. It is also significant that those who claim that their children travel outside of the catchment area in order to obtain Welsh-medium primary education are almost exclusively in the middle classes, whereas when it comes to secondary education the class difference is not significant (Tables 5.8, 5.9).

Table 5.8. Language of primary education, by social class of parents (%)

	Welsh	No choice available	No preference	English	No.
Professional	75	20	3	2	170
Managerial	69	29	0	2	45
Skilled non-manual	62	26	6	6	174
Skilled manual	59	32	5	4	114
Semi-skilled	37	50	8	5	62
Unskilled	36	57	5	2	61

Table 5.9. Language of secondary education, by social class of parents (%)

	Welsh	No choice available	No preference	English	No.
Professional	73	21	3	3	150
Managerial	72	23	3	3	39
Skilled non-manual	57	24	8	11	157
Skilled manual	56	28	7	9	98
Semi-skilled	42	36	14	8	59
Unskilled	33	56	7	4	54

Above we implied that there remains a suspicion about the adequacy of Welsh for the teaching of science. In order to explore this issue parents were asked about the medium through which their children were taught the different school subjects (Table 5.10). Our suspicion in this respect is sustained by the data. The figures show a strong tendency for arts-based subjects to be taught through the medium of Welsh, with science being more evenly distributed between Welsh and English. The discursive construction of the two objects 'Welsh' and 'science' remain in contradiction for some educators. It is also interesting to note in this respect that, despite the insistence on bilingual education, the so-called 'foreign languages' are still taught either through the medium of Welsh or English rather than by recourse to the language being taught. That is 'foreign languages' are still constructed as subjects rather than media. It recalls the recent past when students were barred from studying Welsh at the University of Wales because of a lack of English-language competence. Welsh was taught through the medium of English!

Table 5.10. Language of school subjects (%)

Subject	Welsh	Welsh and English	English
Welsh	85	5	10
Religion	66	9	25
History	65	8	27
Geography	61	9	31
Art	60	9	31
Physical education	60	12	27
Business	52	8	40
Foreign languages	52	10	38
Mathematics	46	11	43
Science	45	12	43

In order to explore the interplay between the family and education it is possible to examine language use among siblings and the language of education and parental language ability. This is important in that within diglossic contexts there is a tendency for children approaching adulthood, rather than conforming with family norms, to follow peer-group practice and the dictates of the normative order which invariably conforms with dominant language use. That is, certain activities and the associated construction of subjects and objects are destabilized by reference to language use for certain age groups. Despite the limited number of cases of second-language speakers, such an investigation will also allow us to investigate the relationship between family and education in language use by reference to those who are part of the production rather than the reproduction stream, that is, those children who learn the language in school rather than in the home.

Table 5.11 indicates that the vast majority of children whose primary education was entirely through the medium of Welsh speak Welsh exclusively together. This is in contrast with those who received their education through the medium of English of whom only a quarter speak Welsh exclusively together. Interestingly, the figures for those children receiving a bilingual education fall between these extreme values.

Table 5.11. Language children speak with each other, by language of primary education (%)

Language with each other	Language of education			No.
	Welsh only	Bilingual	English only	
Welsh always/most often	80	55	25	349
Equal Welsh and English	8	5	7	37
English always/most often	12	40	69	111
No.	371	65	61	497

Where one or both parents spoke little or no Welsh and the children attended a Welsh-medium school, 58 per cent of the siblings spoke Welsh at least half of the time together. This compared with only 38 per cent of those from the same background who attended bilingual primary school and 7 per cent of those who attended English-medium schools. Clearly education does have some bearing upon language use. When one or both parents speak Welsh 'very well' or 'quite well' the difference is significant. The difference between Welsh-medium and bilingual educational results in this respect is far less when there is a use input from the home (Table 5.12). The relationship is brought home when we recognize that children with parents who speak little or no Welsh who attend a bilingual school are as likely to use Welsh together as those children whose parents are fluent but who attend an English-medium school.

Turning to the same relationship, but by reference to the language of secondary education (Table 5.13) we find the same kind of relationship, but with a somewhat stronger tendency to use English. The low incidence of use of both languages suggests that there is a strong separation of the respective languages as objects and the meanings that they signify. The main difference, however, is that at this age there is little difference in the effect of Welsh-medium and bilingual education. These data suggest that the medium of education does have a bearing upon the institutionalization of language use among the young.

Table 5.12. Parental Welsh-language ability, medium of education and siblings' language of interaction (%)

| | Siblings' language together | | | |
	Welsh or Welsh/English	Mainly or only English	Welsh or Welsh/English	Mainly or only English
Child's education				
Welsh-medium	91	9	58	42
Bilingual	77	23	38	62
English-medium	39	61	7	93
Parental ability	very/quite good		little/none	

No. = 498.

Table 5.13. Language children speak with each other, by language of secondary education (%)

| Language with each other | Language of education | | | No. |
	Welsh only	Bilingual	English only	
Welsh always/most often	76	77	36	338
Equal Welsh and English	9	7	5	34
English always/most often	15	16	59	101
No.	187	223	63	473

4. Conclusion

It would appear that the majority of the respondents, in one way or another, have been directly involved in the growth of Welsh-medium and bilingual education during the past fifty years. As provision has expanded, they have increasingly taken advantage of it. There remains a small percentage of this group who seek English-medium education for their children from personal preference, and not because of the absence of Welsh-medium or bilingual provision. There are also those who are drawn into Welsh-medium or bilingual education without reflecting upon its value, this merely being normative practice in their area.

There is a clear relationship between the family and education in the propensity to transform competence into use. In this respect, given the increasing tendency for language group endogamy to decline, it is of paramount importance that attention should be given to integrating the competence gained through schooling into social practice across context. In this respect, what we have considered here is the optimal context associated with a cohesive group of highly competent Welsh-language speakers. Yet the evidence does indicate that there are profound problems to be confronted once we move away from this context to consider those who achieve competence through schooling but without the support associated with familial use of Welsh.

Within the provision it is disturbing to see the continuation of the distinction between the functions allocated to the respective languages and how it reflects the science–arts distinction. We view this as a manifestation of how languages are constructed in terms of reason and emotion, even though the extreme of this construction where only one language is worthy of inclusion in educational practice has, by now, been overcome. In this respect, it is evident that the link between education and the world of work which is the primary structural referent of education must be consolidated.

Historically, schooling has been constructed with two goals in mind. First, the creation of 'good' citizens within a highly normative understanding of 'citizenship', and second, the creation of a labour force which services the labour markets. Both of these processes are currently undergoing a profound restructuring. As we discuss in detail in the concluding chapter the current process of globalization, when linked with neo-liberal discourse, results in the demise of the homogenizing ideology of the state that derived from the advent of modernism and the creation of the modern state. This shift opens up space for diversity, including the reorientation of minority language groups within normative space. By the same token, the inability of the state to regulate the economy within its boundary and the shift of regional development prerogative to the European level obliges us to rethink the nature of labour markets. The associated focus upon regional and local economies corresponds to a new awareness of the significance of local and regional labour markets. The primary goal of a proactive language planning within this new context must be to integrate education with work, employment and labour. Thus far this has not happened. Rather, we have seen a series of piecemeal policies, often formulated as reactions to public pressure and bearing no relationship to the economic order. It is with this in mind that we turn to a consideration of the relevance of the Welsh language for work and employment.

6
Language Use in the Workplace

1. Introduction

It should be evident from what we have said in the preceding chapters about the relationship between motivation and language prestige that the entry of minority languages into the relationship of production, and thereby into the factors of labour markets, is crucial to the renewal of the associated language groups. We have argued with reference to Wales that the cultural division of labour, which largely derived from the modernist regulatory regional development policies of the state, was responsible for limiting the entry of Welsh into the relationships of production in the private sector. The current restructuring process suggests a different organizational structure, one which favours the potential of diversity. Whether the opening of this space leads to reactions favourable for the promotion of minority language groups remains to be seen.

The exclusion of minority languages from specific economic practices is linked with modern capitalism. The argument in favour of languages of reason, as opposed to those which remained in the realm of the emotional, was linked with the emergence of economic science as that which made economics part of the rational order. The centrality of the market relied upon the idea of rational actors sharing a common understanding of market principles. Such developments excluded minority languages from the practices of capitalism.

In our theoretical consideration we emphasized the importance of language prestige by reference to the value of a language for social mobility. There is no doubt that within capitalism social mobility plays a highly significant role in that it is part of the ideological order that promises self-improvement to the industrious and able individual. On the other hand, language segments the labour market, while also opening the entire system to anyone who can operate by reference to all of the relevant languages. Thus prestige must involve not merely social mobility, but also the lateral access to particular segments of the labour market. In this respect it is important to consider both social and occupational mobility. Modern capitalism has been constructed out of the link between modernity, the economic order and the political order that focuses upon the state. For this reason there has been a tendency to relate labour markets to state languages. It is the manner in which, and the extent to which, Welsh has been brought into this structure that becomes the focus of this chapter.

Our work on language and class fractioning in Gwynedd (Morris, 1990, 1995) suggested a close relationship between the economic structure and language-related community activity. That work focused on the discussion of the new middle class of managers, which, by reference to the Marxist focus on class as involving the relations of production and access to the means of production, would be expected to align either with the proletariat on account of their being employed workers, or with the bourgeoisie on account of their control over capital. The work demonstrated that language played a crucial role in this fragmentation of social classes. Welsh-language competence gave access to community resources conditioned by language, and created status groups which focused around language. These integrated the new Welsh-speaking middle class with the proletariat. In contrast, those of the new middle class who had moved into the area and who did not speak Welsh affiliated with the bourgeoisie.

Interesting though such findings are, they should not be surprising. Hechter has suggested an association between interaction patterns and occupational structure. He states: 'Social relations within the workplace will determine much about the course of interaction in other spheres of social life as well. Occupations shape interaction patterns by influencing residential location and by promoting divergent life styles and social identities' (1978: 298). Indeed, he goes further, claiming that 'Occupations can be an important domain for intragroup interaction and tend to have distinct economic interests' (1978: 300). If this claim holds true then it is reasonable to expect that the language of work will also have an influence upon language use in other social contexts.

The historical context of the exclusion of Welsh from specific relations of production dates to at least the sixteenth century. The Act of Annexation of Wales in 1536 sought to integrate Wales and the Welsh language into the English state (Williams, 1987a). One of the consequences was that the Welsh language was restricted to civil society – by and large, to the family, community and religion. Its use in public life was severely restricted over a period of four centuries, and it is only in the last half of the present century that there has been a tangible increase in the use of Welsh in the public sphere. Such developments were partly pragmatic, involving the streamlining of social administration. Even so, they did have consequences in the relationship between occupational places and language competence. It was the same concern with a form of pragmatism that was behind the discursive link between law and language. During the nineteenth century, the political turmoil and uncertainty associated with the consolidation of the modern state gave rise to a paranoid concern about its existence and its link to social and political order. The importance of constructing a normative order premised upon the link between cultural homogeneity, political order and legality that was at the heart of the discourse of political democracy and social stability gave rise to comments about the link between language and a knowledge of the legal basis of social order. Politicians argued that an ignorance of English prevented many Welsh people from having access to the very legal strictures which confirmed their existence as British citizens. The entry of the Welsh into the world of reason was through access to English, and the reward for such entry was entry into the Commonwealth of Britain. However, it was not merely any English that had to be seized, since it was argued that there was a link between 'good' language and rational behaviour, the very basis of social order. The claim that a commonality of language led to a commonality of a reason-based agreement meant that the avoidance of conflict was firmly linked to fostering a common language that united all of those within the realm. In a sense language and cultural homogeneity was at the heart of social order. Within this discourse is a deep-seated suspicion of language, and an uncertainty about the ability of the state to create, contain and sustain social order. These are the foundations of the modern order, an order that, as we discuss in Chapter 9, is in retreat.

The industrialization of Wales during the nineteenth century had a profound effect on the production and reproduction of Welsh, as the turnover of population linked to economic developments undermined the salience of Welsh in many areas. This was associated with the tendency for universal functions to penetrate local markets, with service provision deriving from a British level, being offered within local central places. The operational practices, and often the personnel of such service providers, were invariably linked to English. In the predominantly agricultural areas, however, the reproduction of the language remained high until the advent of the post-Second World War phase of economic restructuring in Wales. There has been a systematic inability among analysts to recognize the relevance of the penetration of economic functions from core locations to the periphery for language use. The differences identified above have tended to be accounted for, not by reference to the control and ownership of capital, but rather by reference to the inherent features of what are claimed to be 'rural' and 'urban' societies. Despite the insistence of sociology that only a single society exists in each state, the existence of a rural and an urban society is taken as axiomatic, and the persistence of minority languages in rural areas while they disappear from urban situations is claimed to be a manifestation of the rural/urban differences.

The recurrent crises of the capitalist world economy necessitate a periodic restructuring of capital in order to access new areas of location where production costs are cheaper. Since 1950, the restructuring of European economies has been in response to this need for capital to find cheaper production costs, and new markets for their products. Wales has been one of the locations where capitalist enterprises have relocated, and the large pool of unorganized, cheap, unskilled, mostly female labour has been one of the attractions for the new firms relocating from the British core. In parallel, there has been a process of decentralization of the public sector, with subsequent movement to Wales of personnel and jobs. The established division of labour in Wales has therefore been fragmenting, with a decline of the heavy industries (coal, steel, iron and slate) and a relocation of light industry and decentralized branch plants to the old industrial areas and the hitherto under-industrialized areas. It is a process that has been complicated by the drive for inward investment and the intensification of the shift towards a service economy. As we have indicated in Chapter 2, these developments have had a profound effect on class structure and the Welsh language.

Over the years we have consistently argued that the regulatory force of regional development policy has generated a cultural division of labour in Wales. Certainly the data indicates that there is strong case for such a claim by reference to the private sector. Some may claim that this is a consequence of the absence of the manner in which 'Welsh' culture has inhibited the growth of entrepreneurialism among Welsh speakers (Menter a Busnes, 1994). In contrast, we argue that this is a consequence of the spatial division of labour, and the manner in which core establishments use peripheral labour. Undoubtedly, this pattern is repeated elsewhere within the UK, but in Wales it is marked by language difference. Industries locating in Wales have tended to do so in search of a labour force. Managerial staff and key workers come from outside Wales, many of them locked into spiralist mobility patterns where company careers are organized in such a way that social and geographical mobility are linked. The temporary nature of the spiralists' residence in any one particular area militates against their social and linguistic integration into the local community. They tend to avoid Welsh-medium education for their children by using private-sector provision. Within the work environment the presence of monolingual English speakers in positions of authority sets constraints upon the use of Welsh. In Gwynedd, for example, half of the managers are non-Welsh-born (Jones and Jones, 1994). It is argued that recruiting local managers is difficult on account of the 'different' cultural context. At the same time the Welsh Development Agency, quite rightly, goes out of its way to ensure that the children of in-migrating employees of inward-investing companies receive education appropriate to their country of origin. There is also evidence that local women and Welsh speakers employed by outside firms frequently undertake managerial tasks and responsibilities, but are denied managerial status (Williams and Morris, 1995). It is widely claimed in Gwynedd that one study commissioned by a state agency was not published because the results clearly demonstrated the denigratory and racist perception of Welsh workers among the managers of external firms.

The situation is somewhat different in the public sector. There remains a tendency to recruit senior management from outside of Wales, but there are also burgher social mobility routes where career promotion occurs within the agency. What are missing are organized career paths for managers that transcend local institutions. Often managers in the public sector are obliged to relocate outside of Wales in order to obtain promotion. This is not to argue that labour should not be mobile, nor that labour mobility should be restricted. However, if the concept of the Learning Region is that of a region which must seek its growth and development from within its own resources, it must be obliged to facilitate local mobility. The greater level of local democratic control in the public sector means a fluency in Welsh is made a requirement for many appointments, particularly at a professional and managerial level (Lewis, 1987: 23-4). When Gwynedd County Council was formed in 1974, it adopted a bilingual policy, while Dwyfor District Council in the west of Gwynedd adopted a Welsh-only internal-administration policy, leading to a surge in demand in both counties for suitably qualified bilingual personnel. Other councils in north Wales adopted a variety of different bilingual policies. Installing a bilingual principle into the committees, departments and services structure of local councils meant that in a relatively short period of time the use of Welsh within the work context was institutionalized in new contexts associated with education, social services, library service, planning and housing. In turn, this led to an increase in consumer demand for services in Welsh from other public bodies including electricity, telephone and water services. The creation of the Gwynedd Bilingual Forum, with a membership drawn from a variety of public bodies, is indicative of the increasing salience of Welsh within the public sector.

These limited examples indicate the complexity of the local situation. They point to how the structure of the workforce and the practices of work restrict the relationship between the world of work and the community. The emerging developmental discourse which is premised upon neo-liberal or Third Way principles opens up new conceptions of relations of production, conceptions which move away from the rigidity and hierarchical structures of orthodox, modernist practices exemplified by Fordism and post-Fordism. The Learning Company demands diversity and flexibility, concepts that have a direct relevance for language use. In this respect we suspect that it will open space for a new role and valorization for Welsh in the organization and operation of work. For this reason alone we argue that the data we discuss below have significant relevance.

The new demands set on employers in the public sector with the Welsh Language Act 1993 may signal a change in the use of Welsh in the workplace (Jones and Morris, 1997: chapter 2). Public-sector organizations are now obliged by law to prepare Welsh-language schemes which detail the measures taken by the organizations to use Welsh in their provision of services to the public. While this may mean that for certain posts the organizations will have to appoint bilingual staff, or to train present monolingual staff to speak Welsh, it will not necessarily lead to a greater use of Welsh within the working environment, as the presence of a non-Welsh speaker means that the common language of communication is usually English. Nonetheless, the provisions of the Act will undoubtedly lead to a boost in the prestige value of Welsh, and this in turn may have an effect on demands by parents for Welsh-medium education for their children. The parallel increase in the status of Welsh may also lead to a greater use of the language by those Welsh speakers who have hitherto made a limited use of the language.

2. Social Mobility of Respondents

The first issue which we wish to consider concerns social and occupational mobility. It is important to distinguish between these two concepts. The distinction is based on the difference between occupation and social class. It is also relevant to recognize that there are different conceptions of social class. The Marxist conception is based upon the relations of production and how one social class relates to other social classes is conditioned by the nature of capitalist economic production systems. On the other hand, the Weberian conception of class focuses upon the market and power, and especially upon the power to gain access to scarce goods within the market. Market power determines life chances, which, in turn, determine class position. The Durkheimean conception places far more emphasis upon values and their relationship to consumption patterns, these values constituting a distinctive moral realm in society that relates to social status. Despite the recent shift towards an awareness that social classes are discursively constructed, the predominant tendency is to relate knowledge about individuals to scales of occupational prestige or socio-economic status. However, different class typologies organize individuals in different ways. While most of them focus upon occupations in one way or another, they organize these occupations in different ways. Some will group occupations on the basis of the differentiated employment qualifications and/or status associated with each group of occupations, whereas others will group occupations by income or the function of the occupations. In our survey we used two measures: the Registrar General's categorization of social class, and a classification by socio-economic groups.

Sociologists are interested in 'social mobility' for a number of reasons, among them the idea that when the rate of social mobility is low, class solidarity and cohesion will be high. On the other hand, social mobility is one of the cornerstones of the capitalist ideological order and the embourgeoisement thesis (Goldthorpe and Lockwood, 1969) claims that it is not so much the inter-generational change in class position that is operative here, but the manner in which economic growth and the associated dispersal of the 'national' wealth creates the impression of inter-generational social mobility. Nonetheless, the importance of the data we present below relates to our claim that the prestige value of Welsh is a crucial element in motivating people to retain or to learn the language.

In Table 6.1 we make a general observation concerning the inter-generational mobility patterns of the respondents by reference to the difference between middle and working classes. The first thing to notice among middle-class males is that almost a third (30 per cent) have not experienced any inter-generational mobility, while 11 per cent had been downwardly mobile. On the other hand, of those whose fathers were in classes 4–6, i.e. the working classes, almost a fifth had been upwardly mobile into the middle classes. Among the women, 61 per cent experienced no inter-generational mobility, while 22 per cent experienced upward social mobility and the remaining 18 per cent had experienced downward social mobility.

Table 6.1. Inter-generational mobility of respondents

	Males		Females		Total	
	%	(N)	%	(N)	%	(N)
Social class mobility of middle class						
(classes 1, 2, 3)						
No mobility (1/2/3–1/2/3)	30	(83)	31	(62)	30	(145)
Downward mobility (1/2/3–4/5/6)	11	(31)	18	(35)	15	(66)
Social class mobility of working class						
(classes 4, 5, 6)						
No mobility (4/5/6–4/5/6)	40	(110)	30	(59)	35	(169)
Upward mobility (4/5/6–1/2/3)	19	(53)	22	(44)	20	(97)

By reference to the middle-class/working-class distinction, 65 per cent of the sample had experienced no social mobility: 30 per cent of these had remained in the middle classes across generations, while 35 per cent had remained in the working classes. A further 15 per cent had experienced downward inter-generational mobility from the middle to the working classes, while 20 per cent had been upwardly mobile. In Tables 6.2 and 6.3 we turn to a more detailed analysis of this data. It is apparent from the survey that there are high rates of 'absolute mobility' among the sample – in no social class category did more than 50 per cent originate from the same class category. The ranges of mobility are somewhat limited, however – for example, only 5 per cent of men and women with semi-skilled or unskilled fathers had become managers, although slightly higher percentages of both men and women had experienced mobility from a semi/unskilled background to a professional position – 9 per cent of men and 14 per cent of women. It appears that, while there are professional niches for Welsh speakers, especially women, managerial positions are more difficult to access.

Table 6.2. Social mobility of male respondents (%)

Respondent's class	Father's class										No.
	1	**2**	**3**	**4**	**5**	**6**	**7**	**8**	**9**	**10**	
1	20	20	18	6	3	5	4	9			46
2	2	7	2		4		4	1		25	12
3	40	27	35	24	17	9	16	11			100
4	4		6		2	11	8	3			28
5	7	13	13	12	18	15	16	12		50	74
6	4	13	5	12	12	26	8	8			66
7					1			1			2
8		7		6	2	3	12	13			21
9					1	2	12	17	100		19
10	9		2	6	2	3		1			16
11	4	7	8	35	35	26	20	23		25	115
12	4		6		2	1					11
13											0
14	4	7	5			2					9
No.	45	15	85	17	123	129	25	75	1	4	519

1 = managerial	8 = self-employed without own firm
2 = professional self-employed	9 = farmer
3 = professional employed	10 = unemployed
4 = skilled non-manual	11 = retired
5 = skilled manual	12 = full-time education
6 = semi- or unskilled	13 = family care
7 = self-employed with own firm	14 = other

Among the higher class categories, there is a large degree of class stability, with approximately two-thirds of fathers from the managerial class producing sons who are either managers themselves or professionals. On the other hand, just over a fifth of men from a manual background had become managers, although there was a slightly higher rate of mobility to a professional status, affecting 30 per cent of the male respondents from a manual background. A further 30 per cent from a manual background stayed in the same class category. It appears that the most mobile group consists of men who come from a skilled or self-employed family background, and the general tendency is for upward rather than downward social mobility. It is noticeable that a higher proportion of the older respondents come from manual, or lower white-collar, backgrounds. This indicates the changes in the Welsh economy towards more service-sector jobs, and the creation of Welsh-medium positions in the professions.

Table 6.3. Social mobility of female respondents (%)

Respondent's class	Father's class										
	1	2	3	4	5	6	7	8	9	10	No.
1	13	11	4		5	5		5	50	20	26
2		11	2		2		4	2			9
3	16		44	20	17	14	23	27		20	108
4	13	11	11	7	8	5	15	6			43
5	4	11	5	13	13	3	8	9			36
6	7	5	5	20	7	20	4	3		20	41
7			3					2			3
8	4		2	7	4	3	4	6			17
9											0
10	6		4	7	5	4	2				16
11	27	47	12	20	39	45	33	34		20	154
12	9		6		1	1	2		50		14
13		5	4		1		4	5			10
14	2			7		2				20	4
No.	55	19	84	15	109	80	48	64	2	5	481

1 = managerial
2 = professional self-employed
3 = professional employed
4 = skilled non-manual
5 = skilled manual
6 = semi- or unskilled
7 = self-employed with own firm

8 = self-employed without own firm
9 = farmer
10 = unemployed
11 = retired
12 = full-time education
13 = family care
14 = other

It is clear that a smaller proportion of Welsh-speaking females than Welsh-speaking males become managers, and this situation reflects the general UK-wide patterns of gender occupational segregation. Almost half the Welsh-speaking professional women come from a professional, managerial or non-manual background, while a third come from a manual-class background, and this is a similar pattern to that found among men. A recent study of women and work in north-west Wales (Morris, 1997) indicated that most professional women worked in the education sector, mainly as teachers at the primary level.

There is a greater tendency for females than males to experience downward social mobility, and there is also a greater fluidity in the inter-generational mobility patterns – once again this reflects a more general trend. It has long been a criticism of social-mobility studies that they do not take the social-class positions of women into account, and one of the few studies to do so (Heath, 1981) showed that women from class categories 1 and 2 (based on their fathers' occupations) were more likely to be downwardly mobile than men from the same class origin. This is evidently also the case by reference to our data. Similarly, it is evident that more females from the higher class categories enter class 4 (white-collar workers) because of the preponderance of female employment in clerical and secretarial positions.

3. *Occupational Mobility of Respondents*

We measure the lifetime mobility of the respondents via a consideration of the difference between their initial occupation and their current occupation. Clearly this is conditioned by age – those who have recently entered the labour market experienced less mobility than their older counterparts. We begin by presenting the general picture across all age groups (Table 6.4). Almost 60 per cent of both men and women had experienced no change in occupational category during their life. Of course, this does not mean that there had been no social mobility within these categories. When we isolate the respondents by age, this incidence of mobility absence declines from 95 per cent for those in the youngest age category to between 50 per cent and 60 per cent for the older age categories. Furthermore, almost three-quarters of the mobility moves were upward.

Table 6.4. Lifetime mobility of respondents

Present social group	Social group category on point of entry to labour market									
	1	**2**	**3**	**4**	**5**	**6**	**7**	**8**	**9**	**10**
Males										
1	**10**	0	24	6	3	1	1	1	0	0
2	0	**3**	4	1	1	1	0	2	0	0
3	0	4	**78**	7	3	6	0	2	0	0
4	0	0	3	**15**	4	3	0	3	0	0
5	0	0	1	4	**48**	15	2	4	0	0
6	0	0	0	0	10	**53**	0	3	0	0
7	0	0	0	0	2	0	**0**	0	0	0
8	0	0	1	0	7	6	2	**5**	0	0
9	0	0	9	0	1	1	2	14	**0**	0
10	0	0	1	1	5	5	1	2	1	**0**
11	3	2	42	11	22	23	1	11	0	0
12	0	0	2	0	1	1	0	7	0	0
13	0	0	0	0	0	0	0	0	0	0
14	0	0	2	0	1	2	0	4	0	0
Females										
1	**2**	0	11	4	5	2	1	1	0	0
2	0	**1**	7	0	1	0	0	0	0	0
3	3	1	**84**	7	3	10	0	0	0	0
4	0	0	9	**22**	3	6	0	2	1	0
5	0	1	4	1	**22**	5	1	2	0	0
6	0	0	0	5	5	**29**	0	2	0	0
7	0	0	1	0	0	1	**1**	0	0	0
8	0	0	7	3	3	1	3	**0**	0	0
9	0	0	0	0	0	0	0	0	**0**	0
10	0	0	3	2	3	4	1	2	1	**0**
11	2	2	43	18	16	53	4	15	1	0
12	0	0	1	0	1	1	11	0	0	0
13	0	0	2	0	0	1	2	0	1	0
14	0	0	2	0	0	0	0	2	0	0

Burgher mobility within the public sector has tended not to be unusual. That is, workers have entered local government and similar institutions at a low employment level and have moved up the ladder to managerial positions within the same enterprise (Williams and Morris, 1995). This can be recognized among the larger groups of respondents who had experienced upward mobility – those moving from professional employed to managerial status. It also involves moving from non-manual and skilled occupations into managerial positions. For both men and women the main change was from a professional to a managerial status. Of the male managers 22 per cent had started their careers in managerial positions, compared with just 7 per cent of women. In professional jobs, however, approximately three-quarters of men and women had entered the career structure in a professional capacity. This is reflected in the different mobility routes. On the other hand there were proportionally more women than men who had moved into managerial positions from a lower starting-point on the occupational scale. Very few had worked their way up to managerial level from the shop floor – only 2 per cent of male managers had started work in a skilled occupation, while a further 2 per cent had started off as a semi-skilled or unskilled worker. In none of the cases was there long-range mobility within the respondents' careers – the moves were within one or two class categories to their entry point into the class structure.

The preceding information on social mobility cannot be effectively compared with the more general data from UK studies (Goldthorpe, 1980; Marshall et al., 1988) since the economic structure of Wales is different from that of the UK, with considerably less economic diversity. Unfortunately, there is no comparable social-mobility data for Wales as a whole. Thus we can do little more than consider the position of Welsh speakers within the occupational and class structures in Wales, and the perceived relevance of the use of Welsh for their occupations among the respondents. This will allow us to make tentative links between the social-mobility patterns and the value of Welsh in such patterns. Thus we move to a consideration of the employment contexts of the respondents.

4. Employment Context

Given our claim that the restructuring process has tended to involve the entry of non-Welsh enterprises into Wales, and that it is in such firms that the use of Welsh is likely to be absent, we sought information from the respondents about their employers: 75 per cent of the economically active respondents work for local firms or organizations, and a further 10 per cent work for companies whose head offices are located in Wales, but are outside the immediate vicinity of employment. Only 15 per cent of the respondents were employed by externally owned firms or externally controlled organizations. There is no significant variation in this pattern by the social class of the respondent. The size of the enterprise varied considerably (Table 6.5). Given the heavy reliance of the economy in Wales on small- and medium-sized enterprises (SMEs), it is hardly surprising that most of the respondents worked for enterprises that employ fewer than twenty-five workers. Such companies already employ some form of flat management principles as a feature of the necessity to be flexible in order to survive. It is these very same companies which will increasingly be exposed to intensifying their reliance upon the human capital of their workers. On the other hand a substantial number of the respondents work for relatively large enterprises.

Table 6.5. **Size of employing institution**

Location	Number employed locally				
	2–4	5–24	25–50	51–250	More than 250
Gwynedd	30	44	15	14	27
Clwyd	13	28	16	9	9
Powys	2	6	5	2	1
Dyfed	28	37	19	11	16
West Glamorgan	7	9	8	5	9
South Glamorgan	2	5	2	5	4
Mid Glamorgan	6	16	4	8	3
Gwent	0	2	1	3	1
TOTAL	88	147	70	57	70

One of the main debates within the literature about regional development and economic restructuring in Wales has involved the desirability of inward investment. State agencies, most notably the Welsh Development Agency, argue in favour of a vigorous policy of encouraging inward investment. This is echoed by some social analysts who claim that the linking of local firms as satellites to the larger inward investors can only be of advantage to the economy in Wales. Others have been sceptical about such regional development strategies, arguing that the quality of the jobs tends to be low and that the increasing competition between European regions results in a limited life for companies which, by and large, tend to have low relocation costs. In many respects, some of these arguments retread the ground associated with the dependency arguments associated with state's regulatory regional development policies of the 1960s and 1970s. Certainly, the recent collapse of the Asian economies has made most people think twice about such strategies, while the current discourse on regional development emphasizes indigenous development rather than inward investment. In this respect, the fact that so few of our respondents worked for these enterprises may be seen as advantageous. The main reason for this low involvement is the location of such enterprises in key locations along the M4 corridor and in north-east Wales. Few of these 'advantages', if indeed this is what they are, have accrued to the areas where most Welsh speakers live.

5. Language of Respondents' Employment

Employer's language policy

Clearly, our main concern is with the language of work. This involves establishing the competence of co-workers, the language policy of the employer and the extent to which one language or another is used. Such issues extend to encompass the language of the relations of production. Thus, one of the main issues associated with a cultural division of labour involving different language groups is the ability of the workforce to interact in one language or another across class positions, and the tendency to use one language or another when both languages can be used. Such a concern should extend to encompass management structures and styles. We can only touch on such issues, whereas the current debate about diversity, flexibility, innovation and flat management insists upon a more detailed approach.

The data in Table 6.6 indicate the relationship between the language competence of the managers of the firms or institutions for which the respondent worked, and the location of head office of that enterprise. In one sense it is hardly surprising that external employers are more likely to have non-Welsh-speaking managers than are local employers: while 72 per cent of managers of local firms/organizations can speak Welsh fluently, only 19 per cent of managers employed by externally owned firms can do so. On the other hand it is not inconceivable that a firm that is sensitive to the relevance of language for worker relationships might have recruited managers locally. In this respect the tendency to recruit managers from outside of Wales, the associated spiralism and the absence of management training in many parts of Wales contributes to the scarcity of qualified personnel (Jones and Jones, 1994).

Table 6.6. Language ability of managers by location of organization's head office (%)

Head office	Fluent Welsh	Learner, not fluent	Understands Welsh	No Welsh	Don't know	Total
Local	71	6	5	16	2	449
Wales, not local	54	3	3	25	14	63
UK, outside Wales	17	1	4	64	13	76
International	0	0	0	100	0	6
TOTAL	365	29	28	143	29	594

Unsurprisingly, it is not so much by reference to the relations of production and their relevance for efficiency or innovation that there has been any significant development in the expansion of Welsh as the language of work, but rather by reference to public relations. In order to tap the importance of a Welsh-speaking public for the enterprise, we found it necessary to establish the nature of the market for the products or services which the employers produced or provided (Table 6.7). Most of the locally based firms serve the local population.

Table 6.7. Respondents' employment: location of head office by employer's main markets/consumers (%)

Head office	Markets/consumers				
	Within local area	Within Wales	Outside Wales	Within and outside Wales	N
Local	79	10	1	10	426
Wales, not local	35	47	2	16	62
UK, outside Wales	21	12	8	62	78
International	0	0	0	100	6
TOTAL	373	82	11	106	572

On the other hand, the external UK-owned organizations have a much smaller interest in the local markets, and target larger markets, both within and outside Wales. The task is that of ascertaining whether or not this difference influences language use. We begin by considering the language of administration of the employer (Table 6.8). The majority of the local employers and those employers whose head office is located in Wales use Welsh in their administration, almost a third of them using Welsh exclusively. The figures for those companies which derive from outside of Wales, on the other hand, use little Welsh in their administrative practices. Despite this comparatively extensive use of Welsh in administration, few of the employers have developed a fully operational Welsh-language policy (Table 6.9).

Table 6.8. Respondents' employment: language of general administration by head office of organization (%)

Head office	Language of administration			
	Mostly Welsh	Both Welsh and English	Mostly English	*N*
Local	31	28	41	448
Wales, not local	33	24	43	63
UK, outside Wales	9	17	74	78
International	0	0	100	5
TOTAL	165	155	274	594

Table 6.9. Language policy of respondents' employers (%)

Fully operational language policy	29
Partly operational language policy	11
Language policy, but not operated	3
No Welsh-language policy	29
Don't know	28

It has already been noted that the 1993 Welsh Language Act requires public-sector organizations to prepare Welsh Language Plans outlining the ways they intend to provide services to their Welsh-speaking clients and customers in Wales. The relevant legislation does not refer to the private sector. Nevertheless, there is some evidence that a few companies, especially in the Cardiff area, are becoming increasingly sensitive to the desirability of promoting a bilingual image, and are adopting bilingual names, logos, slogans, publicity material and so forth. Indeed, the Welsh Language Board has been canvassing the larger private-sector companies with reference at least to extending their awareness and use of Welsh.

Not unexpectedly, it is the organizations and companies serving the local area who are most likely to have an operational language policy – fewer than one in five organizations with markets outside Wales have a language policy, compared with more than half those which serve local markets and consumers. Given the Welsh Language Board's requirement on monitoring policies, even if they largely involve self-monitoring practices, the issue of having a 'non-operational' or 'partly operational' language policy is likely to disappear in the future for public-sector bodies.

Language ability and use at work

We now turn to consider the language competence of the people with whom the respondents work or their work clients (Table 6.10). Given what we have said about the location of the company, and the extent to which it has a Welsh-language policy, it is not surprising that such a high proportion claim to work with colleagues all or most of whom speak Welsh. To a great extent such a pattern is the consequence of the manner in which Welsh speakers selectively use the labour market. Many of our respondents worked in public-sector environments where the use of Welsh was normative – county councils and schools, for example.

Table 6.10. Language ability of colleagues and clients

Proportion of colleagues with ability in Welsh	All	More than half	Half	Less than half	None
Supervisors ($N=527$)	49	9	8	11	23
Colleagues ($N=570$)	45	16	11	14	14
Subordinates ($N=363$)	41	15	12	12	19
Customers ($N=473$)	18	22	25	23	12

In Table 6.11 we consider the language used with these colleagues and clients as it relates to the competence identified above. What is revealing here is the uniformity of the responses, with the tendency to use Welsh decreasing with the perceived proportion of colleagues or clients able to speak the language. To a very great extent this must be the normative effect of asking one question followed immediately by a related question. That is, this is another way of saying, 'If they speak Welsh I will speak Welsh with them, if they don't then I won't'. Nonetheless, there are deviations from this pattern. In all four dyadic contexts the deviations favour English, but to differing degrees. This suggests that the interlocutors we have constructed for them are also differently constructed by the respondents, or at least by those who deviate from the normative tendency. There is least tendency to favour English by reference to the client, and the greatest tendency to do so with supervisors. It is also with clients that English is used least, and with the supervisors that it is used most.

Table 6.11. Welsh-language competence of colleagues and clients by language used with them

Extent of language competence	Language used				
	Welsh	W > E	W + E	E > W	English
Supervisors					
All or most	237	9	3	2	6
More than half	1	34	6	4	0
Half	3	1	29	5	2
Fewer than half	6	2	2	36	9
Few or none	3	0	1	3	107
Colleagues					
All or most	234	12	1	2	3
More than half	2	79	3	3	3
Half	2	6	42	10	3
Fewer than half	4	1	5	52	16
Few or none	3	2	3	9	52
Subordinates					
All or most	138	6	0	2	1
More than half	1	40	7	3	3
Half	0	4	34	4	0
Fewer than half	1	0	4	29	9
Few or none	3	0	2	1	59
Clients					
All or most	72	6	1	3	0
More than half	2	82	10	7	2
Half	3	5	104	6	1
Fewer than half	9	3	8	78	10
Few or none	3	1	2	7	37

Importance of language skills in work

A substantial number of respondents consider a knowledge of Welsh to be essential in their work, while a further number consider Welsh to be useful (Table 6.12). Of the different language competencies, oral competence is rated highest, followed by comprehension. Literacy skills in Welsh are not considered to be as important. Literacy skills in English, on the other hand, are twice as likely to be considered essential. Clearly this has relevance for the current emphasis upon literacy and numeracy for work. While it is not inconceivable that the emphasis given to this argument in the media may condition the evaluation, we feel that the relative absence of Welsh from work practice is much more likely to account for the difference between the responses to the two languages. If there is a relationship between these evaluations and actual practice, then the reported rise in the general perception of the prestige of Welsh is not unfounded (Welsh Language Board, 1995: 8). We can now consider the use of Welsh at work.

Table 6.12. **Importance of knowledge of Welsh and English at work (%)**

	Welsh			English		
	Essential	Useful	Neither	Essential	Useful	Neither
Understand	39	24	37	61	8	31
Speak	44	20	36	66	5	29
Read	35	19	45	59	8	23
Write	39	16	45	64	6	30

Use of Welsh at work

Having established the level of perceived relevance of Welsh for the employment of the respondents and the extent of use, the question arises of the context of this use. The preceding data suggest that Welsh is widely used in work with a variety of different interlocutors, and that this amounts to much more than casual social interaction. Table 6.13 begins to extend this information by comparing the respondent's evaluation of the importance of Welsh in their workplace, and their employers' recruitment practices of employing Welsh speakers for certain work contexts. There is a consistency across the figures for policy, public relations, face-to-face and indirect customer relations, with the majority claiming that the employer does recruit Welsh speakers in these contexts. This figure drops to a third for selling and supervision, and to less than a quarter for travelling company representatives. Furthermore, across all contexts, those who claim that a knowledge of Welsh is essential for their work tend to argue that Welsh is important for recruitment more than do those who do not make such a claim. What is surprising is that there are so many who claim that Welsh is essential for their work, yet claim that the employer does not refer to Welsh in their recruitment practices.

Table 6.13. **Context of importance of Welsh at work**

		Essential	Useful	Neither	Not applicable
As general policy	Yes	212	46	10	539
	No	77	73	43	
Direct public relations	Yes	164	51	12	600
	No	73	61	39	
Answering the phone	Yes	167	48	15	580
	No	77	74	39	
Customer relations	Yes	145	53	11	612
	No	74	64	41	
Using Welsh to sell products	Yes	54	20	5	772
	No	56	53	40	
Supervision of staff	Yes	106	17	1	639
	No	104	86	47	
Travelling representatives	Yes	19	14	4	834
	No	52	41	36	

The spatial distribution of the responses is interesting. Where language density is highest we find the highest proportion of respondents who do not consider Welsh to be of importance in their work. This holds across the three measures of competence that were used. It is tempting to relate these figures to the prestige of Welsh within the local labour market. On the other hand, prestige is more significant within the regional labour market in that many of the occupations within which Welsh has any purchase are not tied to specific locations. It is much more likely that it is a manifestation of labour-market segmentation at the local level. There are contexts within high-density areas where Welsh is of value in the labour market, but there are many other contexts in which it is not. On the other hand, in areas of low density where Welsh does have a high prestige the limited numbers of Welsh speakers are more likely to be employed within enterprises for their language attributes. Cardiff is a case in point where, even though only 7 per cent of the population speaks Welsh, the language has considerable prestige within high-profile enterprises which employ people at least partly for their Welsh-language competence.

6. Conclusion

In this chapter we have made some tentative suggestions about the relationship between mobility patterns of fluent Welsh speakers and the use of language in work. We have consistently argued for a link between the struggle to establish Welsh as the language of work and the increase in its prestige value. As long ago as the mid-1970s, we argued that this was a major motivation associated with the expansion of Welsh-medium education and its appeal to non-Welsh speakers (Williams, Roberts and Isaac, 1978). Among the group of Welsh speakers in the present sample, it is apparent that there are high rates of 'absolute mobility', with 50 per cent originating from a different class category, and the general tendency is for upward rather than downward social mobility. The most mobile group of all are men who come from a skilled or self-employed family background.

The ranges of mobility are, on the whole, somewhat limited, and it appears that there is an interplay between factors of gender and language that affect social mobility. Women in general experience lower rates of social mobility than men, and there is also more of a tendency for women to experience downward mobility. As we noted in Chapter 2, the 1991 census data show that Welsh-speaking women are more prominent in professional occupations than non-Welsh-speaking Welshwomen, suggesting that a knowledge of the Welsh language assists social mobility – a third of Welsh-speaking women workers are professionals, compared with less than a quarter of non-Welsh-speaking Welsh-born women. The survey data appear to concur with this proposition, in that a third of professional Welsh-speaking women come from a manual-class background, and this is a similar pattern to that found among men. Education obviously plays a crucial role in this mobility pattern, and the extension of Welsh-medium education over the past twenty years has been an important factor.

The high proportions of Welsh speakers in managerial and professional positions in Gwent, Powys and South Glamorgan suggest that
there is a considerable degree of geographical mobility associated
with social mobility (Morris, 1998: 40). Less than half the present
sample of Welsh speakers who live in Powys were born there, and
the respective proportions for South Glamorgan and Gwent are 40 per
cent and 8 per cent. Aitchison and Carter (1994) have previously
drawn attention to the fact that a considerable number of Welsh
speakers in the Cardiff area will have moved to the capital to take up
work in administration and the media. There is also evidence that this
is extending to accommodate at least the larger, recently privatized
conglomerates which are very sensitive to public opinion.

The danger is that this extension of an acknowledgement of the
relevance of Welsh for work in some companies and bodies will be
limited to a token status involving the 'token Taff in the corner' who
is called upon whenever anyone asks for a Welsh-language service.
Such a development would be entirely counter-productive in that,
while it will temporarily increase the prestige value of Welsh, it will
do little to sustain the increase, nor will it be very effective in linking
linguistic diversity to the relations of production and to the innovative
capacity of the enterprise.

The data on use in the workplace indicate that there are contexts in
which the use of Welsh is widespread, but that there are also contexts
where it is used only to a limited extent. It also shows that for fluent
speakers the use of workplace Welsh, whatever form it may take, is
not a problem, and that when it is possible to use the language in
work, they do so. Yet, the use of Welsh is currently structured in
such a way that it is those in professional, non-manual, skilled and
semi-skilled occupations who use the language most. It is used to a
far lesser degree by those in managerial and unskilled occupations.

There is a danger of generalizing from this small part of the Welsh
population, implying that this is the general picture of Wales as a
whole. It must be recognized that we are referring only to that part of
the population that has a high level of Welsh-language competence
and who, according to the preceding analysis, are most likely to have
Welsh as part of their qualification portfolio that bears relevance to
their current employment. It is also relevant to recognize that among
this particular group there is a high proportion of those whose
employers barely acknowledge the existence of Welsh, let alone
recognize its relevance and value for their enterprise. Fewer than a

third work for enterprises which have a fully operational language policy, these being mainly those enterprises that serve the local environment. It is in this sense that we await the effects of the 1993 Welsh Language Act.

7
Synopsis

1. Introduction

In this chapter it is our intention to integrate our findings. We do this by considering the details of the data, and also by subjecting the data to a latent variable analysis which allows us to consider the relationship of the different contexts of language use when taken together rather than being considered individually. Thus far we have considered the data that derive from the survey by what we consider to be the essential components of the relationship between the production and reproduction of competence on the one hand, and language use on the other. Latent variable analysis allows us to take this a step further and to consider the data by reference to the relationship between these variables.

Before proceeding to the results of a factor analysis, we would like briefly to consider the data deriving from the part of the survey that pertains to what is customarily treated by reference to attitudes. We elected to pursue this avenue of analysis for one reason. A fundamental premise of the Welsh Language Board's language-planning strategy is that the attitudes of Welsh speakers are such that they are unable to engage with extending language use – that is, that there is at present insufficient 'demand'. Thus, they argue that if they are to extend the enabling principle it must be accompanied by an attempt to change attitudes. Our own response to this involves questioning the entire validity of attitudes as a relevant concept, but more specifically we point to how psychologists underline the tentative relationship between attitudes and behaviour. This being the case, it would appear to undermine the claim of the Welsh Language Board. On the other hand, our own emphasis on institutionalization maintains that the stabilization of language use within discourse bears no relation to the orthodox psychological conception of identity and attitudes. Thus, even though we had no intention of proceeding with the customary form of attitudinal analysis, where measures of attitudes are correlated with measures of behaviour, it was, nonetheless, important that we did proceed with the process of establishing the attitudinal configurations of the respondents, if only to enable us to engage with the argument of the Welsh Language Board.

2. Opinion and 'Attitudes'

Opinion

Thus far, the focus of the discussion has been on the constitution of individuals as a special kind of subject in relation to a particular object – as Welsh speakers. We have discussed the structural constraints that limit the opening of the space that can accommodate such a subject place. In this section we wish to do two further things. First of all to consider how the individual constructs the 'other' in relation to the same object – the Welsh language. In considering this task, we have constructed the subject and the object, and asked the respondent to engage with this construction in linking them in different ways. Second, we seek to uncover how the respondents construct the object themselves by reference to a series of preconstructed conditions.

We begin with the responses to a question which asked for the opinion of the respondents concerning the interest of a variety of different bodies and individuals in Welsh. They were asked to express this opinion on a scale extending from a low of 1, where there was a minimum interest, to a high of 9 which was maximum interest (Table 7.1). The goal here was that of establishing how the different individuals constructed the relationship between two objects – on the one hand, Welsh and the agency as object, or between Welsh as an object and, on the other hand, either a collective subject 'friends', or the individual as subject 'self'.

At the time of the survey the Conservative government was in power, the government that was responsible for steering the Welsh Language Act onto the legislation books. There is a long history of relationship between Wales, Welsh and the Conservative Party, a history which played its role in stabilizing the Conservative Party as an 'English' party opposed to promoting 'Welsh' interests. The recent defeat of the Conservative Party in the general election, when Wales refused to return a single Conservative representative to Parliament, has led to an awareness of the need to change this construction.

Nonetheless, at the time, the trace of this historical discourse undoubtedly played a role in the answers we obtained. Certainly, of all the objects and subjects presented to the respondents, it was 'the government' that was constructed most negatively in relation to having an interest in Welsh. It was followed by the Welsh Office, as the arm of the state and the government in power. On the other hand, a more positive relationship is established between local government and Welsh, suggesting that, at least in some cases, central government and local government are constructed in such a way that they bear opposite relations to Welsh. However, of all the 'agencies', it is religious bodies which come out as having the most positive relationship with Welsh. Private business tends to have a negative link to Welsh.

Table 7.1. Interest of various bodies and individuals in Welsh

| | Minimum interest ———————► Maximum interest | | | | | | | | | No. |
	1	2	3	4	5	6	7	8	9	
Present government	528	182	116	66	89	12	5	0	2	1000
Welsh Office	178	171	172	146	210	44	28	28	23	1000
In-migrants	126	127	153	141	281	83	57	17	15	1000
Private business	123	158	166	149	256	70	53	11	14	1000
Local authorities	82	74	98	106	222	95	125	117	81	1000
Other public bodies	61	118	137	168	313	91	71	25	16	1000
Religious bodies	21	9	17	29	210	71	99	188	356	1000
Friends	17	27	26	38	147	66	156	198	325	1000
Family	14	11	20	23	66	47	109	196	514	1000
Self	7	7	4	6	48	44	81	160	643	1000

Among the individuals and collective individuals, friends, family and self are all constructed as having a highly positive interest in Welsh. This contrasts with 'in-migrants' who are constructed as having what is, by and large, a negative interest in the language. Comparing these two sets of data, it is tempting to construct fluent Welsh speakers as operating within an institutional vacuum by reference to their concern about the language and its implications for the language group. They stand in opposition to most of the official bodies and private enterprise in seeking to promote their interests. There is, indeed, a sense in which these totalities constitute the construction of an 'us' and 'them' that demarcates social space *vis-à-vis* 'Welsh'. It is not a contested space, nor one that the 'them' as 'other' engages with. Reinforced by historical discourse and economic structure, this duality becomes the basis for a moral discourse constructed out of loose conceptions of rights that accommodate 'fairness'. It is the very discourse which neo-liberalism is currently seeking to extirpate. Evidently, this is too stark a polarization but, none the less, it does contain an element of truth that is implicit in the amount of energy that must be drawn up in order to gain minor concessions from the power base.

'Attitudes'

It should be evident that the rational, psychological concept of 'attitudes' is alien to our own orientation. Thus we suggest that attitudes should be seen as statements offered to the individual. As statements they construct subjects and objects, but this construction depends upon two things: first, the willingness or ability of the individual to take in charge the statement by operating as a subject that it constructs, and second, the subject position into which the individual is interpolated. Thus a statement incorporates a number of possible subject places which relate to objects in different ways. For example, the statement 'Welsh is a dying language' contains an object 'Welsh' which is related to another object 'language'. In taking in charge the statement, the individual acknowledges the existence of this type of object relationship. In responding to a range of other statements – 'Agree strongly' . . . 'Strongly disagree' – the individual who takes in charge the statement is obliged to occupy one or another subject position which bears a particular relationship to the objects under consideration. These subject places are in effect what the orthodox perspective refers to as 'identity', but which, in contrast to our position, is interpreted as a feature of the rational, cognitive activity of the individual. Within these subject places, the 'objects' signify different things and the signification process assumes a particular context.

The attitude scales which we presented to the respondents are the customary Likert scales. They were constructed by reference to the following dimensions – instrumentality, status and relationship to other objects, most notably 'Wales'. It is in this symbolic representation that links or relates objects that the space for emotional commitment opens up. Clearly we do not wish to pursue any causal analytic linkages between these and the measures of behaviour. Rather we merely present the results with a minimum of comment (Table 7.2). In line with much of what we have encountered with reference to the behaviour of the respondents, these scales suggest that the same respondents construct 'Welsh' in a highly instrumental way, rejecting attempts to construct it as a language unsuited for the material world. Despite this tendency, it is obvious that there are variations among the respondents, and there is room for different constructions of what the Welsh language means. Thus, the statement concerning the exclusivity of Welsh for administration does relate to more than 'Welsh' in that there is an implicit link to a conception of that which is administered – Wales. It pertains to those who construct the relationship between 'Welsh' and 'Wales' in terms of Welsh-language exclusivity.

Table 7.2. 'Attitude' scales (%)

	Agree strongly	Agree	Neutral	Disagree	Disagree strongly
It is essential that children in Wales learn Welsh.	54	39	4	2	1
Wales would not be Wales without the Welsh language.	46	43	5	5	2
Everyone working in the public sector should be able to speak Welsh.	38	40	11	9	2
It appears to me to be a good idea that some councils in Wales administer in Welsh only.	22	37	13	26	2
Speaking Welsh helps people get promotion in their jobs.	10	54	22	13	1
You are considered to be a person of lower class if you speak Welsh.	2	9	6	48	35
Other languages are more valuable than Welsh.	5	39	14	26	16
Welsh has no place in the modern world.	3	3	5	44	46
Welsh is a dying language	3	15	10	45	27
Most people think that Welsh things are too old-fashioned.	2	21	13	51	13
Welsh cannot be adapted for the purposes of business or science.	2	7	13	49	30

Given this instrumental construction of 'Welsh' and the link between instrumentality and status, it is hardly surprising that it is also constructed as an object that 'holds' status that is released to the speaker. It also tends to be constructed as a flexible object, capable of modification for specific needs. It is this flexibility that gives it life. Nonetheless, its symbolic significance relates to the other object ('Wales'), and in this respect it is this that links the Welsh speaker as subject to 'Wales' and 'Welsh'.

3. Latent Variable Analysis

The questionnaire which we constructed in order to explore the use of Welsh contained more than fifty questions. Some of these questions were constructed out of several items. Thus the question pertaining to 'attitudes' to which we have referred above contained eleven items. This creates a problem for the analyst in that if, for example, a simple binary variable such as gender was to be compared with responses to all items on all questions, over 280 separate analyses would emerge. If this in turn was compounded by reference to other independent variables, such as age, social class or location, the number of separate analyses would be multitudinous. Evidently, some means of resolving this complexity must be used. The solution involves appropriate data reduction that leaves only the major dimensions which underlie the data to be the focus of analysis. Such a process not only raises the reliability and validity of the variables but also leads to a more parsimonious analysis. This is the rationale of what is known as latent variable analysis.

The multivariate statistical process to which we have resorted involves submitting similar items on the questionnaire to a latent variable analysis. The outcome of this analysis indicates whether there are one or more dimensions to the scale. It also produces a latent variable score for each person on these dimensions. This score is based upon a weighting of items which leads to increasing consistency, discrimination and validity. The goal is that of ensuring the unidimensionality of individual factors while ensuring that the items measure the same entity. Our analysis involved producing the following 'reduced' variables: inter-generational competence, family interaction, local and national community use, language of education, language of work, language of media use, attitudes, transactional language use and literacy. The results of such an analysis confirm much of what has been already discussed above. On the other hand there are also some new results:

Gender

It seems that women tend to use more Welsh at work than do males. They also use more Welsh-language media than do males. These are the only significant differences by reference to gender. It is of course, difficult to account for these findings without further analysis, although it is possible to speculate. Thus there is evidence which suggests that gender plays a role in the use of the media, but in order to be meaningful this information would have to link with an analysis of the trends of use by type of media and the nature of the media content. Similarly the reference to the use of Welsh in work requires considerably more information than that provided by this survey. Again we point to the different roles played by men and women in the labour market, and the opportunities for the use of Welsh within these relations of production (Jones and Morris, 1997).

Age

Age plays no role in differentiating the use of Welsh in interaction within the home, at work nor in transactional contexts. In some respects this is encouraging in that it indicates that language reproduction, or inter-generational transmission, tends to involve the extensive social use of Welsh. On the other hand the older Welsh speakers do tend to read more Welsh, to come from a family background which is more likely to be focused on the language and also to use more Welsh-language media. Of course, this may be merely a measure of the tendency for the older age group to use these services regardless of language. The only other aspect that pertains to age is the higher tendency for the youngest age group to construct Welsh as a 'modern' object and, conversely, to reject attempts to construct it as 'old-fashioned' or 'outmoded'.

Mother tongue

There is a range of influences here. Put simply, those with Welsh as their mother tongue tend to use the language in a range of contexts far more than do those who have accessed Welsh through the production channels. These contexts include the family, the community, exposure to Welsh-medium education, the media and certain transactions. On the other hand there is no difference when it comes to the manner in which Welsh is constructed as an object: the respondents construct the language positively regardless of their language background. Perhaps this is not unexpected if the motivation for acquiring Welsh, either as adults or through parental influence, depends upon a positive evaluation of the language as an object. Nonetheless, there is room for concern here in that, if the proportion of Welsh speakers acquiring the language through reproduction is declining, these findings would suggest that the use of the language will also decline.

Competence level

The picture here is remarkably consistent. By reference to all four self-report measures of competence, those with high competence derive from a high incidence of inter-generational competence, tend to use more Welsh at home, at work and in the community, tend to have received more Welsh in their education, are inclined to construct Welsh as a highly utilitarian entity, are more likely to use Welsh-language print media and to use Welsh in professional transactional contexts. The exceptions to this pattern involve the higher probability of using the Welsh-language broadcasting media among those with lower levels of competence, and, for those with lower levels of literacy competencies, of using more Welsh in transactional contexts.

Social class

Interestingly social class plays no significant role in determining the extent of Welsh used at work. There is an argument that most of the positions which carry a Welsh-language qualification tend to pertain to the professional classes and that the concept of language prestige is therefore irrelevant to the working classes. It seems to us that here again there is a need to investigate the distinction between the use of Welsh in work and the use of Welsh for work. The most interesting distinction is between the professionals and the semi-skilled, with the former being more involved with national institutions such as the eisteddfod, but using the Welsh-language print media less, and having a more positive conception of the utilitarian value of Welsh; and the latter being less reluctant to construct Welsh as an outmoded object. It would also appear that the self-employed are most likely to use Welsh within the community. To a great extent these patterns are self-explanatory.

Location

There are significant variations across Wales. This largely relates to language density, with Gwynedd respondents using Welsh more in the community. However, it also relates to policy, with Gwynedd respondents also using more Welsh at work, and having a greater exposure to Welsh-medium education than respondents from other parts of Wales. Also respondents from South Glamorgan tend to use more Welsh within national institutional contexts such as the eisteddfod. Evidently, these factors which relate to policy and density also pertain to the transactional use of Welsh, but not to the extent one would expect, suggesting that language-structured networking is prominent in low-density areas.

Interesting and important as these internal variations are, they do not obscure the impression conveyed by the analysis that the part of the Welsh population which has a sufficiently high degree of competence to use the language in a range of social contexts is highly motivated to use the language, and will do so wherever and whenever possible. The number who do not feel strongly about the reproduction of the language, and who reflect this commitment in their accounts of their language use behaviour are few in number. That is, the negative identity has receded and Welsh now carries considerable status, a status that bears a direct relationship to its prestige. Despite the implication that is inherent in the policy approach of some key institutions, and the research focus of our academic institutions, what are referred to as 'attitudes' are not the causal link between competence and limited language use. This is not an attack on the lack of imagination of those who resort to such mechanical, taken-for-granted research parameters, but rather a simple observation that there is no empirical, explanatory causal relationship between 'attitudes', however conceived or measured, and language use. It is evidently futile to claim that changing attitudes will lead to increasing language use.

However, there are many aspects of their day-to-day activities in which it simply is not possible for fluent speakers to use Welsh. Many of the constraints on the use of language are structural in nature. It is these same constraints which have an effect on the production and reproduction of the language. Again this leads us to emphasize that those associated with policy must come to terms with the intricate processes associated with institutionalization rather than resort to outmoded psychologistic paradigms.

4. *Conclusion*

A study such as this one which only investigates the language use behaviour of part of the population that claims competence in Welsh serves to draw attention to that part of the Welsh-speaking universe that has not been investigated. Given the focus on the relationship between level of competence and use, and given the existence of data which facilitated developing an appropriate sampling frame for those who we felt were capable of using the language in a socially effective context, a conscious decision was made not to include those with a lower level of competence. The preceding analysis makes it clear that the degree of erosion that derives from a negative identity is small, and that the population has a very positive orientation towards the language as a symbolic quality, and also as a medium for expression. Such Welsh speakers go out of their way to use the language wherever and whenever possible. In this respect their behaviour constitutes a form of militancy in that English is very clearly the normative language in Wales. On the other hand there are a range of contexts where the use of Welsh simply is not possible. Some of these are localized whereas others are universal. However, we would not discuss such a situation by reference to the structural concept of domain, but rather by reference to the language ability of the individual interlocutors. In this respect the work of the Welsh Language Board may well lead to an increase in the use of Welsh within the public sector. It is unlikely to have the same impact in the private sector where most of the deficiency exists. It is also clear that, as the density of speakers declines, there is an increasing indecision concerning the appropriateness of using Welsh in certain contexts. In such situations it is only the most militant who will persevere with attempts to establish whether or not it is an appropriate action. Most will resort to risk avoidance with reference to embarrassment.

It is in such claims that we recognize the relevance of the concept of institutionalization. We have argued throughout that an understanding of this concept is central to any attempt to extend the use of any minority language. It involves the difference between those contexts where there is no doubt about the appropriateness of using Welsh. This may involve knowledge of the individual interlocutor, in which case the term institutionalization is hardly appropriate. Rather, we refer to those repetitive situations in which there is a relationship between context and use potential. Developing such situations involves hard work, especially if the interlocutors lack confidence in their ability. Furthermore, any situation in which only 17 per cent at most are fluent in the language would suggest that the probability of encountering contexts in which the use of Welsh is possible throughout Wales is unlikely. However, as we have indicated, the spatial variation in density, and the segmentation of the labour market by language means that such probability contexts are not unilinear. This, in turn, means that there are some contexts and some places where the use of Welsh is unlikely to be possible. It is clear that, as things now stand, the task of interpreting the possibility of using Welsh is a puzzle.

We have also indicated that there are structural conditions that are more and less conducive to producing and reproducing Welsh in such a way that the result is the effective social use of the language. Thus the increasing incidence of language group exogamy has an impact upon the tendency to use the language. Similarly the change in the relevance of the community, both as a focus of social interaction and for the use of Welsh, for those speaking the language and for those seeking to learn it, also has its effect.

In addition, variations in educational provision play an important role in determining the extent of Welsh used by speakers. In this respect we do not simply refer to the provision of education as the basis for producing competence, but also as a radical reconceptualization of the relationship between education and bilingualism. This involves moving away from the modernist focus upon linguistics as the guarantor or an arbitrator of language purity. Modern linguistics has been constructed on the basis of generating 'correct language', this correctness being measured by reference to the rules of grammar. There is a persistent failure to recognize that these rules are nothing more than politically established normative contexts. We have argued for an orientation to pedagogy which expresses the link between language and education, not by reference to this modernist understanding of competence, but rather in terms of the relationship between social constructivism and the range of dialogical competencies. We suspect that the current dialogical focus emphasizes a single dialogical relationship, that between teacher and pupil, and that while it is adequate to generating a grammatically defined competence, it ignores the dialogical relationships that will guarantee a wider range of social use. This includes the use of Welsh between peers, something that is becoming very rare in our schools, even in those which do succeed in generating a high level of competence as measured by educational indicators. If we are correct, then the consequence will be that those without the requisite family background will lack the confidence to enter into new dialogical relationships, leaving the planning agents with the massive task of transferring competence into use. We believe that this is a task that they are currently ill-prepared to confront. Furthermore, the data from the census indicate that the proportion of Welsh speakers from homes with a universally high competence across all family members is rapidly diminishing.

We feel that language use surveys such as this one retain value. They have obvious value as monitoring devices, not only for planning agencies, but also to indicate what is happening to language use in terms that should inform the work of the planning agencies. This of course implies that such agencies must themselves be flexible and must not be encumbered by the limitations of existing legislation. If language use is social in nature, and if social practice is a dynamic process, then the link between the legislature and the agencies of social policy must be equally flexible and dynamic. We can ill afford to await another quarter-century for a new Language Act, or at least, for policy-related developments that will be socially and politically effective. For these reasons we strongly advocate the periodic repetition of this exercise. Unlike other language-planning contexts such an exercise has not been the starting-point of developing a relevant social-policy framework for Welsh, but this does not mean that it cannot, and should not, be integrated into current social-policy practice.

This means that the findings of this study must be associated with a study of the remainder of the Welsh-speaking population. Such a study should seek to establish the extent and context of the relationship between the two groups, the extent of Welsh language use and the factors which intervene in determining the relationship between level of competence and language use. In many respects such a study carries a degree of urgency. It should be the basis for developing coherent language planning strategies that go beyond the framework of the Welsh Language Act. For the moment we turn to a consideration of the planning context of that Act.

PART III

Language Planning

8
The Planning of Welsh

1. Introduction

As we have suggested in the Introduction, the advent of language planning agencies and the use of language use surveys have tended to go hand in hand. We also suggested that this has not been true in the case of Welsh, and that the Welsh Language Board has not availed itself of a detailed language use survey of Welsh, preferring to commission attitude surveys by opinion pollsters and individual community-based surveys by geographers. Another interesting relationship is that involving the link between implementing legal action in favour of a language or language group, and the establishment of a language planning agency. Once again this has not been true of Welsh. The initial Language Act of 1967 was not accompanied by the creation of a planning agency. Clearly, given these preliminary insights, any discussion of language planning must be related to both administration and politics. It is such issues that we wish to address in this chapter.

Evidently, in confronting language planning (LP) we are obliged to address organizations theory, and the way in which it relates to constraints and opportunities generated by organizational environments. Such constraints and opportunities derive partly from institutional or organizational structures, but also from the context established by discursive formations with reference to what can and what cannot be said from a given place. As we shall see, the 1993 Welsh Language Act, and the establishment of the Welsh Language Board, derive from the market approach to public management which emphasizes the neo-liberal assumptions that relate to creating a technical issue out of administration, rather than viewing neo-liberalism as a discourse which simultaneously enables and prevents. The legal discourse of the 1993 Act has a similar relationship with organizational environments. It is essential, therefore, that we treat neo-liberalism as a meta-discourse which has to be understood and analysed in relation to the administrative unit, within the context of what is currently referred to as governmentality.

One essential difference between organizational theory and the goal of this chapter is that, whereas the former is concerned with the efficiency of the agency, our focus is very much upon the rationality of the agency and its practical implementation. While we are interested in whether the agency's mission does lead to the desired effect, whether or not this is achieved in an efficient way is of secondary importance.

Every planning agency must begin from a clear understanding of the nature and cause of change in the phenomenon which they are seeking to plan. This is the starting-point of the debate. Such perspectives relate to models that serve to link the change orientation with the planning orientation, with these models, in turn, focusing upon the customary social-science focus of such work, involving the community, the market and the state. These three dimensions often tend to be addressed by the principles of spontaneous solidarity, dispersed competition and hierarchical control. The nature of the mix between them determines the particular configuration that motivates planning action. A further dimension which has been labelled 'organizational concentration' focuses upon interaction and the allocation of resources. Such factors have become increasingly important in social administration, and are of particular importance to the analysis of the Welsh Language Board and its activities because of the way in which bargained interest accommodation and policy concentration have become key factors within European society and administration since the 1970s.

One point we will argue below is that the current status of language planning in Wales breaks with the more orthodox conception of language planning and the way in which it has been grounded in the orthodox social-science conceptions of change. This orthodoxy means that most language planners have been trained in the social sciences and draw upon them in implementing their work. In contrast, the Welsh Language Board draws upon a conception of change which not only does not derive from the social sciences, but in many ways refutes it.

2. The Legal Context

Before proceeding any further it is imperative to consider the 1967 Welsh Language Act. Prior to this Act Welsh had no legal status other than that which derived from the Acts of Annexation of 1536 and 1538 which established English as the sole language of administration and law, and precluded Welsh speakers from holding office. In some respects, it can be argued that the absence of a legal status is preferable to the limited status conferred by the 1967 Act, if only because, at that moment in time, the absence of a legal status was one of the major driving forces for a sense of justice among Welsh speakers. Indeed, in many respects that Act can be seen as the response of the state to a rising dissatisfaction among part of its constituency to the manner in which the minority status conferred on the language and its speakers over centuries was the antithesis of the claim of the state to represent the will of the people. It can also be seen as a response to a concern, some might say a moral panic, among the same population about the manner in which the process of economic restructuring was undermining the ability of the language group to produce and reproduce the language. Legislation was seen as a salvation. The evidence for this change in the demographic incidence of Welsh speakers derived not only from experience, but also from a comparison of the 1951 and 1961 census. It contributed to the emergence of the Welsh Language Society, a pressure group dedicated to achieving its goal of language promotion, where necessary by civil disobedience. It was also claimed at the time that the fortunes of Plaid Cymru, the Welsh Nationalist Party, were closely related to the same change in the incidence of Welsh speakers within the general population. Furthermore, parallel action elsewhere, most notably *vis-à-vis* French in Canada, was also significant in serving as a model for developments in Wales.

The absence of a legal status does not mean that language planning did not exist. Thus, it should already be evident that what we have referred to as legitimization applies as much to social policy as to the legal framework. It may be claimed that a coherent social policy that is effectively implemented is more important than conferring a legal status upon a language, especially if it involves a strong basis of institutionalization. Indeed, it can be claimed that the need for legitimization derives from an absence of institutionalization. This has a great deal to do with the relationship between legitimation and normativity. In some respects legitimation refers to the manner in which law confirms the normative, whereas institutionalization refers to the manner in which social practice manifests the normative. The problem arises when there is no coincidence between legitimation and institutionalization, that is, when the legal is not acknowledged in social practice. Legitimation can only be effective when it is acknowledged and translated into social practice. If this is not the case, legitimation will either be ineffective or coercive. It can lead to institutionalization contradicting legitimization. We will argue below that this is part of the problem of the Welsh Language Board as a language planning agency which is finding difficulty in translating the current Welsh Language Act into effective social practice.

The implementation of corpus planning in the form of standardization has been a central feature of European policy for centuries. Certainly the manner in which the written word stabilizes or standardizes language has a long history. The translation of this stabilization into a normative structure relates to the manner in which a universal orientation is given to the written word. However, it was claimed that there was a relationship between language and reason, and that good language led to good thinking, a conception which conditioned the drive for standardization at the turn of the nineteenth century. The formation of the modern state at this time, and the manner in which it was premised upon such ideas, led to a coherent attempt to standardize the language which was conceived of as the language of reason. As we have seen, it was the basis for distinguishing between languages of reason and those languages which were deemed unworthy of anything more than use as a *patois*. The issue of the codification of Welsh had been largely resolved by the translation of the New Testament in 1567 and the Bible in 1588, and their employment as the model for correct use. Furthermore, since the end of the nineteenth century, various forms of political pressure were asserted to increase language status. However, in the 1960s the argument in favour of legal status was a new departure, one that involved official recognition at the state level of the existence of a language other than English as an official language. It was in this respect that a commission of specialists was asked to address the issue prior to the publication of a White Paper.

This development was characteristic of the framework of liberal democracy at the time, and of the manner in which the liberal state addressed its relationships with its constituency. The official discourse was based on the assumption that concessions to minority groups are possible and even desirable, but only in so far as they do not prejudice the nature of the dominant/subordinate relationship. However, given that these concessions were made in the face of the demands of members of the minority, it is inevitable that two discourses were involved, and that the report of the Commission was to be found at the intersection of the discourse of the state on the one hand, and of the minority group on the other. Despite the outward claim that such committees which advise the government and the second house in reaching a decision represent the 'democratic process', it is inevitable that they primarily represent the interests of those in power, even though it is difficult for such interests to disregard the interests of their constituency. Nonetheless, they will also be obliged to judge any other interests within the broader populace which will be affected by any decision.

On the other hand the process was consistent with the manner in which more general social policy had conceded an independent status to Wales on the ground of cultural difference. This was evident in the 1927 Education Act, which made specific reference to the relevance of the Welsh language for culture, and a need to address this difference within educational policy. This was a dramatic shift from the situation in the preceding century when this difference was acknowledged but was seen as a negative force in need of purification in the goal of establishing a unitary culture for the British state.

It could be claimed that the Welsh language had no official status prior to the Welsh Language Act of 1967. In some respects, this was an advantage in that it became the basis of struggle on the assumption that Welsh was THE language of Wales, having the same status as English in England. In other respects it left the use of the language open to interpretation, and led to what was perceived as injustice. In 1963, the government established a committee 'to clarify the legal status of the Welsh language and to consider whether any changes in the law ought to be made'. The main recommendation of the report, which was published in 1965, was that whatever was done through the medium of Welsh in Wales should have the same validity in the eyes of the law as if it had been done in English. It was also suggested that official forms should be made available in Welsh, and that the language should be allowed in the court of law without prejudicing the proclamation of English as the language of court records as established in the Act of Annexation. A weak version of the recommendations was the basis for the Welsh Language Act of 1967 which has been interpreted as legitimizing Welsh as a minority language within Wales (Williams, 1987b). The committee, which sat under the chairmanship of Sir David Hughes Parry between 1963 and 1965, was chosen by the government and consisted of Welsh speakers who had reached positions of prominence, either in public office or in a professional capacity. Their prominence had been achieved within the formal state structure and without recourse to the Welsh language. Thus, while their interests lay in the existing power structure, they had the attributes which conveyed an impression of representing the Welsh minority. Any position which represented a contradiction between the 'Welsh minority' and the 'power of the state' was precluded. The only acceptable position was one in which the interests of the two parties overlapped. This committee, in turn was responsible for selecting its witnesses, and thereby the evidence that was considered. In many ways, its procedure was not far removed from present-day quangos such as the Welsh Language Board – the state sets up the Board, appoints its officials as civil servants and the Secretary of State appoints lay members of the Board.

From the outset, the 1967 Act was seen as inadequate by the more radical Welsh speakers and a concerted campaign which lasted for a quarter of a century was initiated to establish a new Act. By the time a new Bill was presented in 1992, the nature of politics and policy had changed. The goal of the 1992 Act was to 'promote and facilitate the use of the Welsh language in Wales, and in particular its use in the conduct of public business and the administration of justice on a basis of equality with English'. It was an enabling Act rather than one which ensured that rights could be guaranteed. This was commensurate with the political climate where the role of the state was assumed to diminish, and citizens were to assume greater responsibility for their actions, assuming that they could be enabled to do so. A Welsh Language Board was established to administer the Act. It consisted of civil servants and a non-governmental body of selected individuals. This Board was to ensure that all public bodies prepared plans showing which services they would provide in Welsh. The Act also repealed the language clauses of the Act of Annexation.

The Act has been severely criticized on several counts. All plans are to be vetted by the Secretary of State for Wales and the Board has no powers to sue a public body which does not comply with its demands. More importantly, the private sector has been entirely excluded from the Act. Whereas it established the principle that Welsh and English should be treated on a basis of equality, this was only to be operationalized 'wherever appropriate in the circumstances and reasonably practical', carrying the danger of it being a means of confining the language to certain locations where the percentage of Welsh speakers was high. There was no right for people to use Welsh or English as they wished, nor to have court cases heard by a Welsh-speaking jury, and no right to Welsh-medium education.

3. Local Language Planning

Before proceeding to a careful consideration of this latest Language Act and its implementation, we would like to turn to a consideration of local planning initiatives. Social policy is capable of being developed at the different levels of local government and the associated bodies have developed language policies. In the absence of a unitary agency responsible for language planning across Wales, the space opened by this absence was occupied by the local authorities. Until recently the autonomy of local authorities was considerable, and many such authorities developed policies in relation to Welsh whereas others declined to do so. At the moment there is considerable variation across Wales in the relationship between language and social policy. Some authorities conduct a large part of their activities through the medium of Welsh, and respond to non-Welsh speakers in deviation from this norm. Instantaneous translation facilities have been established to facilitate public debate. Other authorities have been reluctant to pursue such developments.

Within Wales most of the implementation of central policy is in the hands of local government who can also develop their own policy in such implementation. Thus, in administering the various central Education Acts, local authorities receive finance in order to ensure that the demands of the Act are implemented, but can develop their own language policies in respect of the education delivered within schools. The entry of Welsh into public administration on a considerable scale derives from the 1970s. Such developments have raised people's expectations and also their familiarity with the use of Welsh in public administration to the extent that it has become institutionalized. This has not been an easy process, and in many parts of Wales it has still not occurred. A major problem involves the manner in which the current climate obliges a shift from a public-service-orientated public sector to a market-orientated private sector. The limited number of speakers of minority languages are hardly likely to benefit from this trend. It has meant that the power of local authorities which have operated through the medium of Welsh has declined. Thus the social services which had emphasized the need for social workers and others to interact with their clients through the medium of Welsh have receded in importance in the public sector, and commercially orientated community-based organizations, not all of which shared this belief, have played a more prominent role. The client as consumer is supposedly given more choice but that choice does not extend to language (Morris and Williams, 1994).

The positive extreme of what has occurred is the situation where a local authority prioritizes Welsh in offering a bilingual service. All documents are produced in both languages, with Welsh being given symbolic priority. All members of the public have a right to expect service in the language of their choice. Staff are encouraged to use Welsh in internal administration. However, such staff retain the right to choose which language to use in internal affairs, providing it does not 'significantly affect the effectiveness of internal interaction'. This means that, despite giving staff every opportunity to learn Welsh, it only requires one non-Welsh speaker in a department to ensure that English will be the language of interaction and thereby of administration. At the level of discussion in a formal context the picture is different, with instantaneous translation facilities affording the possibility of speaking in either language. This has been of great assistance in institutionalizing the use of Welsh in official capacities.

A major problem in the use of Welsh at work, both in the public and private sector, is that many if not most of the managerial class come from outside Wales. This tends to determine the language of interaction. Often this has led to the establishment of a bilingual intermediary between the English-speaking management and the Welsh-speaking workforce. Attempts to ensure that management and staff speak Welsh has often been hindered by accusation of racism. The current tendency to promote flexibility and flat management in work is severely impeded by the inability of management to speak Welsh. Nor does the need for public bodies to enable the public to use Welsh, as denoted in the 1993 Welsh Language Act, help language planning in this respect in that it merely leads to the employment of a small number of individuals to deal with 'things Welsh'.

There has been a reluctance to concentrate upon work as a focus for the use of Welsh. However, it has become an issue in relation to housing. This relates partly to the massive increase in the ownership by English people of Welsh housing for use as holiday homes. It has also related to the significant amount of in-migration from England since the 1960s, and the manner in which this undermines the language practices of local communities. Central government has opposed any attempt to influence this process since it would be against the needs for a capitalist economy to have an unrestrained, mobile labour force. Nonetheless, the demand for some form of control in Wales has been strong. Some degree of compromise has been reached wherein the Secretary of State for Wales is willing to consider the influence of housing developments upon the language context.

4. The 1993 Welsh Language Act and its Implementation

Neo-liberalism

Inevitably, perhaps, given the need to resort to new measures in order to resolve the problems of recession and the need to generate a more competitive infrastructure, there has emerged a distinctive orientation towards development. In many respects this orientation is not new but draws upon the focus on human capital that has been at the heart of our understanding of the relationship between economy and society for well over a century. The main thrust of this orientation involves what is referred to as neo-liberalism. Its focus is upon the relevance of human capital for economic development, an orientation which was restricted to Third World development during the 1950s and 1960s. Thus, in many respects, the emergence of language planning in Europe and its relationship to language use surveys as a means of establishing a baseline and benchmarking function *vis-à-vis* the desired outcome of planning go hand in hand with the focus upon human capital in the sense that, until recently, they were both the central focus of conceptions of Third World development. However, there is a difference between earlier theory and practice in the Third World and that currently operating in Europe. Much of the orientation in the Third World involved an argument that autochthonous culture had to be eradicated and replaced by its western or modern equivalent, an argument that has a long history in the sociological literature. In contrast, the European practice claims a value for cultural diversity and places planning and development within the context of development through diversity. This is partly because the same principles apply across all of the European regions. We return to this issue when we discuss the context of regional development in the concluding chapter.

Central to the arguments of neo-liberalism is a critique of the manner in which state welfarism has created a paternalistic, dependent relationship between the individual and the state, a relationship which has fettered individual creativity. Thus, the relationship between the individual and the state must be adjusted, and a new conception of democracy developed, one based upon responsibility. This democracy is based upon the principle of enabling rather than upon some inherent idea of rights as citizen, or even upon universal ethical principles. This has profound implications for such concepts as 'language rights'. It is claimed that such developments remove all ethical principles from political action, leading to a technicist emphasis on individual action. The enabling principle focuses upon the idea of non-directionality, or the claim that states should respond to the needs and expectations of the citizen, rather than directing them towards certain ends. It involves a focus upon the animator state that responds to problems via organization, co-operation and confrontation between public services, elected administration and associations, leading social actors to play a more active role in the solution of social and economic problems. A regulated, reordered, space is created, within which agents participate in the amelioration of their own social problems. It involves embodying the metaphor of network, encompassing an emphasis upon the political, economic and cultural importance of mobility. Clearly, these are important developments worthy of close scrutiny.

As a political discourse, neo-liberalism derives from orthodox liberal arguments which envisaged two natural orders: on the one hand an individualistic, egocentric, interest-motivated economy; and, on the other, an associational, communitarian civil society. In this respect it paralleled the modernist tendency that fed into the social sciences, and which tended to divide economy and society into separate but related endeavours. The reality of the market is seen as a quasi-natural domain with its own form of self-regulation. Thus, individuals are involved in certain relations, the economic relations, which are indifferent to membership in any particular society. Within the liberal conception the individual is a premise. It is conceived as the only observable reality to which we can refer when we observe society. Power can be mobilized in order to condition people's decisions. When such a constraint is not used, the individual is socially free to choose from alternatives as a function of his or her judgement regarding the consequence of that action. The individual is rewarded or punished for his or her action; that is, s/he supports his or her actions, and in this respect is a responsible person. Thus the individual in this conception is a unity which possesses a personal identity. Society is conceived of as a collection of individuals, each carrying interests to which s/he seeks to assign value. They are also involved in the variety and scope of the social relations which characterize any particular, localized civil society. Whereas market activity divides, the social activity of civil society fuses. The general problem of liberal government involves the relationship it should establish with the complex quasi-natural reality over which it presides but with which it cannot do just what it likes. To a certain extent this dilemma has hitherto been addressed via the creation of an overlap between state, society and nation, deriving consent through the relationship between these concepts and the principles of 'democracy'.

Liberal government also addressed the issue of the techniques, procedures and regulations that were necessary in order to achieve an optimum effect in the production of wealth and the simultaneous promotion of well-being. This has tended to be achieved through paternalistic relations between state and citizen, something which reached its apogee in the form of state welfarism. Thus power and liberty are opposed. Political and legal institutions exist in order to counter the threats of absolutism and the arbitrary, in effect, to ensure that certain individuals do not extract power for their own ends. Power is conceived of as that which an individual can exercise over other individuals. By the same token the modernist distinction between reason and emotion was projected onto the reason of economic markets and the potential irrationality of culture and society. In contrast to the view of government as the art of acting on the action of individuals in order to modify the way they conduct themselves, liberalism tended to withdraw from the paternalism of the state and simply let people get on with things. This was linked with a faith in the human capacity for reason in all areas of life.

In contrast neo-liberalism does not accept the market as an already existing quasi-natural reality. Rather it argues that the market can only exist under conditions that must be actively constructed by government. However, it also claims that this is only possible by denying the concept of society, which is displaced by a focus upon the individual, the family and the community. The liberal understanding of society as one of two natural, self-governing orders involving spontaneous relationships of power, authority and subordination is cast aside. Society is relegated to a construct of government, shaped by an imposed authority in the form of the various elements of welfarism and imbued with an associated dependency. As an invention of government, society cannot be the spontaneous order of liberalism. Furthermore, neo-liberalism claims that welfarism is not only costly, but that it is also counter-productive to the economic order in that it is a source of 'irrationality' that generates a new form of 'serfdom' (Hayek, 1974), or dependency.

Clearly neo-liberalism is not only anti-society, but it is also opposed to excessive government, and preaches the rolling back of the state. This raises the issue of how such a position can be compatible with the essential goal of governing. Whereas the political economists of the late eighteenth century saw civil society as the natural correlate of the spontaneous market, such a stand is regarded as impractical on account of the disruptive consequences of dismantling the apparatus of the welfare state. An attempt is made to embed a proliferating variety of models of action based upon liberal conceptions of the self-regulating market in the various apparatuses of the welfare state. These are invariably models of self-regulation or self-government leading to what Donzelot (1984) refers to as autonomization – the governing of society via self-government. It is this that lies at the heart of the concept of enabling or empowering which strives to undo the effects of dependency.

The fundamental principles of such action derive from the concept of an economic enterprise, with autonomy directly relating to the freedom to be economically enterprising. The more freedom is exercised, the greater the autonomy. Furthermore, subjecting to the models serves to create autonomous and enterprising subjects. In implementing this idea, the state develops technologies of government which aim to generate a new and different autonomy based upon the logic of the economic market, leading to what Donzelot (1991) calls 'contractual implications', involving the procedures linked to an 'enabling state', which contrasts with the welfare state. The enabling state encourages citizens to take a more active role in the solution of their own economic, health and social problems. It is here, of course, that we witness the emergence of the concern with a bottom–up or a grass-roots approach that links with the overriding need to ascertain the needs and expectations of the citizen as consumer within the provision of services.

The concept of order has now assumed the meaning of 'the order of a market' that guarantees an equitable outcome. It relies upon the idea of bilateral transfers for general welfare. In practical terms it involves the individual subsuming personal interest in the interest of the greater good of the community. This includes a concern with morality and ethics, elements which hitherto were integrated in the concept of state welfarism. This is despite what has been said above about the manner in which neo-liberalism negates moral issues. What we encounter here is not so much a social morality as a morality premised upon the relationship between the individual and an ill-defined community. Thus, this morality is of quite a different order to that in which society itself as a social order is premised upon the idea of ethical principles that determine the associated normativity. Individualism is channelled in the direction of the greater good as a moral crusade. Similarly, since the market creates unemployment, there is another moral dilemma to be confronted. In market terms, waste is viewed as immoral and efficiency is seen as the antidote. Since the market is viewed as the most efficient way of managing resources, it is seen as a moral order and the transfer of its hegemony into the world of what was previously the world of the social is part of a moral campaign. The effects of neo-liberalism are held to be that people govern themselves in a liberal and efficient way, involving an emphasis upon quality assurance, and a focus upon innovation in practice. Welfarism is relegated to the community and is operated through the principle of the greater good.

Clearly, a central issue associated with this conception involves the extent to which society can, and should, be conceived of in terms of the market. It involves what Dodd (1995: 150) has referred to as the 'conceptual boundary', the interconnection between economy and society. In many respects it is not unlike the boundary between language and culture, or language and society, to which we have already referred. However, given that the relationship between the market and society has assumed an axiomatic context, being far more than an analogy, it has far-reaching implications. It ignores the difficulties of the concept of a perfect market, which has never existed in practice (Gilpin, 1987: 18). It focuses upon what Granovetter (1985: 56) has referred to as the difference between the undersocialized model of human behaviour and decision-making of neo-classical economics, and the oversocialized model of Parsonian structural functionalism. While this is not the place to pursue this issue, it certainly is not something that should be ignored.

The rationale associated with many of the concepts and principles currently driving much policy applications in the European Union are by now evident. Neo-liberalism is not merely a theory, it is also a method, in the sense that strict processes are involved in ensuring the application of the theory. These often operate at the community level as guidelines of good practice in development. It is these mechanical principles which have been absorbed into language planning by the Welsh Language Board. There is a focus upon non-directionality in the sense of action responding to the needs and expectations of the population, rather than directing them towards specific goals. This non-directionality is linked with the idea of enabling or empowering. However, it also refers to the totality in the concept of participation, and community development work focuses upon involving the entire community or, at least, obtaining an understanding of the needs and expectations of the entire community. It also focuses upon integrating the individual with the community through cohesion in such a way that the individual operates by reference to the greater good of the community. Only in this way can the value of cohesion be positively harnessed and operationalized, and the devil of dependency expurgated.

This has profound implications for the orthodox understanding of language planning. It can no longer be conceived of in terms of the modernist conception of state benevolence, acting on behalf of the language group within a general framework of democracy and rights. It also means that language planning can no longer be viewed as an already constituted sociology of language or sociolinguistics. In common with other forms of planning it is far more likely to be seen in terms of the strategic planning of the business enterprise, with a focus upon forward planning, prioritizing, evaluating strengths, weaknesses, opportunities and threats. It will involve seeking to replicate in other locations the success obtained in one location. This will entail involving local personnel in achieving such a goal, and responding to the needs and expectations of the local personnel using marketing. This is the essence of the grass-rootism of neo-liberalism. In a sense, it will be obliged to acknowledge that there is a contradiction between planning and the idea of a market, and will have to develop flexible strategies in its practices.

While we are uneasy about the possibility of understanding human behaviour by referring to a market model, we also recognize the strength of discourse in directing human behaviour. In this respect the market model cannot be ignored. What this means is that language planning, as a discipline, which has largely been constructed on a moralist platform involving local rights, is obliged to reassess its enterprise. It also means that the search for a rationale for the relevance of diversity must accommodate this orientation.

The 1993 Act and agency creation

A distinction has to be made between the development of linguistic policy through legislative means and as a measure of social policy. Within the UK, legislation is the responsibility of central government, and the only reference to Welsh within such legislation is in the Welsh Language Act. Although the Welsh Language Board has been established to administer the latest such Act, it is not a language planning agency in the usual meaning of the term. It consists of civil servants rather than people trained in issues relevant to language planning. Its brief is limited. However, it has of late been given the responsibility of administering the monies allocated to promoting the language which, hitherto, had been administered by the Welsh Office, the main agency of state administration in Wales. These monies include those relating to publications and the financing of cultural activities, but with limited innovative scope in that these funding activities tend to be a continuation of what was previously administered within the Welsh Office. They also play a role in education in the sense that they are responsible for funding the locally based peripatetic Welsh-language teachers which service the various education authorities. Most importantly, as we will discuss below, the implementation of the Act means that they have a degree of authority over many agencies within the public sector who are obliged to address how they intend to conform with the demands of the Act via the Welsh Language Board.

The Board's financial accounts indicate that in 1996–7 it had a budget of about 3 million ECU, of which 1.25 million ECU was earmarked for 'grants', and 1.6 million ECU for salaries of the staff and Board members. Two things stand out – the small budget that, on the surface, appears to be devoted to language planning in Wales and the absurdity of a public-sector body which, in a time of the rolling back of the state, spends more on its staffing than it distributes in grant aid. Whether or not an awareness of this context was responsible for the change, by the following year, we find that the Board is also responsible for distributing a further 3 million ECU in grant aid, this being mainly those monies which were previously administered by the Welsh Office. Of this sum about 80 per cent goes to four institutions associated with pre-school education, print media and youth and cultural activities. These four institutions are firmly stabilized in the social and institutionalized life of Wales. In the same year, the Board was responsible for administering a further 3 million ECU to the local authorities 'for the promotion of education'. Two relevant points emerge. First, that if these last two sets of figures are earmarked, then the Board's role in their allocation is essentially administrative rather than determinist or allocative. Thus it would appear that the only way in which the Board can achieve the financial allocation which would allow it to play a more direct planning role would be by reorganizing, that is, by diverting the funds allocated under these headings, primarily, one would imagine, from the four institutions which receive the bulk of the funding, or from the local authorities. Such an action would, inevitably, produce conflict and concern. Thus, the impression is conveyed that the Board appears to be a poorly funded agency which has little more than a legal obligation to promote and implement the 1993 Act and to administer other funds associated with the language. Its planning function is limited, in the sense of promoting the kinds of changes which it might understand as of value in promoting the language. This leads to the second point. The funds to which the Board has access for innovative language planning initiatives pale in comparison with the resources which the local authorities and agencies such as S4C, the Welsh-language television channel, have at their disposal. Yet such agencies are obliged to defer to the Board's insistence on policing their language plans. This may be particularly irritating for elected bodies which view the Board, thus far, as undemocratic and unaccountable to the public (although it is accountable to the Welsh Office).

Furthermore, there is a massive contradiction between an agency which operates with reference to a neo-liberalism that advocates the removal of dependency by reducing the extent of public funding to a minimum, and the massive support given to the four bodies which absorb so much of the available resources. The Board operates most of its plans by matched funding principles and by the principle of a gradual reduction of support over a relatively short period of time until the supported body is capable of self-support. The recent case of a high-profile adult learning centre is illustrative. This was audited by the Board and found to be incapable of sustaining itself on the income which it generated, largely on account of the entry of competing activities within other bodies, some of which were publicly funded. In accordance with the neo-liberal principles, the natural outcome would have been for this centre to yield to its competitors who were more cost-effective. However, this suggestion led to a public outcry, which merely demonstrates the difficulties facing the Board in the future.

The following statement prefaces the Welsh Language Board's document *A Strategy for the Welsh Language*. This document is set out in characteristic neo-liberal terms, following a set format of establishing needs *vis-à-vis* expectations:

> The Welsh language is the common property of all Welsh people, whether they speak the language or not. It is part of a cultural heritage of all the people of Wales, indeed of Britain, of Europe and beyond. The same is true of the English language.

> The Board aspires to see the day when those in Wales whose preferred language is Welsh will have the same rights as those whose preferred language is English. In a world and continent which are still divided by ethnic and national differences, this is an ambitious aim. But there are encouraging signs as well, as multilingual and multicultural frameworks are increasingly accepted in society. It is within such a framework . . . that we must now consider the future of the language.

A number of points have to be made about this statement. While there remains a tendency to reify language, thereby establishing it as an object separate from its speakers, as something which can be operated on, as something which can be given value, it is also seen as a property. That is, it is placed within an economic context of belonging and of being capable of being evaluated and incorporated into an economist discourse. As such, Welsh has been commodified, something that goes hand in hand with reification. As a commodity it is given value by reference to its owners – as a common property it does not pertain to individual ownership as do most properties. While establishing the language in reference to the Welsh people marks its dominion, it is also claimed that, like the environment, it is of relevance to the entire world. This claim for the value of diversity and of the relevance of language for such diversity is contextualized by making a similar claim for English – the 'Other' of language in Wales. That is, an implicit claim is made for an abstract equality between these two languages within a universal sense of difference, thus sustaining the idea that this diversity which includes Welsh is in the interest of everyone. It is impossible to lie outside of a field of interest.

Welsh and English in Wales are related to speakers who are conceived of as having both preferences and rights. However, the relationship between preferences and rights is not the same for the two groups. Those who opt for one preference have different rights from those who opt for the other preference. This dis-symmetry between preference and rights is the focus of the Board's concern. We are not told about these different rights, but are obliged to assume that they relate to the language preference rather than to any other context. However, the difference of rights relates to 'ethnic and national differences' which hinder the aim of equal rights. Furthermore, 'ethnic and national differences' are counterposed to 'multilingual and multicultural frameworks', these being frameworks which are 'accepted in society'. What emerges is a picture of 'ethnicity' and 'nation' as divisive. It is not clear whether they are socially divisive, but since the converse of multilingualism and multiculturalism does pertain to society, we can assume that the reference is to social divisiveness. The resolution of social divisiveness involves 'acceptance' of preferred 'frameworks', that is, imposition gives way to persuasion. The deletion of agency through nominalization in the statement means that it is not possible to ascertain precisely who or what operationalizes the negative and positive procedures. What we do know is that there is an opposition between 'ethnicity and nationalism' on the one hand, and 'multiculturalism and multilingualism' on the other. The interesting feature here is that, in supporting the second set, the author refutes any sense of nationalism, thereby negating any explicit political involvement. The opposition also reveals a difference between the subjective elements of ethnicity and nationalism which are conceived of as correlates of identity, and language and culture which are objective dimensions. This serves to distance the author from the emotive context of the topic under discussion.

The reference to 'ethnic and national differences' is particularly interesting. Clearly they are not synonymous. If we assume that ethnicity involves the construction of deviation from the normative, that nations pertain to the perception of commonality constructed out of subjects, space and time, and that the modern state seeks to construct such a commonality as a feature of its legitimation in the form of the nation-state, we find that a normativity defined by a state incorporates the sense of nation that implicates everyone who is a citizen. This would explain the use of both concepts. Ethnicity is non-normative, and 'national differences' can only involve challenges to the conception of the nation-state. However, the reference is not to the state, but rather, to a 'world and continent', both of which, implicitly, include states. Thus, whereas it would appear inevitable that both the concepts of ethnicity and nation would involve the state as referent, there is a distancing and associated non-implication of the state.

The philosophy of the Welsh Language Board is a direct manifestation of the more orthodox neo-liberal orientation of regional development, with its focus upon community development and planning. The focus is on forging partnerships that reflect and promote local initiative partnerships which will, in so far as is possible, involve the private sector, and will persuade enterprises of all shades to involve themselves in promoting the language. In some respects, it echoes the shift from what is seen as a 'dependency culture' towards a self-promotion orientation which draws upon local human capital as is characteristic of the rhetoric of community development. Thus, it involves the rolling back of the state and the vesting of responsibility in the community which can no longer look to state subsidies as a form of cultural welfarism that sustains the language. In this respect it 'enabl[es] the language to be self-sustaining as a communication medium in Wales'.

What is strange is that side by side with the neo-liberal rhetoric is an orthodox description of the current state of the language group, a description which is couched in terms of the orthodox sociological paradigm. Thus, we find reference to socio-economic factors in relation to sustainable economic development at the community level. This can be seen as an attempt to stretch existing data into the conceptual framework of neo-liberalism, focusing upon community development without entirely succeeding in extrapolating the orthodox sociological input. On the other hand, as we explain below, the orthodox account of social geography premised upon the ethnolinguistic vitality framework of social psychology merely serves as a backdrop, and the socio-economic reference is very much linked to the market analogy.

The strategy developed by the Board has the following general objective: 'To enable the Welsh language to be self-sustaining and secure as a medium of communication in Wales'. Again the reification of language is notable, as also is the restriction of their geographical terms of reference to Wales. This is to be achieved by:

- increasing the number of Welsh speakers;
- expanding use opportunity;
- changing 'habits of language use';
- 'encouraging' people to avail themselves of the opportunities;
- strengthening Welsh as a community language.

Again there are interesting issues for discussion. The conception of a 'community language' stands alone, separate from the other processes. That is, there is a conception of language use by reference to the conception of community. We are not told what the nature of this community is, and it is difficult to evaluate from the text. It would seem that what is involved here is a conception of communities where Welsh is widely used, and that the aim is to sustain this pattern. It is in this context that there is a distinction between language use as a first and second language. That is, family and community use is referred to as 'first language', and the exclusive use of language in other contexts becomes 'second language' use. Unfortunately, this distinction is not conceptualized by any theoretical orientation to language, and would appear to derive from the conventional distinction of sociolinguistics. However, what is implied is that community plays an important role in sustaining the language group and is categorically different from extra-community processes, whatever they may be. Presumably, the other elements operate at this extra-community level, and it is there that the focus is on changing language behaviour. This change is to be achieved via the punish/recompensation principles of neo-liberalism which relates to the reasonable subject. The enabling process focuses upon using 'the language naturally when conducting their business or when receiving bilingual services from bodies or companies operating in Wales'. This throws more light on the reference to 'community language'. Enabling people to use Welsh in relation to formal institutions is distinguished from the interactional use of language, and presumably the means of 'persuasion' varies accordingly. There is constant reference to a 'natural' use of language which contributes to, but is not the same as, language as 'a living medium of communication'. It also contributes to the 'natural life of Wales'. It derives from the regular use of the language in 'everyday life'. This seems to be cumbersome way of coming to terms with the concept of normalization without referring to the associated sociological concept of normativity.

Monitoring is partly by reference to the decennial censuses of 2001 and 2011 which should allow the Board to establish targets for its main aims, an essential feature of the total quality management of neo-liberalism. Monitoring also involves preparing and reviewing corporate plans on an annual basis. Yet it is claimed that setting targets for most of the proposed work is not possible. The only reason we are given relates to community use, where this is held to rely on developing a socio-economic context that would appear to link with principles of community development. That is, there will be an attempt to integrate language with the fundamentals of community development. We will address the difficulties of such a process below. What is most surprising is that, given the emphasis upon stimulating and promoting language use, no reference is made to language use surveys as a basis for monitoring, especially as this is the conventional way of approaching monitoring in more orthodox language planning contexts. Furthermore, as we have emphasized in Chapter 2, the decennial census is a very crude measure of competence and tells us nothing about language use. To rely on this as the basis for monitoring appears to be futile. At best it can throw light on the number of self-reported 'speakers', but any increase or decrease may well have little to do with the actions of the planning agency. Indeed, any gain may be in spite of the agency's actions and activities.

Implementation

The Board presents six priority areas for its work, areas which are a more specific manifestation of the objectives set out:

- Ensuring that the language achieves equal status with English within state administration. The concern here seems to involve making the state approach compatible with European law by reference to the inclusion of Welsh in official documents. Beyond this technical issue, it will have to operate as a pressure group in normatizing practice. It relates to the way in which Welsh is conceived of as the language of Wales, and English as the language of Britain, conceptions which limit the implementation of equal status to the two languages.

- To ensure that Welsh-medium education is available within easy access of all households in Wales in accordance with parental wishes. To ensure that necessary resources are available.
- Standardization of Welsh through standardizing terminology.
- Translating the enabling principle into use via a wide-ranging publicity campaign. This is conceived of as an exercise in changing attitudes in the belief that it leads to changing practices.
- To integrate the promotion of language use with economic principles of community development.
- To expand the information about the Welsh language by putting pressure on the state statistical office to include a question on Welsh-language ability in other regions of Britain.

The operationalization of these objectives relies on establishing partnerships, that is, in persuading other agencies and institutions to collaborate in pursuing these ends. Some of the 'partners' are government agencies, while others rely either on the state, or even on the Welsh Language Board, for financial support. Thus, one of the main aspects of the Board's work is that of persuasion or lobbying. The related role is that of fostering networks or partnerships between agencies as a collaborative venture. As we have noted, it does have some financial resources whereby this goal is made easier to achieve than it would be by merely relying upon the market argument outlined above. This persuading role extends to the general public who must be persuaded to use the language, to encourage others to use it, to send their children to Welsh-medium schools. This influencing is strategically targeted.

Beyond these two rules and the unspecified context of 'research', the activities, despite a relatively elaborate rhetoric, would appear to be limited. The enabling activity involves operating the language-plan scheme of the Act within public bodies, and persuading private companies to take the same action. At the other end of the equation are the actions which persuade people to avail themselves of these services. There is some finance available for the development of information-technology-related developments – for example, Cysgair (Welsh thesaurus) and Cysill (Welsh spell-check) software packages – but beyond this, there does not appear to be any more involvement than that which was associated with the Welsh Office prior to the formation of the Board. Indeed, in these activities, it would appear that the Board is under strict instructions not to deviate from the previous funding equations.

The 1993 Act was established in this context of market-driven forces and neo-liberalism. By the same token, the Welsh Language Board was established in order to administer the Act. Of late, the function of the Board has extended to include Welsh-language-related actions hitherto administered through the Welsh Office. These developments have profound implications, not only because of the rolling back of the state that is implicit in the administrative shift and the way it influences democratic principles (Touraine, 1994), but also for the conception of language change and the forces that influence it. It raises the question of the need for competencies beyond those involved in the civil-servant functions of public administration, and the relationship of such competencies, or the lack of them, for the foresight that is implicit in the conception of language planning.

The Welsh Language Board was established, and its personnel appointed, with little academic understanding of language planning or issues of social and cultural change as being remotely associated with the relevant positions. Indeed, the impression is clearly conveyed that the general principles of neo-liberalism are transferable across context with the implication that specialist knowledge is not only unnecessary but counter-productive in what amounts to 'language management'. It was essentially an administrative body of civil servants. Thus, the Board is almost completely devoid of personnel with the requisite training in the disciplines that are relevant to language planning. By the same token, as a quango, the members of the Welsh Language Board consist of the 'great and the good', sometimes representing different bodies which are held to have an interest in the Welsh language (for example, S4C). This again means that the necessary language planning expertise is missing. Initially, even the need to draw upon an expertise from outside of the Board was also ignored. Fortunately, of late this has been modified: for some research projects 'experts' are used in an advisory capacity, and at least one Board member has been drawn in specifically for his academic interest and expertise in matters of bilingualism. Whether this will lead to developments which run counter to the conception of language planning as nothing more than the implementation of an Act is questionable. However, it does appear that the Board is already being obliged to give the Act a liberal interpretation in order to achieve the results it desires, suggesting that there exists a conception of language planning as more than the original Act could achieve. It would be puerile to relate this intellectual omission to arrogance; rather, it is the consequence of establishing language planning as an enterprise constructed out of neo-liberalism. In this respect it is quite different from the orthodox conception of language planning. There is another aspect that must be made clear. The current situation involving the Welsh Language Board, as with other state bodies or quangos, is fluid in the sense that we are locked in a political developmental process involving the shift from state-centred to proto-European structures. This process appears to have an air of inevitability about it, but it is also tentative in the sense that the direction of development can be subject to reversal. The inevitability derives from three main factors – globalization, the advent of the Single Market and the common philosophy that drives political decision making. We feel that it is important to emphasize this tentativeness since it must have an impact upon the manner in which any state body views the process of change. A state governed by a political orientation which is sceptical about the globalization process and about the need to encompass a global political structure will inevitably tend to conceive of planning in an inward-looking way, rather than the broadening ethos which encompasses the European dimension, and sees Europe as the context within which such planning occurs. That is, the planning agency is not independent, either of current politics, nor of the broader philosophical problematic within which it is incorporated as a planning agency. We are not denying that there is a pan-European dimension to the current thrust of neo-liberalism, but it is an orientation that is capable of accommodating both a broad and a narrow conception. This becomes possible through the deregulation of economic function which gives neo-liberalism its broad thrust while restricting the socio-political to the existing state context. That is, while the economic deregulation does limit the relevance of state activity, there may be a reluctance to conceive of planning in its socio-political context as pertaining to the same geo-political context. Consequently, social policy and planning tends to be disarticulated from the agenda which is set at the European level. In some respects this a manifestation of the local–global relationship. On the one hand, there is the global context which demands deregulation, and on the other hand there are the various policy initiatives which establish the local context for such global developments.

Operationalizing the enabling principle

The implementation of the Act by the Welsh Language Board is consistent with neo-liberal principles. Public companies have been obliged to develop plans for the implementation of the demands of the Act as policies. These plans are subject to scrutiny by the Language Board prior to being accepted. The basis for the judgement concerning their suitability is the principle of enabling the Welsh speaker to obtain the service rendered through the medium of Welsh. However, whereas this conveys the impression of an authority on the part of the Board, the practice is always subservient to a desire 'not to move too quickly', and not to upset institutions and agencies. Thus a major criticism of both the Act and the Board is that there is no mandate of compulsion and that any proposal can, in any case, be overruled by the Secretary of State.

The commodification of language means that an argument must be presented to the private sector which will induce it to take similar steps, since the Act does not accommodate the private sector, even though the Board can and does put pressure on private-sector companies which are selected as the most relevant for potential co-operation. Thus the argument is presented that language can be treated as a commodity, and that treating it as such in relation to the Welsh speaker will enhance the business potential of the company. Within the market, the cost of developing an adequate policy will pay off by the increase in business. Cost is discussed in terms of the cost of implementing the company or agency's language policy, benefit in terms of language and profit in terms of public satisfaction and effectiveness. Of course there must be a relationship between cost and benefit, and this relationship must result in profit. Therefore, the goal is one of creating a population that is satisfied because there is the presentation of a service with a content that is commensurate with its needs and expectations. If this can be achieved then the outcome will be a satisfied consumer, leading to a service that is more effectively administered and, in relation to the profitability of the company, a bigger and more satisfied market. This conception derived from the rhetoric of neo-liberalism rather than on explored environment. To our knowledge, the only detailed exploration of the relationship between the use of a minority language in commerce and transactional value is by reference to Galician (Rei Doval and Ramello, 1995).

The assumption here is that Welsh speakers operate on the principle of such commodification, preferring to do business with those who use the language than with those who do not. Thus the needs and expectations of the Welsh speaker will be met if the service is provided through the medium of Welsh. If there is no congruence between either needs and expectations or the provision of services, then both are capable of modification. However, the content of both the Act and the Board's documentation make it clear that the belief is that the problem lies with service provision rather than the orientation of the Welsh speaker. It is in this context that language use is conceived of. It entirely misses the relevance of the concept of institutionalization, where language behaviour is stabilized or institutionalized in such a way that the goal of this commodification practice is very difficult to achieve. In some respects this institutionalization can be conceived of as a form of dependency. However, by the same token, it would appear that the principle of non-directionality precludes developing strong bases for changing individual behaviour, something that must derive from grass-rootism.

This blindness is also the consequence of the way in which there is a tendency to ignore the social nature of language, partly as a consequence of rejecting any operable conception of society. Since language planning lies outside of any social conception, it leads to a focus upon the language as a reified entity, rather than upon language groups as social groups. This goes hand in hand with the commodification of language. The pieces of the discourse fit together in such a way that any social conception is excluded.

Equality and normativity

The market in Welsh as a commodity is far from being a global market, and different policies operate for different geographical locations and different sectors. In this respect it has little relevance for anyone wishing to treat Welsh as a 'national' language, with all of the moral and emotive implications, as a language capable of being used anywhere in Wales. Again this is compatible with the need to depoliticize the language by removing it from ethnicity and nationalism, and placing it within the context of multiculturalism and multilingualism to which we referred above. In this way the effect of the Act is to ensure that Welsh has ceased to be a national language, if it ever was. Rather, it becomes an Act which determines that Welsh is a language that can be used with some institutions, in some places, at some times. In this respect it is interesting to note that whereas in Welsh the concepts of Wales and the Welsh are conveyed by the same lexical item 'Cymru', the Board's text marks 'Cymru' as a territorial and not a social concept, but with the spatial dimension being broken up by reference to internal policy action. This is why there is so much more emphasis upon the geographical than upon the social or psychological component. It is also not unrelated to the attempt to divest the language of its moral-political connotation. Geography, not speakers becomes the measure whereby the model of needs and expectations is measured. In this respect it contrasts markedly with the situation in Catalunya where a distinction is made between 'lengua propria', or the language of the people, and the state language. This gives the language and its speakers a territorial integrity that contributes significantly to legitimization. It confers a sense of territoriality without relating to demolingusitics.

It becomes difficult to see how such a conception is commensurate with the idea of Welsh as an autochthonous language within any conventional concept of equality. Indeed, equality is used in the sense of treating the two languages equally, rather than of the equal use of the two languages. This leads to a strange use of the concept of 'equality' since it fails to accommodate the normal context of equality in language group relationships, where reference is to institutionalization and the manner in which it constrains language use. As a consequence, it is impossible to allude to either equality or inequality by reference to language groups as social groups. In this respect it could be argued that the Act, like the previous Act, merely confirms and legitimizes the minority status of Welsh.

Indeed, the manner in which the text refers to equality has little reference to the idea of social interaction, since it lists eleven guidelines which lead to 'equality', none of which refers to interaction outside of the formal context. There are only two subjects within any interaction – the institution and the public. Yet it is claimed that 'equality' involves more than enabling, since it leads to promoting the use of Welsh. This claim is not developed but must rest on the assumption that enabling and meeting needs and expectations lead to increased use.

Given what has been said above, it is hardly surprising that there is a confusion concerning the concept of normativity and its use in the Board's documentation. It lacks its customary sociological conception as the institutionalization of practices as the social norm. Rather, where the term 'normative' is used, it pertains not to any social-science conceptualization but to the goal of 'making normal'. Several references are made to making Welsh normative in this sense, but other references in the policy document make it abundantly clear that, even within this context of the term, English is the norm and English will be the norm. In this respect it is difficult to view the concept of normativity as anything more than rhetoric, or an attempt to introduce a language planning concept into the document as a means of offering the legitimacy of 'the expert'. There is no reference to contextualizing normativity by reference to either territory or context. That is, the explicit referent of normativity is completely absent. The only implicit reference is to the situational. Whereas English will remain the norm in all activities, there will be the possibility of using Welsh over the phone or by letter, but not by reference to the world of work or any similar context. Even here there will be limitations both by location and sector.

Furthermore, as a Welsh speaker, the individual is obliged to mark him/herself as such in order to be enabled. Thus the individual attending a meeting or conference is obliged to inform the organizing body of a desire to use Welsh, leaving the decision as to whether or not this will be possible to that body. That is, it is not conceivable that such practices can be institutionalized in the sense that they can be taken for granted. Nor, it would appear, can the principle of enabling! Of course, in marking oneself as a Welsh speaker by making the request, one is simultaneously marking oneself as a deviant from the norm. Such necessary practices would appear to be the antithesis of normativity. Indeed, throughout the documentation, Welsh is marked either as deviance from the norm, or as a 'first language', but never as a principle. That is, whereas the enabling principle does lead to the goal of establishing the communicational use of Welsh as the norm, the constraints of the Act and the measures taken to implement it ensure that this cannot be achieved, at least not by reference to the sociological concept of normativity. The incessant fear of treading on non-Welsh-speaking toes, and the associated deference that derives from the need to depoliticize language through focusing on enabling, is detrimental to say the least. Of course, the enabling principle implies the existence of deviant practice – it is never necessary to enable the normative – so that the entire Act merely serves to confirm this deviance. There is a confusion of normal as 'not being deviant' with the idea of norm as prioritizing.

Needs, expectations and use

There remains the problem of how to achieve the limited sense of equality that is referred to. It is clear that the Board itself has its doubts since it refers to 'striving towards the principle'. This involves the task of raising the needs and expectations of Welsh speakers so that they will respond to the enabling conferred on them: that is, in our terms, how to reinstitutionalize the language through relegitimization. It is one thing to enable people to adopt a practice, it is quite another to ensure that they take advantage of it. It would appear that this is a massive task. We know that somewhere between 10,000 and 20,000 of the population of Wales make multiple use of the Welsh-language resources such as the eisteddfod, literature, broadcasting, theatre and education on a regular basis. If this is the size of the core, how is it possible to persuade the remaining 95 per cent of Welsh speakers to avail themselves of what is being enabled?

As we have already implied, the feature of neo-liberalism upon which the Board seizes in this context is what is referred to as quality assurance. This is the customary approach within administrative restructuring. For example, within the health service it has been customary to ask service users about their degree of satisfaction with the provision given to them. The goal of the change agent is to increase the needs and expectations of the end user to the point where there is a contradiction between user satisfaction and need provision. This then allows the change agent to press for 'improved service'. Without this change in needs and expectations, its role is redundant. It is an entirely behaviourist approach. It is argued that attitudes lie at the heart of the approach, and that the goal is one of changing people's attitudes. However, it is claimed that attitudes are a manifestation of values so that if these can be changed, then so can attitudes and, thereby, needs and expectations. The human subject is conceived of as a rational being who can be conditioned to operate within a 'market' rationality which, we are told, is the basis for a 'perfect' rationality. It is summarized in the Board's strategy document (Welsh Language Board, 1993) in the following goal of: 'marketing the language in order to change attitudes, raise the confidence of Welsh speakers, or improve the image of the language'.

'The image of the language' is the equivalent of establishing values. That is, it is an argument that falls in line with the associated concept of dependency within the economism of neo-liberalism, where a dependency on welfarism leads to a dependent orientation among recipients. With regard to language, negative identities involve a negative conception of the language and low self-confidence which can be changed by marketing. It views the problem not by structural causality, but rather, by reference to the individual psyche. Change this psyche and all will be well. It is an old theme placed within the market analogy. It is a theme that does little for the self-concept of a people who are told they have a negative self-image, and in this respect carries the danger of being counter-productive.

It is in this context that much of the research orientation of the Board is focused. It involves establishing public opinion and attitudes. Public opinion must be monitored for two reasons: first, the need to establish needs and expectations; and second, to establish consumer attitudes which need to be changed. It should be evident that less emphasis is currently being placed upon measuring public opinion of needs and expectations, except to establish a baseline. That is, it is not used to consider general service provision in order to exert pressure on service providers, since there is a danger that the providers will merely reject such a positive approach.

Despite this commitment to formulating broad partnerships across all interested parties, the action taken in seeking to create a consultation framework for the Board's strategy document (1993) merely left many in Wales with the feeling that the entire process was so selective that it became effectively a process of excluding potential criticism. As we have indicated, the neo-liberal approach insists upon non-directionality which implies ascertaining the needs and expectations of the consumer. In pursuing this goal, a publicity campaign invited the public to respond to a document which they had not seen. The consultative document was sent to a selected 2,000 organizations and individuals within Wales, eliciting 150 replies; an opinion poll of only 129 respondents was commissioned; and a limited number of representative bodies were invited to a one-day conference attended by forty such bodies. This was perceived as a selective process led by the ongoing critical debate about quangos in Wales and especially about the manner in which the incumbent government was using such quangos to pursue policies which were seen to be contrary to 'Welsh interests'. Furthermore, an exercise premised upon a deficiency model, involving the idea that Welsh speakers lack the motivational principles to utilize the language, asks this population to respond to the consultative document as a consequence of a publicity campaign, a document which not only highlights their deficiency, but also implies that they are unlikely to respond to such an initiative! Yet the Board concluded: 'Since every part of the consultation showed a considerable measure of approval for the consultation document, it was totally reasonable, therefore, to accept the consultation document as a sound basis for the strategy itself' (Welsh Language Board, 1993: 3). Many who felt strongly about the issue felt alienated from this process. These were the very people who felt that it was their political actions which had led to the establishment of the new Act. For a process which involved at most around 500 individuals, less than half of whom were Welsh speakers, to be regarded as a consultative exercise seems misplaced. Rather than being an exercise which involved those whom it was meant to serve, it seemed to be a means whereby the interests of the institutions could be guaranteed at the expense of that which the process was meant to serve.

This element becomes the core focus of the Board's research strategy, drawing upon market research in order to establish the nature of values and attitudes among Welsh speakers. It completely ignores the claim of psychologists that the link between attitudes and behaviour is at best weak. It also ignores the implicit assumption in the claim that Welsh speakers are somehow deficient in that they lack the desired values and associated attitudes, an argument that is reminiscent of the customary tendency to treat minority language groups as rationally deficient because of their marginal status *vis-à-vis* the normative. Existing values and attitudes are measured against the desired or desirable. It is the consequence of adopting an approach devoid of any conception of power, domination and deference.

Grass roots

The reference to the socio-economic factors which operate at the community level makes more sense when we recognize that it bears little relationship to the orthodox sociological discourse. Rather it involves operationalizing the integration of language into community development by precisely the same neo-liberal principles as those which refer both to the Welsh Language Board itself and its operational process. That is, it pertains to the same methodology of establishing non-directionality by ascertaining the needs and expect-ations of the target population – in this case the population within a predefined community, setting up local partnerships whereby these needs and expectations can be pursued; exploring the location of the required financial assistance; ensuring that the essential matched funding is raised locally; overseeing the implementation of the project by drawing upon, sustaining and improving human resources at the community level. Thus the Board has an objective of establishing partnership with pre-existing community development projects and agencies such as the various European Leader Programmes, which have been established upon the same neo-liberal principles, in order to guarantee that language is built into community development. In the long run, the goal is the same as that of economic projects: to remove dependency upon the state by allowing and enabling the community to assume responsibility for its own development. Thus we encounter the essential principle of the rolling back of the state.

The rolling back of the state corresponds to creating the citizen as a responsible entity. This operation includes demanding or directing the state to implement its will. However, if minority is conceived of as subordinate then the associated deference and low status are not likely to generate a demand for a realignment of language status and services at the local level. This is why the high evaluation of Welsh encountered in opinion surveys does not correspond with use. There is no conception of institutionalization in the Welsh Language Board's argument, an absence which derives from an inability to acknowledge the existence of society. On the contrary, it argues that all that is required is to raise needs and expectations and the demand for higher standards will follow.

It is easy to recognize how this exercise in social engineering runs parallel to the attempt to create entrepreneurs through promoting what are regarded as entrepreneurial values, attitudes and behaviour. The entire process is based upon competition between individuals, on the model of market or business competition. As we have previously noted, it is linked to a parallel concern with ensuring that the individ-ual drive is not disruptive, but is ameliorated by a concern for the common good in the form of the preconceived community, whether it be a speech community or a different form of community such as the nation. That is, the entire exercise is conceived of as a massive drive for mutual benefit within the wider society. In this respect it is a representation of the eighteenth-century drive for modernity which sought to create a totality in the form of the state that was more than the sum of the constituent parts. Whereas the creation of community development projects premised upon neo-liberalism has deskilled the development process, much as we have claimed language planning has been deskilled, it also means that many community developers, most of whom are untrained in community development, are not aware of the principles of neo-liberalism which are meant to guide their work. This being the case, it is unlikely that they will be in a position to implement the procedures expected of them by the Welsh Language Board.

The experience thus far takes two directions. The model of the Enterprise Agency is used as a basis for developing a series of Language Enterprises which operate at the grass-roots level. Some of the Language Enterprises are associated with existing community development projects such as the European Leader projects, and the various Enterprise Agencies which have been established in order to foster local development. This raises the question of the extent to which community development is not already premised upon the relevance of language for development, and if it is not, why not? However, it does seem to represent a demarcation between the creation of community as a system of interaction and corporate activities within a restricted territory on the one hand, and deploying the human resources of that community for economic development on the other. It also raises the issue of training and development for the agents themselves.

The second approach involves funding applications by already established community development agencies. The tendency is often to treat these as separate activities which bear little or no relevance to the ongoing economic projects which are themselves focused upon fomenting entrepreneurialism. This is an issue we emphasize in the next chapter. By the same token, the local personnel responsible for representing the 'grass-roots' initiative that leads to establishing the Language Enterprise lack any understanding of language planning and of how to use the relevant resources via a coherent model of language planning. As a consequence local authorities often relate the activities of the Language Enterprise with the local authority education departments which are deemed to have responsibility for the language, while also advocating that the resources be used to supplement already existing educationally related language activities. Others adopt the strategy conveyed by the idea that what is required is to promote activities primarily for young people and to ensure that these activities are undertaken through the medium of Welsh, thereby acting as a form of local language police. Such activities are often conceived of as that which is community so that they are an essential ingredient of community development. This may well operate effectively where there is an effective educational policy that promotes Welsh-language competence for the entire age group, the objective being of translating this competence into use. On the other hand, outside of such areas, which are limited in number and scale, such action is in danger of being divisive at the community level.

There is a difficulty in seeking to integrate language planning into economic development principles in this way, a difficulty which derives from the manner in which community development is premised upon human capital, as a result of which community development assumes an orientation which is far more sociological than it is economic. The principles of generating community activity that promotes human capital, among which can be included culture and language, do not necessarily lead to economic development. Indeed, in many respects there is a suspicion that it has more to do with the rolling back of the state, the running down of the local public sector, and diverting funds from local service provision to other ends.

It is necessary to emphasize that the shift away from the social sciences as a body of expertise that is capable of guiding any planning activity is not the consequence of the absence of such Welsh-language expertise, but rather, it is the consequence of neo-liberalism. Given the emphasis on non-directionality, the planning enterprise changes and involves non-intervention on the part of either the planning agent or the expert. Their only role can be guidance, and in many respects they are replaced by the community developer as an enabler and *animateur*. Yet the need to establish needs and expectations by obtaining the grass-roots opinion of those who are being enabled, not merely as individuals, but as entire communities, means that certain social-science skills such as survey research and analysis are necessary. However, the skill level of such expertise is collapsed to the point that it does not require 'the expert'. The consequence is the entire demotion of the relevance of the social sciences for planning to the point of irrelevance. The community developer role is essentially deskilled.

Yet, perhaps the most evident problem that emerges in making language planning a feature of community development is the contradiction between the principle of non-directionality and that of language promotion within a context in which not everyone speaks Welsh. Thus, the need to consult the entire community, often through holding public meetings, means the introduction of the dominant language (Morris, Williams and Williams, 1995). By the same token, the developing of local partnerships and steering committees tends to involve the incorporation of non-Welsh speakers. In many cases it is non-Welsh speakers who take the initiative. Integrating language planning can lead to undermining the very principles of community solidarity and the commitment of individual needs to the greater good of the community. Such problems do not seem to have been considered by the Welsh Language Board.

Taking the language out of politics

The associated principles of enabling and grass-rootism as dimensions of non-directionality link with the political objective of achieving goals through placid means. It relates to the commitment of the individual to the greater good of the community, uniting the essential principles of the individual, the family and the community that we have referred to above. That is, there is no room for protest, nor for direct action, since this will merely alienate those to whom it is meant to apply. Thus, while the Welsh Language Board is seen to be the main language planning agency, it is by no means conceived of as the only relevant agency. Indeed, it is other agencies which are seen as the main providers, leaving the Board with a strong mandate, but a weak involvement. Thus, one of its goals is to formulate a partnership using that mandate. This partnership is conceived of as a means of uniting everyone who is 'working for the benefit of the language', on the assumption that they will agree to pursue the Board's strategy. This is despite the recognition that the Board cannot succeed without such co-operation and that it is, in effect, a facilitator. What is envisaged is a partnership of co-operation which will lead to consensus.

This position is partly a consequence of the manner in which the neo-liberal model adopted as the basis of the Welsh Language Act and its implementation has much in common with the focus on liberty and a concern with the best means of government for achieving that liberty that was characteristic of the American Revolution. It contrasts with the alternative model based upon the moral and ethical principles of a concern with pity that also derived from the eighteenth century. What is involved here is a shift from governance through pity (Boltanski, 1993), to governance for liberty. The two forms of neo-liberalism have quite different orientations to the ethical. However, the state takes a back seat in this respect, since its earlier welfare role is held to have generated a counter-productive dependency. Rather, the focus shifts to the individual and his or her relationship to the community. Self-responsibility becomes the basis of a new form of governmentality. The concern with the best means of the delivery of liberty leads to a mechanistic form of behaviourism. On the other hand, as Boltanski (1993) has shown in reworking Adam Smith's theory of Moral Sentiments, the alternative would involve developing a third person who would act as an uninvolved bystander who would pass judgement on the issue at hand. In this respect, although the Board lacks the expertise necessary to adopt such a position, it does assume the role of judge and jury in implementing the 1993 Act.

As we indicated at the onset of this chapter, in the absence of any agency directly responsible for language planning prior to 1993, the role was taken by the local authorities and independent language activists. Some of these used state funds for these purposes, while also being supplemented by funds obtained directly from the Welsh Office. Others relied solely, either on private funding, or on Welsh Office funding. Those which developed the most positive policies saw themselves as being in the vanguard of the Welsh-language movement, seeking to develop local policies which contradicted what was perceived as the indifference of the central state. The 1993 Welsh Language Act obliges all public bodies to develop a language policy, but evidently some local authorities have a long-standing commitment to the language and go further than the Act demands. This development means that the Welsh Language Board, a Board whose members, until very recently, were nominated by the state, has authority over an elected body. Thus authority and legitimacy do not appear to coincide, and there is considerable tension between the respective protagonists.

There is a sense of naïveté in this approach in that it ignores the entire history of struggle, both in and over the language (Williams, 1987a). In this respect it ignores the entire sociological basis of co-operation and conflict. In a sense this is yet another attempt to achieve simultaneously the same objectives of 'taking the language out of politics', and divesting the language of any moral or ethical context. This is the source of contention. For many years the language movement in Wales has sought to achieve its goals through direct, non-violent action, emphasizing the moral basis of its cause in so doing. This has led to a great deal of sympathy among Welsh speakers for the objectives and methods of the Welsh Language Society who are conceived of as locked in struggle with an alien state. This, in turn, has alienated many Welsh speakers from the Welsh Language Board, which not only openly opposes the Welsh Language Society, but which also can be seen to be serving the interests of an alien government. Its attempt to divest the language of any political context is seen to be contrary to the very methods which have thus far led to the limited success that has been achieved. It is also seen as a ploy to 'take the guts out of the language issue', which, if it lacks a political context, is felt to lack the emotive context or 'heart' which is so essential to the language movement as a moral cause. Of course, the goal of the entire official process is the converse, establishing a system wherein the onus is on the individual, so that the 'rolling back of the state' involves divesting the state of any responsibility: if individuals do not avail themselves of the opportunity implicit in the enabling process, then it is their own fault. If the Welsh speakers do not seize the opportunity, then who can blame the state for the demise of the language? Nonetheless, it is also evident that the enabling principle constructs the Welsh Language Board as an official pressure agency which seeks to persuade various bodies and institutions to integrate with their strategy. In this respect, the Welsh Language Board is in direct competition with the Welsh Language Society, which is an unofficial pressure group operating with different methods and having somewhat different goals. It is one thing to claim that the language has become accepted as a living force in Wales, it is quite different to assign a normative status to it. Until such a status is achieved, polemic will continue to be one tactic of relevance.

It is clear that the danger of alienation from the very constituency which it seeks to represent, and is its *raison d'être*, is of considerable concern for the Welsh Language Board, which is increasingly in danger of being seen as a political tool that will create an easy passage for formal politics while also, as a quango, being remote from the citizen. If this were indeed the case, then it would undermine the entire principle of the rolling back of the state and non-directionality. Indeed, this has developed to the point of being the basis for the Board seeking support from the most unlikely quarters for acknowledgement of its role in sustaining the Welsh Language Group, and the attempted deployment of the Welsh press to communicate this more widely. Such legitimation strategies would appear to be indicative of an inability to persuade the general public of its self-proclaimed significance. If the Welsh Language Board is to take language out of politics, it must first engender some motivational principle that replaces that of moral indignation.

What is clear is that the entire process shifts the debate from the world of ethics to the world of technology. There is no need for debates about the morality of minority status, nor about the responsibility of a benevolent state to respect the rights of minorities. Rather, the entire issue becomes one of establishing the context within which people are enabled to exercise their preferences by reference to goals and values, all of this within an asocietal context. In respect of language planning, the technological capacity no longer relates to a knowledge of sociolinguistics, sociology, economics, but rather to the means whereby self-regulation can be implemented. The entire exercise is premised upon a behaviourist model of action. It is this that is responsible for the Board's attitudes towards external or internal expertise. It is the wisdom of the ordinary citizen as a Board member that prevails.

5. Conclusion

If we do question the work of the Welsh Language Board it is not because of what they do, nor either to doubt the commitment of those who work for the Board with the goal of 'serving the Welsh language'. Indeed, the actions which they propose are valuable and necessary. They constitute a step forward from a situation where Welsh speakers were left to their own limited devices, even if the neo-liberal discourse does imply an eventual return to such a situation, albeit within a context in which these devices are no longer conceived of as 'limited'. It is important to claim a value for Welsh and for Welsh speakers; it is equally important to promote an extension of its use. Rather, our critique is due to a concern about the validity of that upon which the proposed work is premised. We question the validity of a behaviourist approach attempting to change behaviour through changing values and attitudes. It is quite conceivable that the status of Welsh will increase, but not necessarily as a consequence of the Board's actions. In our view it is more likely that the Act will have the effect of increasing employment that segments the labour market within the public sector, a process that is already in operation, and that this will promote an increase in what we call language prestige which, in turn, will influence language status. The dilemma of the Board is that, if this argument is indeed correct, their monitoring procedure will interpret any such change by reference to their own parameters!

Unless there is this kind of scrutiny of the Act and the Board we are left with a slavish conformity with a popular discourse, a conformity that rests on faith. Not that such a questioning requires justification. It is in the nature of enquiry to raise such doubts, and it is in the nature of democracy to question the institutions which govern us. Language planning has always been a feature of governmentality, and in this respect, the Welsh Language Board is no exception.

If we believe that the market analogy will serve to regulate society and will resolve all social problems, then we fall into a serious trap. It involves viewing problems in terms of individual weakness, and solutions in technological terms. The corollary is that we are led to ignore ethical questions, and the issue of rights disappears. This leads to the elimination of the concept of society which is seen as a construct of government shaped by imposed authority in the form of welfarism, and its substitution by processes that impinge on the individual. We already begin to see such a process appearing in the Welsh Language Board's approach to language planning. It is argued that languages can be marketed, and that the solution to the problems of minority language production and reproduction involves creating the right climate for language to be marketed, remote from all political issues and interventions. It no longer becomes necessary to refer to the social contextualization of language use. It is one thing to claim that extending the prestige of a language by inserting it in the labour market at all levels promotes motivation for the use of the language, as we argued in the *Euromosaic* study (Williams, Strubell and Nelde, 1996), it is quite another thing blatantly to commodify language within such asocial parameters. This is no more than the very reification of language against which we argue. We must recognize that, without the ethical debate that was previously subsumed in welfarism, the minority element, based upon a sense of justice and fair play, evaporates.

The very real danger is that an argument premised upon the primacy of attitudes will have an effect counter to that desired. It is quite conceivable that, in one way or another, Welsh speakers will be enabled to use Welsh in new contexts. However, if we are correct, first in claiming that the attitudes of Welsh speakers are already high, and second, that, in any case, it is not possible to change attitudes in the manner implied, the consequence will be that Welsh speakers will not avail themselves of this enabled opportunity. This, in turn, will lead the providers to claim that Welsh-language use was never part of the needs and expectations of Welsh speakers, and that it was all a waste of time and should be abandoned – yet another case of blaming the victim. It is for this reason that we insist that any attempt to extend and recontextualize the use of Welsh must be accompanied by a clear understanding of the process of institutionalization.

While the main tendency is to ignore the relevance of politics, there are those who argue that politics is an essential ingredient of these changes, and that there are significant differences in how these processes develop in Europe that are determined by regional and local circumstances. They argue that there is an increasing penetration of civil society by politics, and that this has a profound impact upon social conflict, competition between social and economic actors, work relations and modes of social and political integration. The Welsh Language Act can be seen in precisely these terms.

Nonetheless, even though we may question the validity of such discourses, we cannot deny their effects on social practices, and perhaps it is only at the level of social practices that discourses achieve any real meaning. Neo-liberalism focuses upon the concept of enabling or empowering, on non-intervention, on a corporatism built around interest groups including language groups. The result is a scenario of participating agents taking responsibility both for carrying out actions, and for their outcomes; of a community that focuses upon the voluntary sector and the individual that subsumes to the greater good, so that reliance upon the benevolent state is eliminated and the community looks after itself. Planning is seen in terms of strategic planning by evaluating strengths, weaknesses, opportunities and threats, the setting of priorities and the measurement of achievements. Local personnel are used to replicate success in one place elsewhere. The enterprise ceases to be thought of as the concrete expression of capitalism, but appears as a strategic unit in a competitive international market, and as an agency of the use of new technologies. It is neither rationalization nor class domination that defines it, but the administration of markets and technologies.

This model of the relationship between people and what might be loosely called the social is simple and mechanical. It is true to the claim of the New Right that there is no such thing as society, merely the individual, the family and community. This stance is also true to the belief that values derive from culture, thereby making any discussion of society redundant since it is values that drive the market. Since language planning derives from the sociology of language, and from the normative focus of linguistics, it is clear why there is no reference to language planning in the Board's documents. The asociological stance perhaps also accounts for the ignoring of the sociological claim for the complexity of values which are conceived as dynamic entities related to the manner in which identity is a social construct. As such it is impossible to isolate and measure. The only reference to the economic is by reference to 'work' and 'community development'. Reference to labour markets and the relevance of language for such markets is missing. By the same token, the discussion of attitudes is devoid of any behavioural context. If there is any lesson to be learnt from the entire body of work devoted to attitudes it is that it is not possible to change behaviour by changing attitudes.

The entire discussion is devoid of any conception of either theory or philosophy, and appears to be entirely ungrounded. As such, it reduces language planning to a technical, mechanical issue, an orientation that leads to the conception of research as a simplistic, mechanical, empirical exercise that merely serves to measure the pace and directionality of the consequences of the planning exercise. Research is reduced to the tool of ideology based on a faith in the market, leading to a failure to understand the very entity that is being acted upon. Since the guidelines of business and a superficial understanding of behaviour are sufficient, there is no need for such complex issues as theory and philosophy. It is one thing to claim that the economy is led by the 'free' market, even though many economists would insist that a 'free' market has never existed, it is quite another to suggest that the same principles are responsible for social behaviour.

In this respect it would appear that if the Board were to expand its activities to accommodate the incorporation of language in the very process of regional development, it would fall foul of other agencies charged with this task. It can oblige such agencies to produce plans for incorporating the enabling procedure *vis-à-vis* the use of Welsh by the public in its activities, but it cannot oblige such agencies to take the relationship between language and economy seriously.

As a consequence the emphasis lies on opinion, an opinion that reflects needs and expectations, without distinguishing between attitudes and opinion. Opinion is coloured by values, and values are influenced by culture. Values or attitudes, in turn, condition behaviour. Thus, if opinion can be measured, then it becomes possible to direct behaviour. Complex processes are reduced to simple generalizations. This leads to damaging claims about how cultural deficiencies inhibit a desirable behaviour, the very totalitarian arguments that involve blaming the victim, and against which minority groups have struggled for decades.

Prior to the establishment of the National Assembly for Wales, it was clear that in administering the Act the Welsh Language Board was, effectively, an arm of the state, even though the state sought to distance itself by creating the Board as an administered quango, Yet the Board was answerable to the Welsh Office and, finally, to the Secretary of State of Wales, that is, to the government. The Secretary of State could veto any developments. This was subject to change following the creation of an elected body in the form of the Assembly. Already the existing government has committed itself to eliminating the tendency for quangos in Wales to serve as a means where the party in power rewards its faithful and powerful members. In the immediate future such positions will be advertised. Presumably it will also make the Welsh Language Board accountable to a democratically elected Assembly. However what is required is a means whereby the Board itself becomes accountable by responding to the needs and expectations of the citizenry. This involves establishing the means whereby the individual and the community have a voice in policy formation and the practices of the Board. It involves a shift from representative to participatory democracy. This is facilitated by the relevance of ICT for such developments. Such developments oblige us to pursue this issue further by consideration of the current emphasis upon the relevance of globalization for governmentality.

9
The Planning of Welsh in Global Development

1. Introduction

In the Introduction, we made a brief reference to the history of language use surveys in Europe and their relationship to language planning. We stated that these surveys served as the basis for an approach which saw state intervention as the essence of planning, and that the model of language planning was premised upon this idea. That is, it was an inherent aspect of a specific conception of governmentality. It should be evident from Chapter 8 that this mode of governance has been subject to considerable change, a change which, at least in so far as Welsh is concerned, has resulted in the emergence of a distinctive orientation towards language planning. If this particular example is representative of the future, this field is now becoming a manifestation of the more general thrust of a governmentality premised upon neo-liberal principles. It raises at least two questions: first, of the relevance of language use surveys for this 'new' understanding of the relationship between state and civil society; and second, of the validity of neo-liberalism for such a practice. This obliges a consideration of the alternatives to the neo-liberal policies as they are currently emerging in Europe.

We also argued that language use surveys and language planning in general should not be understood separately from the more general process of political and economic restructuring, and the associated policy developments. To do so would lead to the danger of reifying language, allocating to it an existence separate from the more general parameters of social and cultural change. However, as governmentality is increasingly conditioned by the market analogy of neo-liberalism, so also is the general understanding of restructuring. We have touched upon this in Chapter 8. Nevertheless, there is a need to take this argument further by exploring the current nature of political and economic restructuring, and the arguments which guide it. This, in turn, should lead to a consideration of how language planning changes, and of the relevance of language use surveys for such a change in orientation. It relates to yet another point which we made in Chapter 8 concerning the need for any planning agency to operate with an understanding of what is responsible for change – in this case, of what is responsible for the change in the circumstances of language production and reproduction. This can be achieved by considering the nature of the neo-liberal discourse and how it conceives of the restructuring process. Once this has been clarified it becomes possible to consider how language use surveys can be of advantage for such a conception. What this means, of course, is that it is conceivable for us to have quite different conceptions of language planning, each one deriving from different conceptions of change which might be expressed as theory or as a general political philosophy, and which relate to different understandings of social change. That is, language planning itself is a feature of discourse (Williams, 1996b). This is an issue which requires discussion and debate if planning is to have any significance. Those responsible for language planning cannot hide behind the existence of an extant Language Act, and politicians must also recognize that language planning should be a dynamic process that is an integral part of a more general social policy, and its relationship to legislation. It involves different conceptions of truth and reality, and obliges us to consider the extent to which the language use survey is compatible with the current flavour. In pursuing such issues we are conscious of the need to extend beyond the limited manner in which the Welsh Language Board uncritically and uncontextually adopts the market analogy of neo-liberalism. In contrast, we would argue that there is a pressing need to consider how the recent trends in regional development are compatible with the goal of incorporating minority language groups as desirable and analysable components of a more general developmental context. That is, language and language groups must be drawn into the regional development frame if language planning is to have an integrative context rather than merely being cast as a residual practice marginal to the mainstream activities of social and economic development. These are the tasks of this concluding chapter.

2. *Language and Regional Development: From Reason to Strategic Enterprise*

We begin with a consideration of the current focus of regional development, and the extent to which language can and should be an integral part of such development. It should already be clear that we are of the view that it is insufficient to discuss language planning without direct recourse to the economic field. This should be evident from the way in which we have referred to language by discussing language groups as social groups, and the way in which sociology grounds the social in economic practice. We sought to operationalize these ideas in the concept of language prestige which addressed the relationship between language and social mobility. Useful though this may be, there is a need to consider the relationship between language and economy in a much broader perspective. However, there has been a tendency, especially in the UK, to refer to regional development in terms of macroeconomic processes and their relationship to neo-classical economics. Indeed, even though the human actor is taken for granted in such an approach, the social rarely surfaces, and economists have a profound difficulty in coming to terms with the social. Of course this is also true of the other kind of economics which comes to terms with the social by dismissing it, implying that everything operates in the same way as the market. In this way, everything can be modified and operationalized according to market principles, as if specific forms of rationalism held a direct one-to-one relationship to such principles, an orientation to which we will return momentarily.

Turning to the concept of enterprise, it is as well to remind ourselves that it also is rooted in rationalism and the normative. Efficient production, responding to market-led demands, the search for maximum profit and investment diversification all constitute the essential elements of enterprises. Yet the enterprise has tended to be left out of the analysis of economic activity. Historically, economics was concerned with capital, economic cycles and the effects of technical innovation on economic activity. This was followed by the analysis of production and its relationship to rationalization. Sociology has tended to address this relationship through the concept of modernization and its link to progress through reason. Thus, during the 1960s, the drive for modernization involved arrogantly exporting western culture to the Third World through community development and regional development initiatives. Deriving from the influence of Taylor and Ford in developing the golden age of the North American business schools during the 1950s and 1960s, the enterprise was seen as the concrete frame of modernization – the idea of rationalism was applied to its functions and its hierarchical structure, to the habitual designing of the circulation of information and ideas, of marketing and humankind; that is, of putting order and clarity onto increasingly complex collectivities. Management was responsible for applying these principles of value to particular situations. Yet, even here the enterprise was not central, but was subordinate to the workshop and the work positions, and the reference was always to organizations rather than enterprises, substituting general principles for the real economic actor. The idea of enterprise was marginal.

Yet there is a longer intellectual history to regional development, and to the relationship between the market and such development. Classical economics is firmly rooted in the Enlightenment project, involving the claim in the importance of reason and rationality for human action. In this respect it was an inherent feature of the state's attempt to exploit the resources within its territory. It was with the mercantilists of the sixteenth and seventeenth centuries that economic thought can be claimed to have started as an autonomous entity, where it is defined as a specific object of reflection. Hitherto, economy was discussed by reference to divine morality. The mercantilists developed a new problematic in trying to demonstrate that the political knowledge of the Sovereign existed in order to enrich the markets controlled by the King. The term 'political economy' was coined at the beginning of the sixteenth century by Antoine de Montchrestien. That is, modernist economics shares with sociology the preoccupation with the relevance of the state. This becomes a problem with issues such as regional development in that it conceives of the 'region' as a referent of, and secondary to, the interests of the state. Below we discuss how it also becomes an issue with the growing tendency for the regulatory powers of states to be curtailed.

The neo-classicists are viewed as the descendants of classical economists, but differ from them on a number of important points. First, they completely ignored the relevance of social groups and the individual rationality, where the individual is conceived of as perfectly sovereign, capable of affecting rational choice in maximizing her/his satisfaction. Rather, they held a subjectivist view of value, and did not seek any objective causality associated with labour. Thus, they argued that the market value of any good does not depend upon its global utility, but on the marginal utility that is procured by the last consumable unit. The rarer that last unit, the higher its marginal utility. Water, which is abundant compared with diamonds, has a more feeble marginal utility, and its price is therefore lower. In reasoning on the basis of individualism and marginalism, the neo-classicists were constructing a theoretical vision of the market. Left to themselves, allowed to be perfectly flexible, markets will lead to an optimal situation of 'general equilibrium'. This was the central argument of Walras and it is also the main thrust of Liberalism.

Today it is increasingly argued that economics is failing to give answers to crucial questions, leading to a tendency for it to be denounced. It is claimed that its predictive incapacity leads to a falling back onto intangible and inoperable concepts such as 'the feel-good factor'. In many respects this is the equivalent of the influence of post-modernism and post-structuralism in sociology, except that it never proceeds to the point of dismissing any role for rationalism and to treating economics as a discourse. Arguments are often made against the effects of the Maastricht Treaty, which is viewed as highly rigid, about how it places a heavy tax on unemployment, how the associated deregulation leads to an intensity of core activities and an associated intensification of peripheralism. Such arguments often lead back to the Keynesian arguments of the 1930s, where it was argued that maintaining the high tax on unemployment involved a rigid structuralism of the economy. Furthermore, in legitimizing a therapy which consists mainly of re-establishing the market, there is a return to the ideas of Walras. There also emerges an argument which emphasizes the freedom of the market to operate at will. However, it is not as simple as pitting Keynesianism against the prescriptions of liberalism or neo-liberalism. Rather, it involves working on a less simplistic conception of economic activity by refining hypotheses in seeking to develop a better comprehension of the diverse mechanisms influencing work in society. Unfortunately, this brand of realism leads to increasingly sophisticated concepts which are further removed from observable reality.

The focus shifts from macroeconomics to microeconomics, with its stress on the logic and co-ordination of individual choice. Evidently, language has a central role in such developments. It also leads to a reassessment of the dogmatic version of liberalism with its idealist conception of the market, with the state respecting the rules of play and allowing the economy to stabilize to the best possible state so that involuntary unemployment is reduced to a minimum. It is the idea of 'general equilibrium' that was formulated by Walras, where the market is the model of reference. The economic subject is discussed by reference to a rational conductor which is presented as a characteristic of human nature as a permanent pregiven that is administered as an active aspect of being, where the economic relations are defined as the modes of co-ordination of predetermined and unchanging channels of human subjects. Rejecting the hypothesis which claims that there is a variability of phenomena based upon an immutable essence, the school of regulation prefers to study the mechanisms whereby contemporary capitalism assures its reproduction. They differ from Marxists in that they assign a passive role to the superstructure.

The standard theory of microeconomics is claimed to have three principal postulates:

- Microeconomics reasons on the individual. All collective phenomena can be understood thanks to the study of individual decisions.
- Individuals are rational. Each person pursues his or her own interests in increasing as far as possible their interests while taking account of all constraints. It is the argument of 'rational optimization'.
- The market is efficacious. The most efficient means of co-ordination among the different decisions of different individuals is through concurrence. Again the market analogy of Walras is evident, with the financial market analogy to the fore.

Current criticism casts considerable doubt about the realism of these three claims. It is claimed that individuals in reality are fully capable of co-ordinating their decisions other than by the market (Williams, 1978). Rather than setting limits by reference to the 'ideal' model, it is now fashionable to try and understand the diverse manners of the co-ordination across all economic actors, a co-ordination based upon rational choice as the *sine qua non* of the market. In a way, this is akin to the manner in which sociologists have tended to abide by the orthodoxy of modernism in constructing a division between rational and non-rational behaviour by reference to the modern/traditional dichotomy, claiming that certain behaviour which, in their view, did not conform with rationality should be labelled as 'traditional' and associated with emotional, rather than rational, principles of behaviour. Minority language groups, as we have emphasized, have been implicated in such discussion within the 'traditional' context which places them within the realm of the non-rational. Such views are increasingly being questioned within sociology (Williams, 1999a).

These lines of argument which challenge the orthodoxies of neo-classical economics have taken a variety of forms. In 1937, Coarse argued that market transactions were eliminated at the interior of the firm, with the head of the firm conceiving of him/herself as substituting for the structure of the market and its exchange transactions. Because of the need to economize transaction costs, internal co-ordination occurs by principles other than those guided by price considerations. The focus shifts to the study of organizations, and to the development of organizational theory. More recently the focus has shifted towards game theory, indicating that individuals, even when operating entirely rationally, take decisions which not only do not lead to their maximum possible individual satisfaction or 'utility', but on the contrary, verge on the catastrophic (Binmore and Das Gupta, 1986). The goal is that of arguing that, despite game theory not being an explicit economic theory, the realities of the contemporary economic world lend themselves more to the explanations afforded by game theory than to the standard theories. In so doing it refutes the premise of classical microeconomics which claims that individual decisions are subject to certain constraints in contributing to the resultant general equilibrium, arguing that such equilibria do not have any *a priori* optimal *raison d'être* – the best possible world is not the natural result of the rational decisions of agents. They also argue that the players can either choose to develop a coalition in co-operative play, or they can choose not to, leaving everyone to act for him/herself. What is clear is that the advantage of flexibility of action which game theory brings into play also places the cognitive composition associated with the reaction of economic agents at the heart of economic analysis. Furthermore, game theory tends to be prescriptive rather than predictive. Economic reality increasingly comes to resemble game theory!

What game theory does achieve is to demonstrate that the orthodox conception of the isolated individual confronting the market, and thereby making no contribution to the general equilibrium, is erroneous. In contrast, it argues that the gain of the individual or enterprise depends, not on isolated decision, but also on the decisions of other actors and, above all, on the complex interactions between them. This extends to a realization that individuals vary considerably in their use of the information that is available to them. Of course such views will proliferate into a variety of approaches. However, what they all seem to share is the persistence with the Walrasian market analogy without rejecting the hypothesis of optimization. Some will opt for a 'limited rationality', arguing that individuals are not only disposed to categories of restrained calculation, but also lack any precise and neat vision of their preferences. Nonetheless, the faith in the concept of the market and in rational optimization means that the decisions of agents have to be placed in their social context. It raises the question of why a pure and flexible market which does not constitute a sufficient explanatory schema should be raised to the status of an ideal type. It is the same type of question that has been raised concerning Keynes's relationship between activity and employment.

The focus shifts to a concern with the anticipation of economic agents. Friedman's monetarist policies argued that increasing the quantity of money injected into the economy involved direct regulation which was contrary to the goal of imposing the rules which limited the progression of prices and the monetary mass. The work of Lucas, the 1995 Nobel prize winner, in this respect appears to herald a return to classical economics in allocating rationality to the anticipating agents, with the individual, prior to making a choice, not only integrating all the available information, but also interpreting the facts of a similar schema of interpretation. We are back in the world of the Walrasian model.

The shift of focus towards microeconomics in the above involves studying, on the one hand, individual behaviour and, on the other, the interaction between individual decisions. Individual behaviour is conceived of by reference to the choice from among alternatives affected by individuals, and tends to focus upon the ranking of choice rather than the decision-making process. The analysis of preferences relates, à la Pareto, to the concept of 'utility' or the satisfaction experienced by the individual. Referring to arbitration, or how the individual arbitrates between alternatives of preferences, leads to the concept of an 'optimal rationality'. Of late the tendency has been to shift from the more orthodox approach of comparing each situation with the ideal model of Walras to considering how and why certain other mechanisms such as the enterprise permit a co-ordination that involves more than individual decisions. It is here that the state enters the picture within a new classicism which not only opposes realism, but links the conception of individual actors operating by an optimal rationality which will not react to state regulation in the anticipated mode.

What is evident from the preceding overview is that economic theory concerns one central question – is a purely contractual society possible? It is also clear that answering such a question obliges a shift in the direction of the social, and of the relationship between social and economic behaviour, and to a flirtation with the intellectual domains of sociology and anthropology. Within economics, such a society is not considered legitimate other than by reference to social links founded on voluntarism, that is, it is based on the reflexive engagement of individuals. For sociology, society constitutes much more than the sum of interacting individuals. It revolves around Durkheim's *conscience collective*, and his claim that 'social solidarity is nothing other than the spontaneous accord of individual interests, an accord where the contracts are a natural expression' (Durkheim, 1912). It would suggest that our understanding of economics and economic development is moving in a direction which can accommodate the kind of conception of language groups which we have presented above.

The question arises of whether or not such a contractual logic is sufficient to meet the needs of the new conceptions of economics. How can it be made coherent by reference to a multitude of private decisions that are taken by each agent independent of one another as a function of his/her predispositions and beliefs? If the market exercises such a fascination for the social sciences, it is because it gives an exemplary response to the impossible question – how is it that the market respects the autonomy of the actors, functioning in a specific economy of means, and leading to a general agreement between members of a society? Furthermore, it is claimed that it has been demonstrated that such an agreement redistributes the available resources in an optimal manner. That is, the social link seems to be spontaneously engendered. It recalls the Hobbesian problem of a state of nature in which individuals are isolated and without contact, concerned only with their personal interests in delicately obtaining optimal and pacific co-ordination. The society could be constructed in some unknown way, without at any moment seeking to affirm either a collective project or a series of collective values. Here lies the image of the 'invisible hand' which imposes the spirit of society. Modernism, imbued with ideas of evolutionism, claims that 'earlier' societies founded their existence on collective beliefs, on respected ethical norms, such a society having a purely formal and abstract mechanism at its heart. This was the community of Rousseau, where social order was vested in the community itself. This claim was subsequently replaced by the claim that social complexity was such that the state had to enter the scene, taking charge of social order and seeking to impose a shared value system or normative structure on a series of communities which came to constitute the state. Minority language groups were implicated in these developments as negative components which had to be eliminated. The current emphasis on the rolling back of the state would appear to reverse this development.

This construction of an 'invisible hand' that sustains society holds considerable problems for the social sciences, and many social scientists refuse to accept it. Following Durkheim, they believe that a harmonious and durable co-operation between humankind presupposes a kind of social cement that is more solid than any contract based upon personal interest. As we discuss below, this point, which is central to orthodox sociology, is increasingly being shared by the heterodox economists, even though they insist on the eminent role played by institutional forms in the engendering of collective action. Without mutual confidence, and without shared ethical norms, co-operative action between individuals would not be possible because it presupposes a minimum of social trust and openness to others.

The orthodox analysis rejects the theoretical pertinence of these social and cultural determinations. Collective action is thought of as the exclusive product of the rational calculation of interests. Thus, the hypothesis of rationality plays a central role in their work – rationality is the only thing that economic actors share in common. In the absence of all other points of social reference that guide their actions, it is the only one on which they can rely for co-ordination. Thanks to it, individuals can put the other protagonists in their place and anticipate their actions. This speculative reasoning allows the issues of play to become compatible with the interests of everyone. In many respects, such a view is both ethnocentric and dogmatic. It leads to arguments in favour of a single and specific rationality that must be exported regardless of cultural differences. It is the cornerstone of the impact which modernism has on the conception of social homogeneity and the demise of diversity. In a sense it can also be claimed that reason serves as the 'invisible hand', and thereby serves as a form of transcendentalism.

The heterodox reflections in their current forms – evolutionism, regulation or conventionalism – insist that this analysis is incomplete, and that actions need to be contextualized. They seek to place individual action within the form of specific institutional contexts that are historically and socially determined, and which assign to them their meaning. This question is fundamental. It involves underlining the necessary articulation between economics and the other social sciences. Without such an articulation, the principle of common rationality leads economic theory to an impasse. Yet it seems to be recognized by a limited number of economists.

The exclusive referencing of the principle of rationality prioritizes those individuals with systematic opportunistic behaviour. It follows configurations of interaction marked by an extreme reciprocal mistrust, leading to unsatisfied equilibrium. Faveau notes that it leads to a microeconomic analysis where the sophisticated agents deploy their ingenuity in order to trick or prevent others in an operation. Experimental studies claim to show that, on the contrary, real individuals are spontaneously much more co-operative than the theory suggests. Taking the contexts of interaction into consideration, the conventions of action and of belief which reunite the actors permit rejecting that vision of a rationality premised upon strict opportunism.

The principle of common rationality touches on a second problem, more focused than the preceding one, of the theoretical difficulties associated with recognizing a purely decontextualized approach to behaviour – the indetermination of equilibrium. One of the main themes of economic theory in recent years has consisted of understanding the principle of rationality of beliefs, involving what is called the hypothesis of rational anticipation. It is concerned with submitting individual beliefs and opinions to the same principles of arbitration and effectiveness as those which pertain to actions – if one prediction is weak, it obliges revision until anticipations and reality coincide. Beliefs are considered as the means and it is then the integrality of the individual carrier that passes under the control of instrumental rationality. This gives a new direction to speculative calculation.

Each belief is examined by the agents as the object of a rational deliberation created by a questioning of its capacity to accept the adhesion of other individuals who all examine the problem from the same perspective. The acceptable representations are then those which, once unanimously agreed, are realized. It is a view that persists in viewing the economy as autonomous from the rest of society. The autoreferential paradoxes become the formal expression of a conception that uproots the individual. In the absence of profound convictions, each individual accounts by mimicking the others in determining their actions. Leaving that *impasse* requires a perspective which resituates the contractual logic in the broader social frame. It is precisely such a development that involves the manner in which regional development is being rethought.

3. Regional Development: A New Approach

The orthodox conception of regional development has been subject to considerable criticism by those who have argued that it does not merely relegate the periphery to a residual role within the economic order, but that peripheralism itself is actively created by the very process of regional development. It is argued that the tendency has been to deploy resources to the periphery for the benefit of core interests, with such interests not merely involving underwriting the periodic entry of core enterprises in search of cheap, unorganized labour, but also locating 'developments' which were not acceptable within the core. The entire dependency argument was constructed around the claim that regional development led to an exploitative spatial division of labour.

The current developments in Europe involve promoting a new politico-economic spatial alignment that makes Europe competitive as a geo-political force. The internal processes associated with this development involve the deregulation of the economy and the removal of many of the regulatory powers hitherto deployed for orthodox regional development from the various member states. Associated with this drive is the goal of eliminating the core–periphery distinction through a regional development premised upon the development of human capital rather than the deployment of fiscal capital. At the heart of the debate about how society should respond to global economic and technological change has been a reconsideration of the nature of learning and its relationship to human capital. This focus on human capital exists within a specific developmental discourse broadly labelled as neo-liberal but involving a range of different approaches and orientations. Evidently, a new conception of regional development is being constructed.

Central to the entire approach is the concept of the enterprise and of the individual entrepreneur. It is as well to remind ourselves that the concept of the enterprise is also rooted in rationalism and the normative. Efficient production, responding to market-led demands, the search for maximum profit and investment diversification, all constitute the essential elements of enterprises. Yet, as we have seen, the enterprise has tended to be left out of the analysis of economic activity.

Schumpeter gave considerable importance to the entrepreneur. He characterized capitalism by a spirit of routine crossing in proportion to, and as a measure of, the concurrent lowering of the tax on profit (Schumpeter, 1954). He argued that this form of capitalism was condemned to die, finally being replaced by a planned economy. It was only maintained by the intervention of entrepreneurs who reintroduced the war values of the aristocracy in a routinized world, and which stood above all the agents of innovation. It was the struggle between the North American and Japanese industrial armies, and the victory of the latter, which accelerated the transformation of our image of the enterprise. While the American enterprise was orientated to rationalization, the market and flexibility, the Japanese enterprise gave priority to the definitions of its objectives and the mobilization of its technical and human resources in order to compete. Research on the integration of the enterprise paid particular attention to the reduction of social distance, without excluding the authoritarian relations of production. By referring to strategies of enterprise rather than general rules of rationalization, the enterprise becomes an essential actor of social life, and the analysis is no longer reduced to the fundamental being of the capitalist system. What emerges from this break with a highly formal macroeconomics is a shift to a microeconomics which overlaps with studies of management, and ultimately, to a sociological approach. The study of system on the one hand, and of actors on the other hand, dissolves, this being as true of the enterprise as for the nation and consumption. It leads to the destruction of our image of modernity and the focus on the idea that actors are defined by their conformity to, or their deviance from, a sense of history which adjoins with the progressive triumph of rationality.

From this shift there emerges much of the current thinking that focuses upon the relevance of human capital for economic processes and development. In this respect our argument revolves around the claim that there is energy, coherence and solidarity associated with minority language groups, either as practice or as potential. Thus, in the same way as a sense of nationalism has been deployed to promote state economies, the human capital, embedded in the structures of minority language groups, can be harnessed for economic goals. In one sense, this is nothing new, as anyone familiar with patterns of labour-market segmentation and their relationship to cultural factors will attest; but, in another sense, the orientation is different. The focus shifts to a respect for the relationship between language and culture, away from the denigration of some languages which are deemed somehow to be outside of the realm of reason. The focus also shifts to a concern with community as an integrating force wherein lies the very human capital that can be harnessed and promoted. There is also the claim that diversity, including cultural diversity, is of central importance for processes of innovation and that, in this respect, the various language groups within Europe represent a key element that is of significant value to Europe as a whole. Before proceeding to a consideration of these issues we would like to consider how globalization has been conceived of in a specific way that links with a deterministic discourse on economic development.

4. Globalization

It should already be evident that we are addressing the fundamental shift in thinking about development that has occurred in recent years, largely as a consequence of the need to adapt to an open global economy. The movement from state-regulated economies of production to an advancing need for states and companies to adapt to increasingly open global markets, which involve a constant growth in competitiveness, and where technical innovation leads to the emergence and/or demise of entire sectors, has had profound implications. This globalization of the market and of production is most directly evident in financial tensions. In Europe the advent of the Single Market and the Maastricht Treaty derive from a need to make Europe competitive as a geo-economic force. Indeed, the acceptance and implementation of the Single Market is symbolic of the passing of state-based political-economic systems to a global economy. Whether or not, as some (Hirst and Thompson, 1992) suggest, this globalization remains dominated by state-level companies, the associated changes are having a significant effect both on current thinking about economy and society and upon actual practice.

The internal restructuring process within Europe carries two aspects that are of particular relevance to our interest – on the one hand, the discourse which drives this restructuring process, and on the other, the implications of the Single Market for the European periphery. The relevant neo-liberal discourse leads to the setting of a particular agenda for the restructuring of Europe. It is responsible for the reorientation of the relationship between economic theory and regional development, and for this reason alone it is of particular relevance to us. Being the dominant discourse associated with current social and economic planning, it sets an agenda that determines associated practices, and for this reason cannot be ignored, even if we choose not to condone it. The central principal of neo-liberalism is the claim that the freeing of the economy and the suppression of the degraded and exhausted forms of state intervention are sufficient to guarantee continued development. That is, the economy should be self-regulating, involving the banks, the lawyers and the various agencies with ranking functions.

The argument is made that the market economy is the most efficient means of removing the political and administrative control of the economy that was encapsulated in regulation. It is argued that such regulation had a negative effect upon the entrepreneurial spirit, large-scale investment, an improvement in living standards, the integration of social justice and individual satisfaction. It argues that social and economic development requires investments; an equitable distribution of production; the mobilization of resources which are increasingly more diverse (education, public and private management) mobility of the factors and systems of communication; and the safeguarding of a social equilibrium increasingly threatened by deepening divisions based upon inequalities that foment conflict. The assumptions of such an argument are indeed questionable. To discuss world exchange, the effect of new technology and the multiplication of the system of production is one thing, to state that they constitute an autoregulating world system, and that thereby the economy escapes, and can escape, political control is something else. An exact description gives way to an erroneous interpretation. Hegemonies persist, and these hegemonies pertain to states or unions. What does seem evident is that what have been created are global finance networks rather than a global economy. This can be seen in terms of imperialism which a long time ago was defined in terms of the predominance of international financial capital over state industrial capital.

Nonetheless, the advent of the Single Market has curbed the customary relationship between the state and 'its region'. The tendency to treat the periphery as a residual entity, where specific strategies could be deployed in order to resolve core problems, or to maximize core interests, is no longer possible. Such strategies tended to involve short-termism and also included the development of dependency relationships between core establishments and peripheral labour, something which severely disarticulated local and regional economies which have lost any integral cohesion. There developed an intensification of fiscal, sectoral and cultural dependency upon the core and its enterprises. This was often associated with a claim that the population in peripheral areas tended not to have the resources and abilities essential for entrepreneurial activity, largely because of their non-normative cultural make-up that focused upon minority languages and cultures. These 'regions' had to be drawn into the rationalism of development through the intervention of the core. The states' 'regions' are in a process of disappearance through redefinition. They are no longer regions of the state but of the force that is capable of regulation – Europe.

These changes have far-reaching repercussions. As we implied in Chapter 1, the concept of dependency has to be rethought. Regulation processes have not only moved from the state, but have also receded and been realigned as a consequence of globalization. The fiscal crisis limits the ability of welfarism to compensate for marginalization, even if it were advocated. This is not to deny the persistence of core–periphery distinctions, nor the tendency for these distinctions to intensify through a core-focused regional development. Rather, it merely recognizes that the conceptualization has to be rethought. By the same token it sometimes appears that sociology as whole must be rethought. Premised as it was upon the idea of rationalism as the basis for normativity and progress, the questioning of such assumptions undermines many of its claims. Similarly, the development of the European Union questions the one-to-one relationship between state and society. If this is brought into question, then so must be the construction of deviation from that normativity as an ethnicity that derives from a state normativity. The drive to generate a European citizenship and, indeed, a European society, might be one response.

On the other hand it does seem as if the entire edifice of sociology is in danger of collapse.

These changes have profound implications for definitions of 'us' and 'them', of the region and its preconstructed referent. Whereas the closure of the state defined the 'us' of the state by reference to the 'them' who did not pertain to the state, within the state the region pertained to the state as preconstructed (Williams, 1999b), permitting the construction of series of internal identities that tended to be encompassed within the 'us' of the state. The construction of the European Union redefines the region by reference to Europe. As we indicated in Chapter 1, it also defines an 'us' of the region that can fragment the regional identities of the state, leading to a moral panic characteristic of 'Little Englanderism'. Similar claims can be made by reference to Wales and the Welsh language. Establishing a degree of political autonomy within what might be seen as a proto-European federalism would appear to have achieved many of the objectives that hitherto were reserved for a nationalism conceived of by generating a drive for autonomous statehood. This drive to a very great extent revolved around the claim for difference constructed around language and culture. The elimination of this need generates the very real possibility that, for better or worse, language and culture yield place to politics as the basis for autonomy. This is not to imply that language is not implicated in politics, but rather to suggest that it assumes second place to an all-inclusive politics as the basis for generating the requisite 'identity' that is a *sine qua non* of democratic integration between the polity and its public. Similarly, information technologies are constructing new communities devoid of state boundaries, making the role of the state in cultural homogenization difficult to sustain. Nonetheless, such communities can sustain the politics of the local, spatially constrained community.

As we have argued in Chapter 8, to fall into the trap of believing that the market analogy will serve to regulate society, and will resolve all social problems, can have serious consequences. It views problems in terms of individual weakness, and solutions in technological terms. The corollary is that we are led to ignore ethical questions, and the issue of rights disappears. It leads to the elimination of the concept of society which is seen as a construct of government shaped by imposed authority in the form of welfarism, and its substitution by processes that impinge on the individual. We already begin to see such a process appearing in the Welsh Language Board's approach to language planning.

5. *The Global and the Local*

Evidently, what we have in mind points towards a specific local feature of the more general debate concerning global economic restructuring. That debate involves how major changes in socio-economic, political and cultural structures in Europe affect the manner in which local issues can be resolved. It assumes a variety of orientations ranging from the focus upon technological shifts (Freeman and Perez, 1988) to how the regime of accumulation is determined (Lipietz, 1987). It includes a consideration of the relationship between social life on the one hand, and changes in the economic, social, political structures on the other. Within this diversity of perspectives, there is an increasing emphasis upon the relevance of mass production and flexible specialization for the significance of alternative forms of the organization of production, and on how they relate to specific historical procedures operating at the global, state and local levels.

It is argued that the increasing uncertainty associated with rapid technological change and changes in demand and market characteristics of economic activity, together with the break up of traditional economic regulatory activity involving the demise of neo-Keynesianism and indicative planning, leads modern corporations to divest themselves of what are seen as secondary activities in order to concentrate upon core activities. That is, such corporations are beginning to disintegrate. This leads to the creation of new networks of smaller enterprises, of localized SMEs (small- and medium-sized enterprises) which form robust subcontracting supply networks for the main business. There is room for such developments within the periphery, providing it does not accentuate the core–dependency structures. The structural interdependence would appear to control for this. The big corporations become more flexible and less bureaucratic, creating semi-autonomous departments and divisions as networks. These new developments do not rely upon the price competition of market contracts nor on bureaucratic administrative relations, but rather they rely upon co-operation and trust between the new semi-autonomous units and subcontracting firms within the network. They also tend to be companies whose activities, regardless of where they are located, are operated with English as the language of work. This has implications for the associated satellite companies.

As we have argued above, it can be claimed that, within these studies of economic restructuring and its effects, there is a tendency to marginalize the political, with the circulation of capital and international market relations receiving considerable autonomy. Restructuring tends to be explained either in terms of market volatility, fragmentation and unpredictability *vis-à-vis* a shifting technology, or in terms of the globalization of competition and money markets. It is argued that Fordist patterns of social and political organization are destabilized through a realignment of the conditions of capital profitability or consumption patterns. This, in turn, leads to smaller production units, a demand for flexible work organization, and an associated shift away from a static relationship between qualifications and employment towards an emphasis upon skills, flexibility and dynamic employment settings. Perhaps this marginalization of the political is not surprising given the manner in which the prevailing neo-liberal discourse makes planning a technical rather than an ethical issue, or, in Europe, how the advent of the Single European Market precludes recourse to politically motivated regulatory practices.

These points are strongly reiterated by Lovering (1998). Arguing from economic data, he claims that the optimism concerning the manner in which economic restructuring in Wales has led to performance improvements in the economy in Wales is misplaced. Thus, the promised prosperity that is associated with the goal of making Wales a 'motor region' has not been achieved, and the evolutionary model involving a transition from dependency to inward investment to endogenous growth is false. According to Lovering, there is no support for the argument that Wales is being transformed from a 'Learning Region' into an 'Intelligent Region'. He proceeds to indicate that the conception of 'development' relies upon the conceptions associated with the 'new regionalism' which lack any theoretical coherence while retaining an ideological appeal. While we would question the implicit distinction between ideology and a theory that harnesses truth, we accept his point.

6. *Competing Perspectives*

It is becoming increasingly evident that there is a clear distinction being made between a regional development orientation that focuses on neo-liberalism, and another perspective which is called 'the Third Way'. The argument is made that current neo-liberal policy is increasing the discrepancy between the European core and periphery. This is not merely the effect of the Single Market, but encompasses neo-liberal policies which strengthen the competitive position of the strongest firms and regions in the core at the expense of the peripheral regions. Simultaneously, as part of that same process, firms in the periphery are drawn into strong competition in emerging markets, while also being involved in the consequences of capacity rationalization when firms reconsider their spatial division of labour within the Single Market. Such regions increasingly have to compete with other regions as the barriers to the mobility of capital are demolished.

One alternative that receives attention is 'the Europe of the regions', involving a structural shift towards decentred economics and a decentralization of a proto-European state. Certainly the transfer of the crucial state functions of security, competition, industrial and regional innovation policies and regional development to Brussels suggests that things might be moving in this direction. It is supported by the parallel transfer of other state functions, including infrastructural improvement and supply-side support for entrepreneurship, to the regional level. Such developments herald a shift from Keynesian welfarism to Schumpeterian workfarism, a shift which involves the emaciation of the state's capacity for promoting a regional development based upon planned industrial intervention and demand management. In this respect it means that all regions will increasingly have to rely on their own resources and those of the European Union.

Whereas there is abundant evidence that neo-liberalism is a central platform of European Union policy, there is also an indication that active intervention through regional, technological and social policies is also of relevance in European Union activity. This much is clear from the support given to SME-based activity, to the drive to promote employment in the periphery and thereby to limit exclusion, in industrial relations and in industrial innovation. It is also evident that such interventionism is part of the more general market-led integration policies for Europe. As such, it constitutes a form of Euro-federalist social democracy that links with the concept of a managed economy.

In this respect it draws upon both Keynesian demand management and the Schumpeterian view of the supply-side. An explicit feature of this approach is the narrowing of regional disparities, alleviating exclusion in the periphery and creating employment in the same regions. It certainly contrasts with the former centralism of state-directed Keynesianism, and leads to a focus upon strengthening the political alliance between the regions and the institutions of the European Union. At the heart of this development is a form of Euro-federalism in which local democracy and institutional strategies develop in a suprastate political setting of open governance. The focus is very much upon local institution-building and local political empowerment.

The other alternative is the 'Third Way', or the managed economy, an approach that derives from what is referred to as 'critical socio-economics' (Amin and Thrift, 1995: 53). There remains a tendency for networks of large corporations and dominant institutions to influence development in the periphery, often in a way that promotes core interests. The Third Way seeks to set up a network of intermediate institutions between the market and the state so that they can counter such decisions and consequences. It seeks to integrate this institution-building with democracy at the local, regional and international level in order to empower the region and give it a voice. This involves reconceptualizing democracy away from the prevailing representative form towards participatory democracy (Putnam, 1993). Digital democracy, or the use of electronic media for promoting debates that cross the represented/representee divide, is a means whereby this can be implemented. Given that the focus shifts to the process of institution-building, policy makers must withdraw from prescribing goals in the modernist sense of planning. Rather, the entire community should be involved, preferably within a learning context, if only to avoid the danger of an emerging hegemonic local statism. It is a process that promises much for language planning.

In some respects this approach involves replacing the abstract market by the concept of social networks. This orientation remains firmly fixed in the modernist conception of the centred rational subject operating to promote interests, but also seeks to incorporate the interpersonal into the debate. The furthest it goes in redefining the subject is in the claim that the participants in a network define one another through interaction, the focus remaining upon the rational constructivism characteristic of much sociolinguistic work (Callon, 1991). Subjects include machines and money (Amin and Thrift, 1995: 50), which merely leads to their reification. We still seem to be a long way from a decentred economics. Individuals rationally construct networks through which they exert a power that is dependent upon their ability to use a network to enrol others to speak on their behalf. It does link with a new thrust in economics in which institutional behaviour rather than the rationality of optimization within reified markets conditions economic behaviour. A concern with the uncertainty of capitalist economies is responsible for links with the current focus on innovation and flexibility. Thus the networks must be flexible, and must link this flexibility to innovative practices. However, the advent of post-structural ideas means that innovation is no longer conceived of as the unlinear process linked with evolutionary developments that somehow replaces the present. Rather, it is acknowledged that the past not only feeds into the present, but is an important ingredient of the present. Thus innovation becomes an essential ingredient of adaptive capacity in the face of adversity. Furthermore, it is conditioned by diversity.

The drive to promote an associative economics involves a shift away from state-driven or command economics towards relationships that are interactive. Thus, there is an openness that replaces the rule-driven thrust of modernist planning, this openness encompassing the possibility that different regions will develop in different ways, with the focus on diversity, and a move away from linear trajectories and uniform progression of the modernist link between development and progress. The outcome is the change in the social consciousness of a community, something that is to be achieved through negotiation and institution construction. Despite the focus on diversity there remains a sense in which the hegemonic principles of the modernization thesis remain part of the argument, largely because of the need to establish links within the networks that extend beyond the community, the region and even Europe. Nonetheless, it is such ideas that drive the focus on supply-side measures such as the circulation of information, training and skill formation, knowledge-transfer network formation, the integration of supply chains between enterprises and the use of effective support systems to ensure the continuity of innovative action.

Evidently, these typologies are constructed out of the polarities of neo-liberalism on the one hand, and Keynesianism on the other. They also incorporate some implications of the demise of the regulatory power of the state, and the way in which this opens the space for a new conception of regulatory policy. Nor is the new technology missing, but this is correctly seen as the means of implementing one or other of the principles of the respective types. In some respects, some of the ideas represent the Left's abandonment of socialist principles while seeking to retain a semblance of commitment to democracy and social equity, if not to equality, in the face of the Right's successful promotion of neo-liberalism. Inevitably the contradictions that arise from the construction of these polarities and the developing of policies which seek to accommodate both will become the site of political struggle in the immediate future. Yet this may well be misplaced, since if the state has lost its power to regulate, no one seems very sure where power lies in an increasingly fragmented world.

What the recent discussions about globalization reveal is an increasing tendency to resort to a discussion of networks and a marked decrease in references to society. This is no coincidence. As we have remarked, society was constructed as a political adjunct of the state and was sustained by the state. It involved striving to create bonds between individuals that would transcend the territory governed by the state. It is the associated state nationalism that has been the bane of minority language groups since the eighteenth century. As we remarked in the opening chapter, the new context has destabilized social theory. It also leads to an argument that if the state has been responsible for the homogenization of society in the name of its nationalism, then the demise of its powers heralds a period of diversity. Yet, this does not deny the existence of the social, for if that social, like the state, is the effect of discourse, then it is very real. What it does mean is that the social does not, as the modernists claimed, represent some external structure that exists as a feature of humanity or as a social order. Rather, it is a dynamic entity that is constantly being created and recreated. In this respect modernist philosophy and the associated politics help to stabilize the social. Together with a range of other organizations and institutions, sociology undoubtedly also plays its part.

In some respects it is not only 'networks' which prevail in current debates about development, but 'community'. Within the relevant discourses it has become the space within which individual and collective existence operates. In political terms it equates with a new form of communitarianism (Touraine, 1997). The community has become the object around which a range of issues are problematized and resolutions are presented. Community becomes the focus for action in relation to economic development and social problems. Within modernism, at least since the demise of the Rousseauian sense of community, the state was conceived of as the sum of all the communities within its territories, with the consequence that state and community could never be in opposition (Williams, 1992b). The state was the means of integrating the sum of communities. The shifting nature of the state has implications for this relationship. The community is now presented in a number of different ways – as the focus of shared interests, as the embodiment of networks, as local interests, as the relay of communications, as the sum of cultural similarity. They rely upon shared identity. The rolling back of the state has shifted responsibility to the community, which becomes the focus of developmental attention. Such attention emphasizes subsuming individual interest to the interest of the greater good, not in the form of the social, but of the community. This is a radical shift in responsibility and accountability, and links with the idea of 'government through community', to be achieved via a participatory democracy that uses electronic means to link the community with the regional site of governance as a basis for community empowerment. In many respects, this links with the individualized ethos of neo-liberalism and its focus upon needs and expectations, choice, empowerment, personal responsibility and control over personal destiny and self-governance, leading to the concept of a self-governing community. Government no longer pertains to a 'national' territory, but rather, to the relations of identification between the individual and his or her 'community'. Individuals are expected to invest in themselves through choice or calculated action, and to maximize this investment according to the codes of their particular community.

7. The Local Model

Our own position on the demise of the social and of the relevance of sociology for an understanding of change relates to our claim that it is discourse that fixes subjects and objects in a stable position. Discourses have a concrete effect upon social practice through the constitution of these subjects and objects as the effects of meaning.

Rational reflexivity is not absent from this process, but does not play the pre-eminent role it is accorded in orthodox sociology. Society is one such object, and we would argue that it has yet to be destabilized to the point that is claimed. Thus, for example, social class for us is not a fixed entity manifested in a person's position in the division of labour or patterns of consumption. Rather, it is a consequence of the way in which subject places are constituted in the relations of production. How these subject positions are constituted will be subject to considerable variation, and for social class to achieve meaning involves considerable work. Changes in relations of production associated with the shift in the meta-discourses of theories of production will have an effect upon the nature of the social. In our attempt to come to terms with a conception of language planning, we do not dismiss the social, but recognize its shifting nature, and the fact that it has to be constructed as a feature of meaning. The question which Adam Smith (1976) confronted remains, 'what is the moral mechanism that creates society out of a collection of separate individuals lacking the solidarity of an emotional community, allowing actors to act in harmony over distance without any sense of dyadic relationship?' This is an issue of normativity, and it is as well to recognize that the normative is not entirely dependent upon the state but is a fluid, contested space. The rolling back of the state and the demise of its regulatory powers does not mean that it will cease to play a role in the generation of normative structures. The answer which Smith developed relied on the 'internalization of the spectator'. His emphasis was upon the well-informed spectator who is not engaged in action, but who contributes to the development of moral relationships. He further showed how this was not dependent upon personal attributes, but could involve anyone, and that in this respect it constituted a structure, a system of places to be occupied by the individual. Today this is an issue that pertains to the information society, and how the interactive force of electronic media is beginning to play such a role. The 'I' is both specific and general in that everyone is an 'I' that is capable of becoming a subject other than the 'I'. This deictic context is central to the construction of society in and through discourse. It is with this understanding that we consider the nature of language planning within the existing context.

   The goal of any language planning must be to dispute monolingual hegemonies through reinstitutionalizing and relegitimizing minority language use. It must involve recognizing these hegemonies through

constructive reflexivity. It also involves undoing the effect of hegemonic discourses upon the general population, not merely of the
Welsh-speaking population, but also those who do not speak Welsh,
if this process is to be of relevance to Wales as a whole. It is point-
less to treat the two social groups as if there was little or no
relationship between them. After all, Welsh speakers belong to both
groups, they are capable of interpolation into subject places that
pertain to either or both associated identities, as well as being associated with the unifying 'Welsh' identity. The preceding discussion
suggests that in many respects this is an opportune time to consider
such actions, since the forces and associated discourses that have
established such hegemonies are being restructured and realigned.
There is an urgent need to ensure that diversity becomes a central
feature of that realignment. However, in Chapter 8 we argued that
there is little indication that the requisite thought is currently being
given to the planning of Welsh.

The creation of the National Assembly for Wales and the subordination of agencies, including the Welsh Language Board and the
Welsh Development Agency, to its authority, represents the kind of
regional political empowerment that should link with regional political practice as a multilingual practice. It leads to democratizing the
economy, the state and civil society, and language must be at the
centre of this development. Such a democracy demands a humility on
the part of politicians and civil servants, and an associated willingness
to engage with the constituency rather than merely to seek its opinion.
This means that a politics of association between civil society and the
state is essential. The dependency that is inherent in the authoritarian
attitude of the Welsh Language Board, which claims an authority
while expressing a confrontational 'leave it all to us' approach, is
obliged to disappear. The shifting political space destabilizes
discourse, leading to the need for the public to be given a voice, but
that voice must be heard in either and both languages. This means
that politics is no longer a spectacle from which people can remain
aloof as spectators, it must become an engagement. The level of
action is quickly shifting towards the region and its capacity for efficiency. The shift from representation to participation in politics that
we discuss below is a move in this direction. It means that the region
must be treated as a collective subject, but in order for this to happen
it must be disassociated from the other collective person of the state.
As we have implied, this process is accelerating.

It is one thing to put faith in community democracy, but the political does not stop at the boundaries of communities, regardless of what is happening to the state. In Wales the link between the community and the proposed Assembly is beginning to be conceived of by reference to digital democracy. Thus far politicians have tended to resort to electronic media in order to test public opinion. Digital democracy must go much further, developing a sense of participation that replaces representative democracy. That which defines democracy is not merely the collectivity of institutional guarantees or the rule of the majority, but, above all, the respect for individual and collective projects which combine the affirmation of personal liberty with a particular, social, national or cultural collectivity. In this respect it should encompass individual liberty, cultural diversity and pluralism. It is evident that democracy is not representative unless it is pluralist. Indeed, the spirit of democracy is nurtured by a constant debate on the mobile interface between unity and diversity, and on the best means of reinforcing the relationship between them. The use of Welsh in participatory democracy is at the heart of the Assembly and its associated democracy. Linking the community and the Assembly must involve the use of electronic technology through the medium of Welsh as a basis for developing a debate which reaches to the heart of the Assembly. The problem is that not all Assembly members nor civil servants are bilingual, and conventional translation is inadequate if an electronic chat or debate is the goal. It is essential to develop the means of machine translation which could adequately facilitate such developments.

What emerges from the preceding discussion is that there is a profound process of economic restructuring in process. It involves an attempt to orientate work practices, to redirect enterprise competition in the direction of collaboration, to make what used to be described as 'training' into an ongoing learning process, to elaborate all of this around the centrality of ICT and its relevance for the harnessing of human capital. A reading of the literature associated with the Welsh Language Board conveys the impression that, whereas language planning is being conceived of by reference to the neo-liberal conception of the economic market, the actual practice of language planning remains remote from the more general principles of regional development within Wales. There is little overlap between the practices and strategies of the Welsh Development Agency, for instance, and those of the Board, other than an insistence that the Welsh Development

Agency develop a language strategy, not in relation to its regional development practices, but by enabling the Welsh speaker to access its offices. This in turn leads the Welsh Development Agency to conceive of their responsibility in this respect as acquiring added finance for translation facilities, rather than as incorporating the language into its day-to-day practices. The two practices of language planning and economic planning remain as far apart as they have ever been!

The one agency that does relate language and economy – Menter a Busnes – adopts a deprecating conception wherein the claim is made that the link between language and culture is such that, for some reason, Welsh speakers lack an entrepreneurial capacity. This is precisely the kind of argument which we have argued lies at the heart of the modernist link between normativity and reason. In this respect it is a definite step backwards, but in other respects there are aspects of its work which are extremely valuable. It seems absurd that this restructuring process does not go hand in hand with a reconceptualization of language and of its relevance for a diversity-led development. Even in the Mentrau, the focus is upon leisure activities, and there is little evidence that those involved in these initiatives have anything remotely resembling a clear conception of the ongoing economic restructuring, and of the significance of their own activities for this process.

In addition there is a need to consider the implications of such changes for education and local and regional integration (Williams, Strubell and Nelde, 1996). Integration involves the realignment of economic relationships that were undone by the core–periphery dependency relationships. It involves inter- and intra-sectoral integration at both a local and regional level. This involves structural and market integration that will lead to the reinvestment of profit at a local and regional level. If the region is increasingly to rely on its own resources, these developments are essential. Clearly educational change relates to the need for a flexible labour force at all levels. Flat management demands such a development. Again this involves structural and content changes. It is customarily expressed in terms of a content that involves a broad-based knowledge for schools, moulded in such a way that the emphasis shifts from standardized, direct knowledge towards systems knowledge and abstract concepts that promote understanding and innovation. The concept of lifelong learning that relates to the need for flexibility and responses to changing economic circumstances leads to an awareness that the distinction between vocational and adult education must be broken down. Telematics in education offer a range of possibilities for educational reform, including the potential of developing a virtual system that can transcend European regions through a network approach to education. If, as we argue, language is central to the social construction of meaning, then the systems of knowledge, when linked with linguistic diversity, can be the source of innovation.

All of this is accommodated and accomplished within what is referred to as the Learning Region and the Intelligent Region. It is claimed that the rolling back of the state implies that any region is obliged to draw upon its own resources in order to promote development. These resources include both human resources and the associated cultural capital. Furthermore, development must be shaped by the needs of the region and the market. Thus, while technology serves the region, it is not the driving force, but rather, it is an enabling force that helps the region to achieve its goals. Also the Learning Region offers a close integration between the sectors which support the bulk of the employment within a region, on the one hand, and the regional education and training sectors, on the other. It will focus upon those sectors which offer the greatest potential for efficient employment and economic growth. Within peripheral areas it requires a vision of the future which is based upon the relevance of niche activities for growth. The Learning Region envisages the relationship between education and training on the one hand, and the regional economy on the other as a two-way process, prioritizing regional and local skill needs. The need for flexibility is highlighted within peripheral regions by the marginal nature of many activities and enterprises.

It is this conception that becomes the cornerstone of regional development within peripheral regions. It involves a high level of fiscal intervention in the form of initiatives that address the need for community development, employment creation, sustainability and training. This integrates with the concept of the Intelligent Region as one which involves the development of inclusive local and regional partnerships, a critical awareness of local and regional labour market structures and a focus upon the relevance of national, transnational and international partnerships for the development of best practice. However, to our knowledge, not a single European region has carefully and methodically considered the relevance of minority language use for such developments. In Wales two processes seem to be in operation. The first involves the formal separation of language issues from these economic developments by the creation of a Welsh Language Board whose function focuses upon an institutionally focused enablement with little reference to empowerment. Second, it is left to the random decisions of involved individuals at the community level to ensure that language is incorporated in community development activities. There is no link between the macro conceptions of regional development policy and community development initiatives.

The main feature of the regional development argument which demands our attention involves the claim that change in work organization is an essential prerequisite of growth for the following reasons:

- the need to remove dependency organizational structures because they lead to negative motivation on the part of the worker;
- rapidly changing productive circumstances and technological development demand a flexible, adaptive labour force and work organization;
- networking principles based around flat management principles and flexibility promote co-operation and trust which contribute to motivation and drive around the issue of loyalty;
- such shifts lead to 'value-added partnerships' which give a flexibility of response to the organizationally autonomous parts of the productive chain;
- this serves to integrate the local and regional economy into a mutually reliant structure that operates for the growth of local and regional economies. This integration focuses upon both sectors and across sectors.

Similarly the argument extends from the focus upon the workplace to accommodate communities, the argument including the following points:

- there is a need to draw upon the energy and cohesiveness of a community operating together, in unison;
- community developers must operate as *animateurs* and facilitators in drawing the community together in order to exploit its potential;
- the community must withdraw from dependent relations with the local and regional state;
- no individual or group should be alienated from this process;
- individuals must be encouraged and helped to subordinate individual benefit to the greater good of the community;

- the resultant community resources must be harnessed to promote flexibility and innovation as a means of withstanding risk.

It can be argued that if this is generally true, it is even more true of peripheral locations where the economic structure has tended to lack any semblance of sustainability, with short-term gains being the basis for capital deployment, leading to cycles of employment and unemployment, often of a seasonal nature, that affect most families within such locations. The various European Commission initiatives currently in place in Wales seek to promote at least some of these developments. Many of the agencies such as Menter a Busnes, Antur Teifi, or Menter Môn seek to focus upon Welsh as a basis for promoting the networking that is part of these community development activities. What is lacking is a development strategy for Wales that is based on a clear understanding of the current debates to which we have referred above. We have argued that language should be a central feature of the relations of production, and that the solidarity factors associated with mutual support and risk-minimization strategies are strongly linked to language, by reference both to how it structures meaning and to how it links subjects in compatible subject places. It can also be argued that in many respects, given the above objectives, coherent community development in Wales is not possible without paying close attention to language (Morris, Williams and Williams, 1995).

What must be encompassed is the awareness that such an approach needs to be contextualized by reference to language and culture. The importance of the way in which meaning derives from the traces of prior structures, while also conforming to the relationship between linguistic form and discourse as social practice, must be retained. It is such forces, rather than a self-controlled rationalism, that condition individual and group identity. Such an identity is central to the relationship between self-conception and the various dimensions of human capital that are claimed to be essential for the promotion of development. The relationship between these dimensions and the various life skills, meaning systems and positive contextualization will vary across cultures and locations, and this variation must not only be understood, but promoted in such a way that they are seen as strengths rather than the negative connotations which they were given within modernism.

The essence of this call for organizational restructuring involves a shift away from the hierarchical management structures of Fordism towards the flexible management practices and structures of post-Fordism, with management and the workforce working side by side as motivated colleagues. This shift, it is argued, will lead to a heightened motivation, increased productivity and a labour force that is sufficiently flexible to be able to respond to political, economic, market, or technological change. The evident consequence of the advent of the Single Market and neo-liberal development principles in intensifying the core–periphery difference makes the need for a flexibility that combats uncertainty particularly appealing to peripheral locations. By the same token, the existence of the language communities constructed out of minority language groups that proliferate in the European periphery should be well placed to take advantage of such conditions.

There is a contradiction between planning and markets, but a firm has to plan and therefore becomes capable of developing flexible strategies for overcoming possible obstacles via flat management. In the periphery, such obstacles are an integral feature of a perpetual uncertainty. In the past this derived from state regulation that generated specific strategies for the periphery, strategies which tended to focus upon relatively short-term capital-intensive strategies which bore little relevance to local or regional economies. The Single Market has eliminated such state regulation, but it has also intensified the core focus, and the associated peripheralization of economic space within Europe. Simultaneously, the fiscal crisis and the attack of neo-liberalism upon the welfare state limits the range of welfare resources available to compensate for such developments. This leads to policies that focus upon the community, the family and the individual as responsible for their own destiny and welfare. Uncertainty within the periphery remains, but compensatory fiscal intervention is also evident, such intervention seeking to promote local economic integration and the integration of both the individual and the economic structure with the European dimension. This is coupled with the argument that integral economic development depends upon structural changes in the organization of work that leads to the harnessing of human capital as the basis for the promotion of a new impetus for growth and productivity.

Whereas, even fifteen years ago, many were talking about monopoly capitalism and vertically integrated companies which increased in size as the competition was eliminated through the monopolization of capital and the economy of scale, things have changed. The development of cheap, centralized power and efficient but costly production machinery did give such an advantage to large companies that achieved economies of scale. However, low-cost computing and communication has tipped the advantage towards partnerships of small companies, each of which performs one part of the value-added chain and co-ordinates its activities with the rest of the chain.

However, the debate clearly extends beyond the single firm, and involves the integration of disparate firms into value-added partnerships linked to a value-added chain. The Third Italy model is a case in point. Such a partnership relies on a high degree of mutual trust and co-operation based upon information sharing as a core feature of increased motivation and flexibility. Whereas diversity is a central component of innovation (Hingel, 1993; Gaffard, 1993), it is conceivable that trust derives from commonality. This contradiction is resolved by linking diversity and commonality through networking within a focus on European integration. In many respects such a conception is the very antithesis of free-market business transactions based upon competitiveness, which treat information as a commodity in need of protection. Companies perceive each other as adversaries and resolve competition via hierarchical integration. Within Value Added Partnerships (VAPs), on the other hand, companies develop a relationship based upon the sharing of information and a related development of mutual trust. Again we would underline the centrality of language for such relationships. Already we find examples of intranets being created to generate the interactive basis for such developments within specific sectors. These can and must operate bilingually, and must link with machine translation that will integrate them with similar intranets in other European regions and other parts of the world. It is these same telematic structures that inform educational developments.

Within VAPs, each small operating company focuses upon doing only one step of the value-added chain – all aspects of the organization are tailored to this single task. This sense of focus translates into low overheads, lean staff and few middle managers. The fact that each company in a VAP is free to be different from the others creates a diversity that can be the seedbed of innovation. Managers share an interest in making the entire Value Added Partnership productive and competitive. They must have empathy for the other organizations with which they deal. VAPs have the co-ordination and scale of large companies, with the flexibility, creativity and low overheads of small companies.

Language is also relevant to the advent of flat management. Given that 50 per cent of managers in Gwynedd come from outside of Wales, and that Welsh is the language of the greater part of the workforce, the tendency is for firms to develop a bilingual middle management that intervenes between management and the workforce. The obvious answer that would facilitate the development of flat management principles, while retaining the value that language affords to work integration and flexibility, would be for the managers to learn Welsh. However, it is also evident that they have a highly negative orientation towards the language and its speakers (Jones and Jones, 1994; Morris, 1990, 1992). This derives partly from the spiralist nature of their occupations, involving a relationship between social and geographical mobility within the same company, and partly from stereotyping. This situation is further complicated by the Welsh Development Agency's drive for inward investment. It is ironic that the Welsh Development Agency appears to devote more attention and energy to providing education for the managers of inward investors in their respective languages than it does to the introduction of Welsh into its own activities.

Knowing how social networks within Gwynedd are structured around both locality and language (Morris, 1989), the issue of inter-sectoral integration assumes a particular relevance. Brokers which can transcend the structures that derive from such knowledge are required to promote the networks which can link sectors for mutual benefit and local and regional integration. There is a need to target specific personnel by means of language learning for specific purposes. This must involve an awareness of the relationship between language and the benefits that can accrue from integration. Clearly, what is at stake here is the promotion of a sense of commonality constructed out of the relationship between language and economy that focuses upon the development of specific structural forms which support and promote economic development.

It is in this sense that Welsh speakers can become a community of self-governance. This implies that language enters the domain of self-responsibility. This is the danger with the current language planning that we have already indicated: Welsh speakers are enabled, and they are now expected to use the language. If they do not avail themselves of the services, this failure becomes an indication of the absence of need and expectation *vis-à-vis* language use and the services are in danger of being withdrawn. This is not good enough. Language must be promoted, not by reference to a policy formulation with the heavy hand of an Act behind it, but as part of the integral policies which are restructuring companies, economies and regions. Welsh must be seen as an asset rather than an obligation. Furthermore, it must be seen as an asset for everyone, not merely for Welsh speakers. The arguments which sustain this position have yet to be framed. Current practice in the public sector, where agencies are obliged by the 1993 Welsh Language Act to present a plan for the enabling of Welsh language use, is for these agencies to submit an enabling plan which falls far short of the integration of Welsh into their day-to-day practices. They may even implement a bilingual development officer responsible for ensuring that they meet the obligations confirmed by the Welsh Language Board. However, in order for Welsh to become the language of work, something more akin to the mentoring activities of management training is required, where employees who speak Welsh or who are learning are tracked by a fellow worker who directs activities towards language action. Where such practices might be seen as draconian by reference to language, they would be perfectly acceptable within more orthodox training measures. It is in this respect that Welsh must be seen as an asset within the day-to-day work context.

Similar practices must be implemented to ensure that the excellent work done by some schools in generating competence is translated into use. Evidence suggests that the main problem is that of a lack of confidence rather than a problem of attitude. In some senses, and despite their ability to generate competence, part of the problem here may lie in the schools. Thus when we consider the nature of competence and recognize the relevance of the dialogical basis of communicative competence, it becomes evident that many schools create competence in a narrow range of dialogical contexts. This has much to do with teaching methods and the relative absence of interactive processes that link with the social construction of meaning in the methods that are used. Again it is possible that the advent of telematic-based learning, where there is a heavy emphasis on interactive learning, may help resolve this particular problem.

If Welsh is seen as an asset within the context of diversity and its benefits, the question then arises of the extent to which it can be sustained via Keynesian methods in a period of neo-liberalism. The current support for the language from state resources via the Welsh Language Board is small compared with that for languages such as Basque or Catalan. On the other hand, there are other agencies which use Welsh and have Welsh-focused activities, and who receive substantial support. That is, there is both direct and indirect policy support for the language and its speakers. It is difficult to envisage this support receding. However, if the argument can be sustained that such support is devoid of dependency connotations, and yields considerable benefit to the community or to business, the rationale for language planning changes, and the associated discourse dovetails with the emerging discourse of regional development.

The argument that has been central to our thesis thus far is that language prestige is a major motivational factor which leads non-speakers to learn Welsh, either for themselves or their children. This valorization of language would appear to be the *sine qua non* of the existence of the language group. In this respect, the commodification of language must become more general, it must extend into the practices implicit in the relations of production. A great deal is made of 'language competence societies' (Tucker, 1991), and the need for this concept to extend beyond reference to occupationally relevant skills in the state language (McGroarty, 1993). Attention must begin to be given to these factors in relation to Welsh, moving the focus away from instruction and classroom-based learning to workplace skill development. This must involve not only developing the requisite Welsh-language skills in the various occupations, but also ensuring that those who lack confidence in their Welsh-language competence are given the opportunity to use the language in contexts where the occupational skills require them, and where they come into contact with other Welsh speakers. Workplace language education (Gowen, 1992) must be developed.

It is also evident that minority language television is becoming increasingly prevalent within the periphery. Its scale is such, as we have indicated, that it has a significant impact upon local and regional economies (Williams, 1989). It is clear that this is the case in such diverse regions as Scotland, Wales, Catalunya, Euskadi, Galicia and Ireland, and that it will soon have a similar impact in the Friulan area of Italy. However, there is a strong argument to be made that it should diversify into multimedia, and that it should also serve as the basis around which telematic activities can be promoted on a regional basis. Such developments should not only serve their own sector, but should also be a basis for promoting integration across sectors and even regions. That is, the media industry should be conceived of as a catalyst around which regional development can be promoted rather than merely involving an injection of activity into the area. In this respect there is a need carefully to tease out precisely what the relationships are between language and economy, between language and economic structures and processes, so that these media can be used to facilitate much more than communication.

It is also important to recognize that the interactive potential of telematics has implications for language. We have already indicated the need for constructivist pedagogic developments that derive from the link between language and the social construction of meaning. We suspect that telematic-based interaction forges a new conception of space within the deictic framework of time, space and person that implicates language in meaning. Again we return to the work of Adam Smith and the need for the bystander to link dyadic structures as they develop within intranets. Beyond the evident aspect of the informality of email construction and how this permits breaking the normative dominance of linguistic standards which may allow some to enter the world of written communication in Welsh, there are other language-related components of such interaction currently under investigation by reference to Welsh.

Evidently, such a local strategy involves areas of activity which have tended to be delegated to community development and regional development. What is required in regional development should be evident from the preceding discussion, that is, inter- and intra-sectoral integration, the formation of Value Added Partnerships through networking principles, and so on. Community development then becomes little more than the flexible implementation of these principles at the community level. Recent years have witnessed the creation of a substantial force of community developers in Wales. While the majority have a good understanding of their communities and some may even operate by reference to the mechanical demands of a neo-liberal-led practice, few of them have the requisite training in community development. Many of these actors are bilingual and form a resource that requires appropriate training to develop their expertise.

The development of networks and support functions associated with inter- and intra-sectoral restructuring and the promotion of Value Added Partnerships is currently being undertaken by agencies such as the different Anturiaethau such as Antur Dwyryd or Antur Teifi or Menter a Busnes, and whatever their philosophy, they are doing adequate work in this respect. They are assisted by the various local partnerships that link them to the formal development agencies and

Training and Enterprise Councils as well as with educational providers. However, these partnerships remain loosely structured and reliant upon personal initiative. Whether or not Welsh becomes a central feature of these networks remains a lottery. Furthermore, regardless of personal commitment, their ability to integrate Welsh into the activities and networks which they are promoting again relies upon factors which are unrelated to any formal initiative. In this respect, the promotion of Welsh within development is very much a *laissez-faire* activity.

The learning component whereby the companies and community are reoriented towards these new structures is in the hands of the Training and Enterprise Councils, and the further education and higher education sector in Wales. There are at least three problems here. First, there is little awareness in the current practices of these agencies of the relationship between telematic-based learning and constructivist pedagogies. Whereas the Digital College is now on the horizon, the learning deliverers are ill-prepared for such developments. Second, there is the added danger that the link between constructivism and interactive learning will focus upon the modernist psychological paradigm, rather than approaches which derive from the social construction of meaning. If this is not the case, then the link between bilingual learning and the social construction of meaning that feeds into telematic-based learning must be given attention, and quickly. There is little indication that this is the case. Third, the institutionalization of Welsh into education has been piecemeal, with the result that the educational sector is ill-prepared to implement a fully effective supply–demand telematic-based learning system such as that proposed by the Digital College, where Welsh plays a central role. Even the current educational system is inadequate by reference to Welsh. The principles of democracy insist that the entry of Welsh into the relations of production is paralleled by the access of everyone in Wales to a bilingual educational provision. Failure to provide this service implies the exclusion of some non-Welsh speakers from the benefits which a knowledge of the language affords.

8. Conclusion

In Chapter 1, we postulated a relationship between state and civil society. Our discussion concerning regional development implies that a process generally known as the rolling back of state has significant implications for that relationship, as does the discourse that drives it. Certainly, the nature of the state and its activities is changing. As we have implied above, neo-liberalism espouses a reduction in state involvement, albeit that we have contested the extent to which this implies a retreat of the political. This reduction has profound implications for the distinction between the public and the private sector. There is an attempt to extend public-sector activities into the private sector by drawing upon human capital in its various forms as the basis for extending privatization, making it responsible for functions which, hitherto, had been the domain of the public sector. At the same time, the welfare state is seen as being transformed into a responsibility that lies with the voluntary sector. While this process should be the cause of disquiet for anyone concerned about extending the quality of life of the underprivileged, it does offer an opportunity associated with the reconstitution of society in areas which have always suffered from neglect through location and marginalization.

On the other hand, it is clear that minority language groups have already been marginalized, at least by reference to their ability to produce and reproduce themselves, to the extent that the absence of state support becomes problematic. We have argued above that it is essential to consolidate the role of minority languages in the community, the family and in education; that it is essential to extend the prestige of the various languages through their integration into the processes of economic production; and that particular attention must be paid to transforming competence into use. The model which we have sketched above seeks to achieve these goals within the context of the restructuring and realignment processes that are already under way by reference to the reconstitution of peripheral economies. The advent of capital in the form of extending the media to encompass minority language groups by the creation of community development projects such as the various Leader projects, must be linked with drawing upon the latest forms of technological development and a clear understanding of how best to promote economic growth from the various resources available within any locality or region. It is our claim that this is only made possible by recognizing the relevance and value of language in such a process.

The data which we have presented indicate that, for those who have accessed the Welsh language via the reproduction process, both ability and attitudes are high. However, it also indicates that the use of language is restricted, and that changing this situation is far from being as simple as improving needs and expectations, as the neoliberal model implies. We argue that language behaviour is an institutionalized facet which is not part of the rational process of decision making associated with attitudes or other mentalist conceptions which are implicit in the Welsh Language Board's conceptualization of the enabling process, and which they are implementing.

However, the future of the language group does not lie with those who gain the language through reproduction. Indeed, census data suggest that the reproduction capacity is rapidly diminishing as a consequence of language group exogamy. The picture among those who benefit from the production process is quite different. The limited number of cases in our sample suggests that their propensity, and sometimes, their capacity, to use the language is subject to constraints additional to the institutionalization of language use. There are problems of competence, not in relation to issues of standardization and purity, but rather, by reference to the restricted dialogical capacity which they possess. Other studies suggest that, even in Gwynedd, where Welsh-medium primary education is the norm, those who learn the language through the production process rely upon highly specific social networks associated with educational streaming and selective employment recruitment for the context to use and improve their competencies (Williams and Williams, 1998). Such factors lie at the margins of the language planning activities and remain little researched.

Finally, if diversity does relate to the innovative capacity that is of importance to economic practices, the Welsh language has a significance beyond any sentiment concerning its survival capacity. The details of these claims must be thoroughly and adequately researched. We suspect that this research would focus upon the social construction of meaning and its relationship to discursive processes as social practice. Variety of meaning practices linked with the relationship between linguistic form and discursive practice then becomes the cornerstone of innovative capacity. Such issues are beyond both the capacity and the conception of the Welsh Language Board. They relate to much more than language and, as things now stand, there is no evidence that language is being constructed as an object that has any relevance beyond that which it has for the subjects who speak it. It begs the question of where we now stand concerning language planning.

It appears that the conception of planning is also obliged to change in the face of the neo-liberal problematic. It is no longer the effect of state intervention as a centralized, co-ordinating mechanism based upon some general conception of allocation of economic good according to needs and expectations, at least as an ideal type. In many respects several conceptions of planning view it as an element of central state management that replaces the market, thereby placing planning and the market in direct opposition. Such a view is inherent in the orthodox conception of language planning, where planning is viewed as the intervention of a state in order to overcome the influence of market forces on the ability of a language group to reproduce itself. From a market perspective it is a highly irrational activity. On the other hand, language planning also seeks to conform with a conception of rational organization, but, given the opposition between planning and the market, the implication is that the market system is irrational, at least insofar as it acts in opposition to the idea of a democratically elected government rationally to control the destiny of those who – presumably on rational principles – have elected it into office. There is yet another view – that language planning is necessary because of the disruption on a faction of the citizenry that derives from a normatively conceived rationality that is implicated in the more general planning process.

The concept of the market is evident in what we have said above about the manner in which regional planning is being rethought, and it would appear that the goal of the Welsh Language Board is that of integrating their language planning activities with this new conception. It involves a kind of neo-corporatism in which interest associations are assigned a distinctive role somewhere between the state and civil society. The goal is that of deploying for public purposes the kind of social order that associations can generate and embody. This becomes an alternative to direct state intervention and regulation. In sum, it involves deploying public responsibilities of a social group with special interests, while ensuring that they are made subservient to general interests by appropriately designed institutions. The neo-liberal focus on the market involves liberating individual self-interest from bureaucratic–regulatory constraints, and rests on a faith that the untrammelled pursuit of self-interest is of benefit to everyone. Devolving state functions to the community involves an attempt to marshal collective, other-regarding interests for social purposes. It rests on the premise that people do hold solidaristic

'values' and coterminous identities that can contribute to social order
without state co-ordination (Williams, 1992b).

Thus the corporative–associative delegation of public policy functions to private-interest government represents an attempt to utilize
the collective self-interest of social groups in order to create and
maintain a generally acceptable social order, and it is based upon
assumptions about the behaviour of organizations as transforming
agents of individual interests. By private-interest government is meant
the 'self-government' of categories of social actors defined by a
collective self-regulating interest. Rather than involving the illegiti-
mate use of power, it involves an attempt to make associative,
self-interested collective action contribute to the achievement of
public-body objectives. This means that it must involve an overlap
between the 'categoric goal' of an organized group and the 'collective
good' of the entire population. It is here that we locate the attempt to
'take politics out of the language' and to promote the idea of 'value in
diversity'. It is certainly at odds with a problematic which views
society as consisting of conflicting interest groups, and which seeks to
represent the interests of the marginal in its presentation and activa-
tion.

It is also here that we recognize the dilemma regarding support
measures for community activities. The Mentrau Iaith which constitute one of the cornerstones of the Welsh Language Board's activity
appear to be minimally funded, involving support for one officer over
a limited period, and although the Board's aim is to increase funding
in this area, it is in the role of an initial facilitator, handing over in
due course the power, and the responsibility for subsequent funding,
to the community. The neo-liberal discourse would argue that if its
function is important enough to that community, it should be willing
to support it. This conflicts with the edifice of language planning
which has been constructed on the principles of funded intervention,
which means that if this is to be the outcome then promoting the
ultimate financial support structures becomes part of the work of
language planning. On the other hand, the argument for a Third Way
would locate Welsh within a European context, arguing that most of
the European minority language groups exist in the periphery, and
that language-related support measures should be an integral feature
of the development funding for these regions. There is little evidence
that the Commission is likely to support such a development. Its own
support for minority language groups is minimal and under threat.

While there are indications that support for minority language-related activities are increasingly becoming acceptable within mainstream programmes, there is little indication that specific support is built into these programmes in a constructive way, either as a feature of community regeneration or the more general developmental initiatives. Perhaps an intermediate strategy that will develop is that of mainstream funding from local or regional authorities supplemented by local fundraising activities which convey the impression of community responsibility.

From the point of view of planning minority languages this would appear to involve both positive and negative consequences. A uniform policy is no longer essential and each community, regardless of its size or of how it is conceived, has its own integrity. Space is opened up for local action to operate on its own terms, or at least on the terms of the structuration quality of the community. It would also appear that the step back from the normativity that is implicit in the orthodox conception of society involves a rejection of the denigratory effect of such a normativity on entities such as minority language groups which, by default, are constructed as beyond the confines of the normative. Yet normativity remains, as does the danger of labelling as deviant that which does not achieve the requisite economic behaviour on account of some deficiency that is measured by reference to the normative. Thus it seems that the space opened up for establishing a positive role for diversity can easily be closed, and will always be qualified.

The changing context insists that the function and nature of language use surveys must change. The former context of monitoring use as the basis of a planning conception of social policy linked to the state regulation of Keynesianism must be reconsidered. This does not mean that such surveys no longer have a monitoring function. Indeed, the heavy emphasis upon monitoring within the new form of governmentality implies that in this respect their function is enhanced. Rather, as we have implied in our analysis, it must be recognized that the orthodox survey has its limitations. It can outline the structure of possible use, and thereby links neatly with the enabling goal of the Welsh Language Board in that it can give an indication of the subjective evaluation of these possibilities. Indeed, we would argue that our own survey could be replicated to coincide with the 2001 census in order to serve as the monitoring measure of the Welsh Language Board's activities to that point. It can also point to where the link between possibility and practice outcomes are high or low, and, in this respect, is indicative, not of an attitudinal problem, but of where institutionalization is limited. It is here that we would insist that such surveys must link with a discursive analysis of the situation, one which clarifies the nature of the subject places that open up in relation to specific objects. If this can be achieved, then a critical analysis of language planning becomes possible, one that relates policy objectives to context and to how these contexts relate to the various associated discourses and the subject positions. Only then can we really come to terms with language use as institutionalized practice.

Wales is entering a new period in its history. The creation of the Assembly promises much, and serves as the basis of hope for many. For others in Wales, the Assembly is either an irrelevance or heralds a change for the worse. Much has been made of the claim that the Assembly will operate from the outset as a bilingual entity. However, the initial desire to achieve such an objective has subsequently been tempered by an awareness of the implications of such a context. The Welsh Office does not have a good record on the use of Welsh. As an arm of the Home Civil Service, many of its staff are recruited outside of Wales and often have no experience of Wales. Their allegiance is to the government and to their heads of department. Its translation section acknowledges that serving a bilingual Assembly will not be easy. The Welsh Office's record in the past has been abysmal. Even today it fails to respond in Welsh to local authorities who seek such a service, its awareness of the significance of electronic translation services has been both late and limited, and the realistic statement to the effect that bilingualism in the Assembly will be limited has not gone down well. If the Assembly cannot set an example in its the use of Welsh, its credibility will be severely undermined.

Clearly, there is a need for nation/region-building within which the former conception of a nation striving for statehood yields to the new conception of a region with a voice within an emerging European federalism. This does not mean abandoning the historic basis out of which the sense of nation is constructed. That is impossible. Current discourse is forged out of prior discourses, the traces of which will remain. In this sense, history is not a quest for 'truth', but for the reality of discursive formations, and the manner in which they affect the social construction of meaning. Given the opening of space for diversity, not merely in the UK, but across Europe, language will play a central role in this construction, but it will do so in a new way. That way will be dictated by discourse. We must recognize that discourses are never equally aligned but hold status, and that some discursive formations construct the same object in different ways, with the status systems playing a role in the salience of these object constructs. It is in social practice, where discourse achieves meaning, that the construction occurs. The new discourse that derives from this debate will be the basis for the reconstruction of Wales. The current period of economic and technical change is crucial for that reconstruction, language must be part of it, but it must be a part that is forged out of understanding and imagination, rather than a slavish dedication to preformed discourses.

Bibliography

Achard, P. (1986). 'Discours et sociologie de langage', *Langage et Société*, 37, 5–61.

Adorno, T. (1969). 'Scientific experiences of a European scholar in America', in Fleming, D. and Bailyn, B. (eds.), *The Intellectual Migration*, Cambridge, MA: Harvard University Press.

Aitchison, J. and Carter, H. (1994). *A Geography of the Welsh Language 1961–1991*, Cardiff: University of Wales Press.

Aitchison, J., Carter, H. and Rogers, D. (1989). *In-migration and the Welsh Language: A Case Study of Tregaron and its Region*, RSRU, Monograph 3, Aberystwyth, Department of Geography, University of Wales, Aberystwyth.

Amin, A. and N. Thrift (1995). 'Institutional issues for the European Regions: from markets and plans to socioeconomics and powers of association', *Economy and Society*, 24/1, 41–67.

Arnauld, A. (1990). *On True and False Ideas* (trans S. Gauknoger), Manchester: Manchester University Press.

Baker, C. (1985). *Aspects of Bilingualism in Wales*, Clevedon: Multilingual Matters.

Baker, C. (1995). 'Bilingual Education in Wales', in García, O. and Baker, C. (eds.), *Policy and Practice in Bilingual Education*, Cleveland: Multilingual Matters, pp.152–65.

Baker, C. (1997). *The Early Life Cycle of the Welsh Language*, Cardiff: Welsh Language Board.

Bakhtin, M. M. (1981). *The Dialogical Imagination*, Austin: University of Texas Press.

Balibar, R. (1985). *L'Institution du français*, Paris: PUF.

Balsom, D. (1985). 'The Three-Wales model', in Osmond, J. (ed.), *The National Question Again*, Llandysul: Gomer Press, pp.1–17.

Balsom, D., Madgwick, P. J. and van Mechelem, D. (1984). 'The political consequences of Welsh identity', *Ethnic and Racial Studies*, 7, 160–81.

Baudrillard, J. (1981). *For a Critique of the Political Economy of the Sign*, St Louis: Telos.

Beck, U. (1997). *The Reinvention of Politics*, Oxford: Polity Press.

Binmore, K. and Das Gupta, P. (eds.) (1986). *Economic Organizations as Games*, Oxford: Blackwell.

Boissevain, J. (1974). *Friends of Friends*, Oxford: Blackwell.

Boltanski, L. (1993). *La Souffrance à distance*, Paris: Metailie.

Boltanski, L. and Thevenot, L. (1987). *Les Économies de la grandeur*, Paris: PUF.

Bourdieu, P. (1982). *Ce que parler veut dire*, Paris: Fayard.

Bourdieu, P. (1987). *Chose dites*, Paris: Minuit.

Boutet, J. (1994). *Construire le sens*. Paris: Lang.

Callon, M. (1991). 'Techno-economic networks and irreversibility', in Law, J. (ed.), *A Sociology of Monsters*, London: Routledge, pp.132–61.

Calvet, L. J. (1974). *Linguistique et colonialisme*, Paris: Payot.

Clarke, M. P. (1997). 'Language, Grammar, and Being', unpublished Ph.D. thesis, Lancaster University.

Coulmas, F. (1992). *Language and Economy*, Oxford: Blackwell.

Dafis, Ll. (ed.) (1992). *Lesser Used Languages – Assimilating Newcomers*, Carmarthen: Joint Working Party on Bilingualism in Dyfed.

Davies, J. (1993). *The Welsh Language*, Cardiff: University of Wales Press.

Day, G. and Fitton, M. (1978). 'Religious organization and community in Mid-Wales', in Williams, G. (ed.), *Social and Cultural Change in Contemporary Wales*, London: Routledge, pp.242–52.

Denney, D. (1991). 'The social construction of nationalism: racism and conflict in Wales', *Contemporary Wales*, 4, 149–64.

Denney, D, Borland, J. A. and Fevre, R. (1992). 'Nationalism and community in north west Wales', *Sociological Review*, 1, 49–72.

Descartes, R. (1970). *Descartes: Philosophical Writings*, London: Nelson.

Dodd, N. (1995). 'Money and the nation state: contested boundaries of monetary sovereignty in geopolitics', *International Sociology*, 10/2, 139–55.

Donzelot, J. (1984). *L'Invention du social*, Paris: Fayard.

Donzelot, J. (1991). *Face à l'exclusion*, Paris: Esprit.

Durkheim, E. (1902). *De la division du travail social*, Paris: Alcon.

Durkheim, E. (1912). *Les Formes élémentaires de la vie réligieuse*, Paris: Alcan, 49.

European Commission (1995). *The Regions' Way to the Information Society*, Unit XIII/A-6, DG XIII, Brussels: EC.

Eusko Jaurlaritza (1997). *Encuesta Sociolinguista de Euskal Herria*, Vitoria: Gobierno Vasco.

Fairclough, N. (1992). *Discourse and Social Change*. Oxford: Polity.

Foucault, M. (1966). *Les Mots et les choses*, Paris: Gallimard.

Freeman, C. and Perez, C. (1988). 'Structural crises of adjustment: business cycles and investment behaviour', in Gosi, D. (ed.), *Technical Change and Economic Theory*, London: Pinter.

Gaffard, J. L., Bruno, S., Longhi, C., Quere, M. (1993). *Coherence et diversité des systèmes d'innovation en Europe*, FAST, Brussels: EU.

García, O. and Baker, C. (1995). *Policy and Practice in Bilingual Education: Extending the Foundations*, Cleveland: Multilingual Matters.

Generalitat Catalunya (1998). *Encuesta del uso de Catalan*, Barcelona: D. G. Politica Linguistica.

Giddens, A. (1973). *The Class Structure of the Advanced Societies*, London: Hutchinson.

Giggs, J. and Pattie, C. (1992). 'Wales as a plural society', *Contemporary Wales*, 5, 25–64.

Giles, H., Bourhis, R. and Taylor, D. (1977). 'Towards a theory of language in ethnic group relations', in Giles, H. (ed.), *Language, Ethnicity and Language Group Relations*, London: Academic Press, pp.307–48.

Giles, H., Hewstone, M. and Ball, P. (1983). 'Language attitudes in multilingual settings: prologue with priorities', *Journal of Multilingual and Multicultural Development*, 4/2-3, 81–100.

Gilpin, R. (1987). *The Political Economy of International Relations*, Princeton: Princeton University Press.

Goldthorpe, J. (1980). *Social Mobility and Class Structure in Modern Britain*, Oxford: Clarendon Press.

Goldthorpe, J. and Lockwood, D. (1969). *The Affluent Worker in the Class Structure*, Cambridge: Cambridge University Press.

Gorter, D., Jelsma, G. H., Plank, P. H. van der and Vos, K. de (1988). *Language in Friesland*, Ljouwert: Fryske Akademy.

Gowen, S. G. (1992). *The Politics of Workplace Literacy: A Case Study*, New York: Teachers College Press.

Gramsci, A. (1971). *Selections from the Prison Notebooks*, London: Lawrence & Wishart.

Granovetter, M. (1985). 'Economic action and social structure: the problem of embeddedness', in Granovetter, M. and Sedberg, R. (eds.), *The Sociology of Economic Life*, Boulder, CO.: West View, pp.53–81.

Griffith, W. Ll. (1976). *Iaith Plant Llŷn: Astudiaeth mewn Ieithyddiaeth Gymdeithasol*, Cyfres Ysgrifau ar Addysg, Cyfrol 6, Cardiff: University of Wales Press.

Gruffudd, H. (1998). 'Young people's use of Welsh: the influence of home and community', *Contemporary Wales*, 10, 200–18.

Harrison, G., Bellin, W. and Piette, B. (1981). *Bilingual Mothers in Wales and the Language of their Children*, Board of Celtic Studies, Social Sciences Monograph, 6, Cardiff: University of Wales Press.

Hayek, F. A. (1974). *Law, Legislation and Liberty*, London: Routledge & Kegan Paul.

Heath, A. (1981). *Social Mobility*, Glasgow: Fontana.

Hechter, M. (1975). *Internal Colonialism: The Celtic Fringe in British National Development, 1536–1966*, London: Routledge & Kegan Paul.

Hechter, M. (1978). 'Group formation and the cultural division of labour',

American Journal of Sociology, 84/2, 293–318.

Hingel, A. J. (1993). *Note on a Model of European Development: Innovation, Technological Development and Network-led Integration*, FAST, Brussels: EU.

Hirst, P. and Thompson, G. (1992). 'The problem of "globalization": international economic relations, national economic management and the formation of trading blocks', *Economy and Society*, 21/4, 357–96.

Hughes, G. and Sherwood, A.-M. (1995). *Economic Activity and Linguistic Characteristics in Wales: Analysis of Census of Population Results*, Aberystwyth: Menter a Busnes.

Humphreys, J. and Rubery, J. (eds.) (1995). *The Economics of Equal Opportunities*, Manchester: Equal Opportunities Commission.

James, C. (1985). *Iaith a Chymuned yng Ngwynedd, 1921–1981*, Caernarfon: Cyngor Sir Gwynedd.

Jenkins, D. (1960). 'Aber-porth: a study of a coastal village in south Cardiganshire', in Rees, A. D. and Davies, E. (eds.), *Welsh Rural Communities*, Cardiff: University of Wales Press.

Jenkins, G. H. (1997). *Y Gymraeg yn ei Disgleirdeb: Yr Iaith Gymraeg cyn y Chwyldro Diwydiannol*, Cardiff: University of Wales Press.

Jones, D. G. (1998a). 'Coleg Ffederal Cymraeg ym Mhrifysgol Cymru', *Y Traethodydd* (Gorffennaf), 138–44.

Jones, D. G. (1998b). 'Problem prifysgol', *Y Traethodydd* (Ebrill), 71–5.

Jones, D. G. (1999). 'Rhagor am y Coleg Ffederal Cymraeg', *Y Traethodydd* (Ionawr), 30–4.

Jones, E. (1992). 'Economic change and the survival of a minority language: a case study of the Welsh language', in Dafis, Ll. (ed.), *Lesser Used Languages – Assimilating Newcomers*, Carmarthen: Joint Working Party on Bilingualism in Dyfed, pp.120–33.

Jones, G. E. (1982). *Controls and Conflicts in Welsh Secondary Education 1889–1994*, Cardiff: University of Wales Press.

Jones, K. and Morris, D. (1997). *Gender and the Welsh Language: A Research Review*, Research Discussion Series, no. 18, Cardiff: Equal Opportunities Commission.

Jones, S. J. and Jones D. R. (1994). *Vacancies and Recruitment in a Peripheral Labour Market: A Case Study of North West Wales*, Research Papers Series, Bangor: School of Banking Accounting and Economics, University of Wales.

Lewis, E. G. (1987). 'Attitude to development of Welsh', in Williams, G. (ed.), *The Sociology of Welsh, International Journal of Sociology*, 66, 11–26.

Lipietz, A. (1987). *Mirages and Miracles: The Crises of Global Fordism*, London: Verso.

Lovering, J. (1998). *Misreading and Misleading the Welsh Economy*, Papers in Planning Research, Cardiff: Department of City and Regional Planning, University of Wales.

McGroarty, M. (1993). 'Second language instruction in the workplace', *Annual Review of Applied Linguistics*, 13, 86–108.

Marshall, G., Rose, D., Newby, H. and Vogler, C. (1988). *Social Class in Modern Britain*, London: Unwin Hyman.

Menter a Busnes (1994). *Quiet Revolution? Language, Culture and Economy in the Nineties*, Aberystwyth: Menter a Busnes.

Mitchell, J. C. (1969). *Social Networks in Urban Situations*, Manchester: Manchester University Press.

Morris, D. (1989). 'A study of language contact and social networks in Ynys Môn', *Contemporary Wales*, 3, 99–117.

Morris, D. (1990). 'Ailstrwythuro Economaidd a Ffracsiynu Dosbarth yng Ngwynedd', unpublished Ph.D. thesis, University of Wales, Bangor.

Morris, D. (1992). 'The effects of economic changes on Gwynedd society', in Dafis, Ll. (ed.), *Lesser Used Languages – Assimilating Newcomers*, Carmarthen: Joint Working Party on Bilingualism in Dyfed, pp.134–57.

Morris, D. (1995). 'Language and class fractioning in a peripheral economy', *Journal of Multilingual and Multicultural Development*, 16/5, 373–88.

Morris, D. (1997). *Women's Role in the North West Wales Labour Force: Report for TARGED*, St Asaph: North West Wales Training and Enterprise Agency.

Morris, D. (1998). 'Minority women in a changing labour market: the case of Wales', *Minorities and Women*, Finland: Åland Islands Peace Institute, 27–44.

Morris, D. and Williams, G. (1994). 'Language and social work practice: the Welsh case', in Williams, R. W., Davies, E. and Williams, H. (eds.), *Social Work and the Welsh Language*, Cardiff: CCETSW/University of Wales Press, pp.123–54.

Morris, D., Williams, G. and Williams, E. W. (1995). *Evaluation of the JIGSO Project: Report for the Countryside Council for Wales*, Bangor: Research Centre Wales.

Nairn, T. (1975). 'The modern Janus', *New Left Review*, 94, 3–31.

OPCS (1994). *1991 Census Cyfrifiad 1991 Welsh/Cymraeg*, London: HMSO.

O'Riagain, P. (1994). A Conceptive Analysis of Four Language Use Surveys. Report submitted to the EC.

O'Riagain, P. (1997). *Language Policy and Social Reproduction: Ireland 1893–1993*, Oxford: Clarendon Press.

Owen, T. (1960). 'Chapel and community in Glan-llyn, Merioneth', in Rees, A. D. and Davies, E. (eds.), *Welsh Rural Communities*, Cardiff: University of Wales Press, pp.185–248.

Poulantzas, N. (1973). *Political Power and Social Classes*, London: New Left Books.

Putnam, R. (1993). *Making Democracy Work*, Princeton: Princeton University Press.

Rawkins, P. (1987). 'The politics of benign neglect: education, public policy, and the mediation of language conflict in Wales', in Williams, G. (ed.), *The Sociology of Welsh, International Journal of Sociology*, 66, 27–48.

Real Academia Galega (1990). *Estudio sociolinguistico da comarca ferrola*, RAG: A Coruña.

Rees, A. D. (1950). *Life in a Welsh Countryside*, Cardiff: University of Wales Press.

Rees, A. D. and Davies, E. (eds.) (1960). *Welsh Rural Communities*, Cardiff: University of Wales Press.

Rei Doval, G. and Ramallo, F. (1995). *Publicidade e lingua Galega*, Santiago de Compostela: Conselo de Cultura Galego.

Roberts, C. (1985). 'Teaching and Learning Commitment in Bilingual Schools', unpublished Ph.D. thesis, University of Wales, Bangor.

Roberts, C. (1987). 'Political conflict over bilingual initiatives', *Journal of Multilingual and Multicultural Development*, 8/4, 311–22.

Schumpeter, J. A. (1954). *History of Economic Analysis*, Oxford: Oxford University Press.

Sharp, D., Thomas, B., Price, E., Francis, G. and Davies, I. (1973). *Attitudes to Welsh and English in the Schools of Wales*, Basingstoke and Cardiff: Macmillan and University of Wales Press.

Smith, A. (1976). *A Theory of Moral Sentiments*, ed. D. D. Raphael and A. L. Macfie, Indianapolis: Liberty Classics.

Southall, J. E. (1895) *The Welsh Language Census of 1891*, Newport.

Tajfel, H. (1974). 'Social identity and intergroup behaviour', *Social Science Information*, 13, 65–93.

Thomas, B. (1988). 'Differences of sex and sects: linguistic variation and social networks in a Welsh mining village', in Coates, J. and Cameron, D. (eds.), *Women in their Speech Communities*, London: Longman, pp.51–60.

Touraine, A. (1994). *Qu'est-ce que la democratie?* Paris: Fayard.

Touraine, A. (1997). *Pourrons-nous vivre ensemble?* Paris: Fayard.

Tucker, G. R. (1991). 'Developing a language-competent American society: the role of language planning', in Reynolds, A. G. (ed.), *Bilingualism, Multiculturalism and Second Language Learning*. Hillsdale, NJ: Lawrence Erlbaum, pp.65–79.

Webster, R. (1982). 'Education in Wales', in Cohen, L., Thomas, J. and Manion, L. (eds.), *Educational Research and Development in Britain 1970–1980*, Slough: NFER-Nelson, pp.203–14.

Welsh Language Board (1993). *A Strategy for the Welsh Language*, Cardiff: Welsh Language Board.

Welsh Language Board (1995). *Public Attitudes to the Welsh Language*, Cardiff: Welsh Language Board.

Welsh Language Board (1999). *Continuity Paper in Welsh-medium Education*, Cardiff: WLB, Adran Addysg.

Welsh Office (1995a). *1992 Welsh Social Survey: Report on the Welsh Language*, Cardiff: Welsh Office.

Welsh Office (1995b). *Statistics of Education and Training in Wales: Schools*, No. 3, Cardiff: Government Statistical Services.

Williams, C. H. (1987). 'Location and context in Welsh language reproduction: a geographic interpretation', Williams, G. (ed.), *The Sociology of Welsh, International Journal of Sociology*, 66, 61–83.

Williams, C. H. and Evas, J. (1998). *The Community Research Project: A Summary of Community Research Conducted in Mold and the Teifi, Gwendraeth and Aman Valleys*, Cardiff: Welsh Language Board.

Williams, G. (1976). 'Differential risk strategies among Welsh farmers in Argentina', *American Ethnologist*, 3/2, 65–89.

Williams, G. (1978). 'Industrialisation and ethnic change in the Lower Chubut Valley, Argentina', *American Ethnologist*, 5/3, 618–31.

Williams, G. (1979). 'Language group allegiance and ethnic interaction', in Giles, H. and Saint-Jacques, B. (eds.)., *Language and Ethnic Relations*, Oxford: Pergamon Press, pp.57–67.

Williams, G. (1983). 'On class and status groups in Welsh rural society', in Williams, G. (ed.), *Crisis of Economy and Ideology: Essays on Welsh Society, 1840–1980*, Bangor: BSA Sociology of Wales Study Group, SSRC, pp.134–46.

Williams, G. (1984). 'What is Wales? The discourse of devolution', *Journal of Ethnic and Racial Studies*, 7/1, 138–59.

Williams, G. (1987a). 'Bilingualism, class dialect and social reproduction', in Williams, G. (ed.), *The Sociology of Welsh, International Journal of Sociology*, 66, 85–98.

Williams, G. (1987b). 'Policy as containment within democracy: the Welsh Language Act', in Williams, G. (ed.), *The Sociology of Welsh, International Journal of Sociology*, 66, 49–60.

Williams, G. (1989). *Multiplier Study of Welsh Language Broadcasting in the Local Economy*, Bangor: TAC/S4C.

Williams, G. (1992a). *Sociolinguistics: A Sociological Critique*, London: Routledge.

Williams, G. (1992b). *The Welsh in Patagonia: The State and the Ethnic Community*, Cardiff: University of Wales Press.

Williams, G. (1994). 'Discourses on nation and race: a response to Denney et al', *Contemporary Wales*, 6, 87–104.

Williams, G. (1996a). 'Modernity, normativity, and social order: the problem of ethnicity', in Bombi, R. and Graffi, G. (eds.), *Ethnicity and Language Community: An Interdisciplinary and Methodological Comparison*, Atti del Convegno Internazionale, Udine: Forum, 517–38.

Williams, G. (1996b). 'Language planning as discourse', in Singh, R. (ed.), *Towards a Critical Sociolinguistics*, Amsterdam: Benjamin, pp.281–304.

Williams, G. (1999a). 'Language and ethnicity, the sociological approach', in Fishman, J. A. (ed.), *Language and Ethnicity*, Oxford: OUP, pp.164–81.

Williams, G. (1999b). *French Discourse Analysis: The Method of Poststructuralism*, London: Routledge.

Williams, G. and Harris, R. (1993). *Consumer Expectations and Satisfaction with the Health Services in Wales*, Cardiff: Consumer Council.

Williams, G. and Morris, D. (1995). *Peripheral Economic Structure, Labour Markets and Skills: Report of the TARGED Labour Survey*, Bangor: Research Centre Wales.

Williams, G. and Roberts, C. (1983). 'Language, education and reproduction in Wales', in Bain, B. (ed.), *The Sociogenesis of Language and Human Conduct*, New York: Plenum Press, pp.497–515.

Williams, G. and Thomas, A. (1986). *The Media and the Welsh Language*, Cardiff: Welsh Office.

Williams, G. and Williams, E. W. (1991). *Reading Patterns among Welsh Speakers*, Cardiff: WDA/S4C.

Williams, G. and Williams, N. G. (1998). 'Language and social networks among young adults in Gwynedd, Wales', in O'Riagain, P. (ed.), *Developing Policies to Improve Conversion of Language Competence into Language Use among Young Adult Groups*, Report prepared for the EC, DGXXII, Brussels: EC, pp.53–75.

Williams, G., Nelde, P. and Strubell, M. (1997). 'Del diagnostic al remei: Euromosaic, llengua i desenvolupament economic', *Revista de Llengua i Dret*, 28 (Barcelona, Dec.), 145–85.

Williams, G., Roberts, E. and Isaac, R. (1978). 'Language and aspirations for upward social mobility', in Williams, G. (ed.), *Social and Cultural Change in Contemporary Wales*, London: Routledge, pp.193–205.

Williams, G., Strubell, M. and Nelde, P. (1996). *Euromosaic: The Production and Reproduction of Minority Language Groups in the European Union*, Brussels: EC.

Williams, H. G. (1999). 'Learning suitable to the situation of the poorest classes – The National Society and Wales', *Welsh History Review*, 19, no. 3, June, 426–52.

Williams, J. L. (1973). 'The Welsh language in education', in Stephens, M. (ed.), *The Welsh Language Today*, Llandysul: Gomer Press, pp.92–109.

Wright, E. O. (1978). *Class, Crisis, and the State*, London: New Left Books.

Glossary

Anturiaethau	community development projects (e.g. Antur Dwyryd, Antur Teifi) concerned with economic regeneration
buchedd groups	status groups
CCETSW	Central Council for Training and Education in Social Work
cerdd dant	traditional Welsh language singing to the accompaniment of the harp.
Digital College	institution devoted to open distance learning using telematic delivery within the context of digital television
eisteddfod	Welsh-language cultural festival of poetry, music and drama
ICT	Information Communication Technology
Learning Company	companies which have the propensity to be constantly adaptable to the needs of economy involving constant process of reskilling and upskilling, flexibility and flat management
Learning Region	regions which have the capacity to generate lifleong learning developments in association with the changing needs of local and regional labour markets.
Mentrau	community development projects (e.g. Menter Môn)
Mentrau Iaith	community development projects concerned with Welsh language promotion
Menter a Busnes	job creation agency dedicated to increasing entrepreneurialism *among Welsh speakers.*
Merched y Wawr	Welsh language women's movement
Mudiad Ysgolion Meithrin	Welsh language nursery group voluntary movement
OPCS	Office of Population Censuses and Surveys
papurau bro	Welsh language community newspapers
S4C	Welsh language television channel
SEGs	socio-economic groups

Talwrn y Beirdd	traditional Welsh language bardic contest
telematics	information communication technology
Urdd	Welsh League of Youth
VAPs	Value Added Partnerships – these are fluid partnerships established between companies which may last for a short time based on specific interest before breaking up, perhaps being reassembled in the future. They rely on a high degree of mutual trust and confidence and constant flow of information across membership.
WDA	Welsh Development Agency – job-creation agency

Note: The counties referred to in the text – Gwynedd, Powys, etc. – are as defined in the 1991 Census of Population.

Index